Politics of Representation
Housing, Family, and State in Baku

After the privatisation of state-owned housing, relationships between states and citizens in former socialist countries have undergone major social, economic, and ideological transformations. This book investigates changes associated with housing in Azerbaijan. It traces the subtle continuities of people's past housing experiences and the role of solidarity and support among families and kin-groups in the quest to secure housing for future generations.

How, in the Soviet period – and in light of overcrowded dwellings in some urban areas – did families manoeuvre through official housing regulations and bureaucracies to raise their chances for being allocated additional living space? How did citizens take advantage of housing sanitary norms and registration practices when approaching administrative bodies? In what ways did these norms shape mutual encounters between citizens and the state not only in public discourse, but also in locally distinct and often informal ways? What are the reasons for the different dynamics and trajectories of the answers to these questions in spatially and historically distinct neighbourhoods? What role did distinct housing architectures play? And how do all these various aspects of the Soviet-era housing regime and related memories of past everyday lives merge with present developments, challenges, and contexts?

Based on ethnographic fieldwork and archival research in the capital of Baku, this book demonstrates that housing cannot be reduced to its economic aspects, but is strongly embedded in wider social processes, distinct political agendas, and moral expectations. By unfolding nuanced cases and ethnography on the rarely considered topic of housing in the South Caucasus, the book amply demonstrates the efforts, challenges, and limitations different groups have been facing amidst times of economic uncertainty.

An anthropological perspective on the phenomenon of housing in people's everyday lives serves as a starting point to illuminate crucial notions of 'house' and 'home' and to explore the manifold connections of these notions with past and present state ideologies of modernisation alongside the perceived continuity of patriarchal 'traditions'. It explores, too, how the role of architecture and materiality in official politics has served socialist and postsocialist states through (mis)representations and the negotiation of state-citizen relations in general. The author argues that most of these housing-related processes, at the level of the state as well as in local neighbourhoods, are shaped by 'façade politics' involving different modes of social interaction between human and non-human agents which serve to handle collective interests and (self-)images among citizens and state representatives alike. Taken together, he argues that various 'politics of representation' serve a better understanding of contemporary processes in post-Soviet contexts and beyond.

D1703514

Halle Studies in the Anthropology of Eurasia

General Editors:

Christoph Brumann, Kirsten W. Endres, Chris Hann, Burkhard Schnepel,
Lale Yalçın-Heckmann

Volume 40

LIT

Sascha Roth

Politics of Representation

Housing, Family, and State in Baku

LIT

Cover Photo:
Partial view of downtown Baku from Nariman Narimanov Avenue
with dilapidated pre-socialist dwellings in the foreground
(Photo: Duška Roth, March 2014).

This book is a revised version of a dissertation manuscript, submitted to the Faculty of Philosophy I at Martin Luther University Halle-
Wittenberg in 2016.

This book is printed on acid-free paper.

Bibliographic information published by the Deutsche Nationalbibliothek
The Deutsche Nationalbibliothek lists this publication in the Deutsche
Nationalbibliografie; detailed bibliographic data are available in the Internet at
http://dnb.dnb.de.

ISBN 978-3-643-90890-2 (pb)
ISBN 978-3-643-95890-7 (PDF)

A catalogue record for this book is available from the British Library.

©LIT VERLAG Dr. W. Hopf   LIT VERLAG GmbH & Co. KG Wien,
Berlin 2020   Zweigniederlassung Zürich 2020
Fresnostr. 2   Flössergasse 10
D-48159 Münster   CH-8001 Zürich
Tel. +49 (0) 2 51-62 03 20   Tel. +41 (0) 76-632 84 35
Fax +49 (0) 2 51-23 19 72   Fax
E-Mail: lit@lit-verlag.de   E-Mail: zuerich@lit-verlag.ch
https://www.lit-verlag.de   https://www.lit-verlag.ch

Distribution:
In the UK: Global Book Marketing, e-mail: mo@centralbooks.com
In North America: Independent Publishers Group, e-mail: orders@ipgbook.com
In Germany: LIT Verlag Fresnostr. 2, D-48159 Münster
Tel. +49 (0) 2 51-620 32 22, Fax +49 (0) 2 51-922 60 99, e-mail: vertrieb@lit-verlag.de

Contents

List of Illustrations

Map

Plates

Sources:
Plates 1, 3, 4, 8: *Azərbaycan Respublikası Dövlət Kino-Foto Sənədləri Arxivi* (ARDKFSA) [State Film and Photo Documents Archive of the Azerbaijan Republic];
Plates 2, 5, 7, 10, 11, 14–18: taken by author [2013-2014];
Plates 6, 9, 12, 13, 19: taken by Duška Roth

Acknowledgements

This book marks the end of a journey which began as a dissertation project in Autumn 2012 as part of two different yet closely-connected and structured graduate programmes: the International Max Planck Research School for the Anthropology, Archaeology, and History of Eurasia (IMPRS ANARCHIE) and the Graduate School 'Society and Culture in Motion' (GS SCM). I am deeply grateful to these programmes for their overall and generous support of my project. At the GS SCM I want to thank Ralph Buchenhorst, Daniele Cantini, James Thompson, and my PhD-fellows for their helpful comments and suggestions during our coursework. I am greatly indebted to the Max Planck Institute for Social Anthropology in Halle (Saale), particularly to Chris Hann and all members of the department 'Resilience and Transformation in Eurasia' for its inspiring work atmosphere, academic input, excellent research conditions, and constant support. In particular, the IMPRS ANARCHIE, its interdisciplinary structure, and scholarly exchange with historians and archaeologists have left a permanent imprint on my academic thoughts and approaches. I want to thank the principal faculty of ANARCHIE for the inspiring conversations, interdisciplinary discussions, and exciting seminars. Thanks go also to my fellow Research School members, especially to my officemate Mustafa Coşkun, for the rich intellectual exchange of ideas and beneficial conversations. Our coordinator Daria Sambuk deserves appreciation and gratitude for accompanying us during this formative period with administrational, personal, and moral support.

Furthermore, I want to express my gratitude to all members of our department and participants in the weekly seminars who gave invaluable feedback on this work at different stages of its formation. I also thank the administration, the librarians, the IT-team, the research coordination, and the student assistants whose constant support in all matters allowed me to concentrate fully on my work. Thanks go also to Jutta Turner for the cartography entailed in this book.

The realisation of the present work was only made possible by the support of many people, friends, colleagues, and institutions. I am truly indebted to my main supervisor, Lale Yalçın-Heckmann, for her invaluable support over the last years, her helpful comments, and thorough reading of previous versions of the manuscript. Her supervision in all stages of my research and writing process was outstanding and perfectly complemented by historian Michael G. Müller and his profound expertise on how to integrate historical sources into the methodological toolkit of anthropologists. I also want to express deep gratitude to my examiners Bruce Grant and Chris Hann whose invaluable comments on the PhD thesis and suggestions for improving the text for final publication will always be appreciated. Special thanks I further owe to Jennifer Cash for her invaluable comments, suggestions to the manuscript, and its final language editing, as well as to Berit Eckert and Michaela Rittmeyer who prepared and formatted the book for final publication.

This work further received valuable comments and feedback from other colleagues and scholars working on the Caucasus and beyond. Many of them invited me to discuss parts of my research in various academic events and conferences. I am grateful to Eva-Maria Auch, Tristam Barrett, Tsypylma Darieva, Susanne Fehlings, Bruce Grant, Philipp Jäger, Ketevan Khutsishvili, Florian Mühlfried, Sergey Rumyantsev, Stéphane Voell, and many others. I owe an enormous debt to Rasim Mirzayev and his wonderful support in a wide range of relevant issues. My initial interest in the region and issues presented in this book gained important impetus from my undergraduate studies at the Department of Social and Cultural Anthropology at the University of Tübingen. There, it was Irmtraud Stellrecht who aroused my anthropological interest in the post-Soviet space and the Caucasus region.

Research for this project would not have been possible without the great number of people and institutions in Azerbaijan who actively and diversely supported me and my family during our stay in the field. Their invaluable support, their great hospitality, and their active role in making our stay pleasant and unforgettable will always be remembered. I owe an enormous debt to Aliagha Mammadli from the Institute of Archaeology and Ethnography at the Azerbaijan Academy of Sciences. Without him, his generous support, and engaging discussions, this research would have been hardly possible. I also thank Maisa Rahimova, the institute's director, for her support in gaining access to local archives. Among the latter, of central importance have been the State Archive of the Azerbaijan Republic, its Baku Branch, and the Azerbaijan State Film and Photo Documents Archive. I want to emphasise my gratitude to all the archive staff who patiently helped me find my way. Thanks go also to the Caucasus Research Resource Center, the Women Crisis Center, and many other NGOs who lent support with accessing relevant information and networks.

I am indebted to many people, friends, and colleagues who shared a great amount of time with me and introduced me to manifold aspects of everyday life and facets of the city which would have remained unknown to me otherwise. For their generous hospitality, exciting conversations, and social support I am particularly grateful to Rufat Ahmedov with family, Mehdi Gadimov with family, Rahilya Geybullayeva, Rustam Gozelov (*Allah rəhmət eləsin!*), Rahib and Togrul Guliyev, Bahar and Hikmet Hacizade,

Zaur Hamza, Akbar Hasanov, Vali Huseynov, Asef Ibrahimov, Samira Karayeva, Joshkun Karimov with family, Hamza Khalilov, Ruslan Khamoyev with family, Kamran Majidli with family, Yashar Mirzaliyev, Nizami Nesibov, Nick Nwolisa with family, Daniel Paul with family, Adil Safiyev, Rail Safiyev, Ramil Safiyev, Bakhtiyar Shabanov, and Jeyhun Valiyev. For their great hospitality, for providing us with a home, and for becoming much more than just a host family, I am especially grateful to all four of the 'Qacarovs' for the time and conversations we had together.

All of the people mentioned above, and many others whom I have not named explicitly, have contributed to the success of this project. Of course, all remaining shortcomings are solely mine.

By far the greatest and most helpful support I received from my beloved wife Duška and our children Kaya and Mika. My wife's immediate readiness to accompany me on fieldwork and the openness to live a different life, in a different setting, equally provided the basis for that research as did my wife's continuous encouragement and support for this project from the very beginning. For my family's constant trust, moral, and emotional backing, and their patience with this project, I am inexpressibly grateful.

Parts of this book have been published previously in different form. Chapter 1 contains sections and arguments which were first expressed as part of an edited volume: 'Ideologies and Informality in Urban Infrastructure: The Case of Housing in Soviet and Post-Soviet Baku', 2019. In: Tauri Tuvikene, Wladimir Sgibnev, and Carola S. Neugebauer (eds.), *Post-Socialist Urban Infrastructures*, pp. 54–71, London: Routledge. Parts of chapter 4 were published as 'Curtains, Cars, and Privacy: Experiences of Dwelling and Home-Making in Azerbaijan', 2020. In: Johannes Lenhard and Farhan Samanani (eds.), *Home: ethnographic encounters*, pp. 45–57, London: Bloomsbury.

.

Note on Transliteration

The transliteration of Russian throughout this book follows the United States Library of Congress System, with established exceptions for well-known figures and places. One apostrophe indicates a soft sign, two apostrophes indicate a hard sign. Names recorded in Russian on archival documents were transliterated as if they were Russian, even if they are Azerbaijani names. Azerbaijani usage follows the Latin transcription adopted by the Republic of Azerbaijan in 1991. Generally, there are exceptions in the text for accepted anglicised terms (e.g. Baku rather than Bakı).

With reference to the International Phonetic Alphabet (IPA), the following table indicates the pronunciation of Azerbaijani letters which are either not used in English or spelled differently:

LATIN	IPA
C/c	[dʒ]
Ç/ç	[tʃ]
Ə/ə	[æ]
G/g	[ɟ]
Ğ/ğ	[ɣ]
X/x	[x]
I/ı	[ɯ]
İ/i	[ɪ]
J/j	[ʒ]
Q/q	[g]
Ö/ö	[œ]
Ş/ş	[ʃ]
Ü/ü	[y]

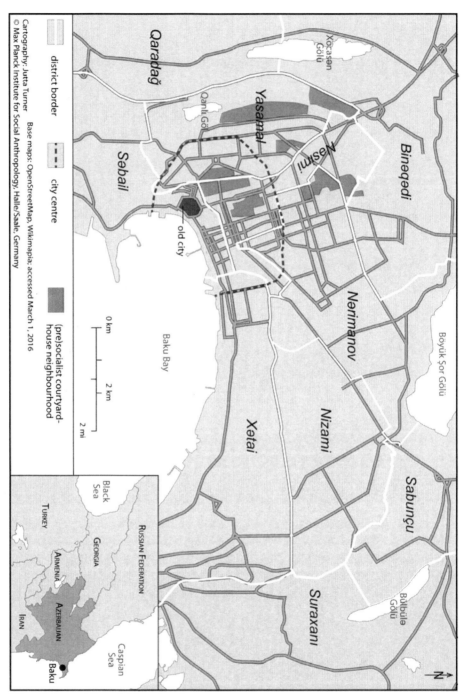

Map. Baku and its neighbourhoods.

To my family – in the widest sense –
who showed me what family is all about

Chapter 1
Introduction: Unravelling the House in Soviet and Post-Soviet Baku

Houses, as property in general, are investments into the future. This holds equally true for businessmen, economic elites, or state leaders who invest their money in assets and engage in conspicuous consumption around the globe, as it does for the many who aspire to an ideal image of a middle-class lifestyle based on more 'homely' images of materiality and consumption. It also is true for the vast majority of people who are less privileged and not well equipped to acquire, maintain, or enhance property but for whom the housing question rather constitutes a daily concern and major challenge. But in each and every case, housing matters are related not only to the financial and economic aspects of the future. Housing reflects a myriad of topics.

In this book, by taking ethnographies and historical accounts of housing as the starting point of my enquiry, I deal with issues such as changing ideologies and state-visions of modernisation, and the role of architecture and materiality in official politics of representation. I discuss the inner workings of the Soviet housing regime; the role of privatisation and its broader impact on different groups of citizens; and on how those groups perceive, experience, and deal with their post-Soviet housing situation in present-day Baku.

Here, it is clear that it is not only economic considerations that play a role in the housing question. Housing is, above all, embedded socially in the practices and moral expectations of support among kin-members. Immediate associations of the house in Azerbaijan invoke the life-cycle event of marriage because marriage is seen as constituting a house and home in material and symbolic terms.

Another central topic is how locals understand and negotiate privacy by architectural means, as well as in everyday social interaction. The importance of private space, along with people's engagement in home-making and renovations, are further aspects of the housing question that invite scrutiny. Here too the Soviet state's approach towards the home and domestic sphere of its citizens has left an imprint.

As housing, property, and the social processes around it can be primary reasons for family conflicts, I finally deal with questions of social and legal contestations of property-related issues. These are discussed with further reference to local notions of patriarchy, power relations, and domination inside families. Furthermore, patriarchy and the fostering of conservative (allegedly national) values characterises the government's post-Soviet approach to representing the nation, and securing the loyalty of its citizens, in terms of kinship. In summary, all these processes illustrate politics of representation at different levels of social and political institutions, up from the state and down to everyday social interactions.

In Azerbaijani, the word for house is (*ev*). It refers to the built structure, and in urban areas, the term *ev* also refers to apartments, so long as the physical differences of such multi-storey, multi-unit structures are not considered important. Otherwise, more specific terms for an apartment dwelling are used (e.g. *mənzil, bina evi*).

As elsewhere in the Caucasus, and in Central Asia, the concept of *house* in its linguistic, socio-economic, and moral senses is inextricably linked with other meanings: family, home, and marriage. *Ev* also describes social groups like families or households (see also Yalçın-Heckmann 2010: 77). It is the central metaphor and symbol for the ritual of marriage and establishing the formalised relation between two families. Similar metaphors are found across Eurasia, if not beyond, with multiple Turkic and Romance languages (e.g. Spanish, Romanian) still encoding an equation between marriage and the house. In Azerbaijan, as in Turkey, the house is regarded as a precondition for marriage. This is expressed linguistically in both Turkish and Azerbaijani. In Turkish, 'Marriage (*evlilik*) is literally the state of being with a house; to marry (*evlenmek*) is to become enhoused' (Delaney 1991: 112). The Azerbaijani[1] verb 'to marry' is nearly the same – *evlənmək*. Thus, marrying and being married is equal to the process of creating a house – symbolically by meaning to create a family and in the ideal case to also materially set up a dwelling separated from the parental household. *Ev* therefore also encompasses the notion of 'home', and there is a strong link to gendered concepts of home-making (see Chapter 4 and 5).

The web of associations with *ev* spread wider. Because house and marriage are so tightly linked, the normative understanding is that living

---

[1] Most scholars use the terms Azeri and Azerbaijani interchangeably, although they have distinct connotations. I have aimed for consistent usage of 'Azerbaijani' when talking about state, citizens/citizenship, society, and language, and of 'Azeri' in contexts emphasizing the ethnic category.

separate from one's parents is only legitimate after marriage. Of course, there are exceptional reasons one might live alone, such as during higher education or work far away from the parental home, but only the transition from an unmarried to married status really endows the legitimate right to set up a separate household. Local expressions for marriage further reflect the norm of virilocal post-marital residence. *Evlənmək* is predominantly used when speaking about getting married from a male perspective. From the bride's perspective, to get married is referred to with the expression *ərə getmək*, which literally means 'to go to the husband'. Such gendered difference disappears when speaking about any person being 'married', which is *evli* ('with house') for both men and women. However, an unmarried person, whether male or female, is not *evsiz* ('without house'), which means 'homeless', but *subay* ('single'). Clearly, the 'house' comprises the meaning of home as a spatial, social, economic, political, gendered, and moral concept.

The wide range of meanings connected to *ev* and its embeddedness in social processes invites further investigation into the role such socio-cultural ideologies have played in the processes of apartment allocation in the Soviet Union. During Soviet times, when the state predominantly owned, allocated, and controlled urban housing, it was the house, too, that additionally gained political priority. It was a constantly scarce and valuable resource for the state and its citizens, and its distribution affected the quality of their mutual relationship. With post-Soviet privatisation, housing experienced a major legal and economic shift. No longer provisioned by the state, and no longer considered a fundamental right of citizenship, the house started to become a commodity in the globalising context of the new market economy. But how has this change been experienced by different groups of urban inhabitants, and how do they cope with recent transformations in society and the housing sector after more than seven decades of socialism?

From a historically-informed anthropological perspective, the present work aims at unravelling the importance of housing and the house in families' everyday life, and its interrelation with their ideas and practices in the urban context of Baku. It equally considers the state's changing approaches, ideologies, and policies as implemented in the sphere of housing. In the comparative framework of the Soviet and post-Soviet housing regimes, I also examine continuities and discontinuities in the social life of citizens and their relationship to the state.

Some of the questions asked are these: What are local notions of the house, its social, architectural, and symbolic meanings? To what extent is housing connected to imaginations of social differences and inequalities? What role do different forms of housing play in socialist and postsocialist discourses on modernisation, and how have narratives of housing changed over time? How does housing contribute to the creation, maintenance, and transformation of collective identities?

Overall, this work engages with many subtle legacies of the socialist housing regime in a post-Soviet urban society. It opens up alternative ways of analysing social change and inequalities in Baku and Azerbaijan, but not only these places. A consideration of the city's consecutive *housing regimes*, understood as 'system[s] for producing and distributing housing, as both a material object and a symbolic meaning' (Zavisca 2012: 11), serves to provide a deeper contextualisation for contemporary questions. The repercussions and ramifications of the Soviet housing regime have moulded with the social, economic, and political transformations following independence. In Azerbaijan, as well as in many other postsocialist Caucasian and Central Asian republics, the neoliberal economy unleashed since the 1990s has combined with an authoritarian political regime with vast economic power and interests, as well as strong ambitions towards the (re)traditionalisation of society. By dealing with the issue of housing, these tendencies can be approached comparatively from a vantage point, as past and present housing regimes have continuously brought these politics and economics deep into the most private space of a couple, their family, and their hopes for the future, though embedded in changing ideological frameworks.

Most material in this book is based on one year of fieldwork in the city of Baku, the capital of Azerbaijan, from August 2013 to August 2014. Altogether, between 2007 and 2014, I spent two years in Azerbaijan. Every time I returned, I was struck again by the pace of urban construction and the number of new high-rises and residential blocks mushrooming in the central parts of the city. This urban change is meant to represent the striving of an independent nation towards a bright, modern, and prosperous future. Simultaneously, the city's past left its imprint on the different housing architectures of pre-Soviet and Soviet times, and hinted at the vividly changing social and material landscape since the mid-nineteenth century. But as is the case with many other 'developing cities', Baku faces problems such as 'a retreat from planning; lack of institutional coordination; poor implementation of laws; chaotic development patterns; suburban sprawl and a surge in informal construction' (Valiyev 2013: 636). Taken together, these factors have supported a vivid transformation of urban space, in which the housing sector, including individual as well as mass housing construction, is characterised by high levels of informality, corruption, and non-transparency. Most of these developments resemble trends in many large cities of the former Soviet Union and have been subject to academic debates on the peculiarities and more recent developments of postsocialist cities in general (e.g. Alexander et al. 2007; Darieva et al. 2011; Hirt 2012, 2013).

Post-Soviet Baku lacks a general development plan. In Soviet times, however, urban development and the construction of housing were based on sustainably designed master plans (*general'nyi plan* or *genplan*), with the last one dating back to 1986. These plans 'served several purposes including functional zoning of the peninsula area; development of residential areas [...] taking into consideration Baku's city limits, establishment of an urban agglomeration provided with improved employment, education, housing, culture and recreation opportunities' (Valiyev 2013: 629). In contrast, the flourishing oil sector fuelled a postsocialist, profit-driven construction boom that lacked legislative and controlling measures and even basic principles of spatial planning. The result was chaotic and inflationary construction in central areas, accompanied by high rates of corruption (UNECE 2010: 37). As I have discussed elsewhere (Roth 2019: 64), in today's Baku, we encounter widespread obstacles in terms of proper documentation, informality, and infrastructural provision (see also Valiyev 2013; Barrett 2014). Interestingly, despite their illegal status, most informal dwellings in the city's suburban settlements are well connected to transport, water, and electricity. State and private companies rarely check the legal status of properties carefully before delivering the requested infrastructure, and bribes are usually involved. In certain respects, documents further complicate the matter. 'In many cases, construction has some document issued by municipalities for a fee (very often bribes). However, subsequent elected municipality members very often do not recognize these documents as legal' (Valiyev 2014: S49). Furthermore, what is officially generalised as informal housing in Azerbaijan subsumes a variety of characteristics: squatting on another person's legal land (including state or municipal property), the absence of legal documentation and/ or construction permits (including extensions of existing dwellings), or unsafe structures and locations (Valiyev 2013: 637–38). Informal practices in the Baku housing sector have always played an important role in order to allow access to housing, land, and ownership.

In summary, as this book will show, the meaning of the house (in its wider sense) entails a myriad of social, economic, and moral, as well as political and ideological dynamics. At another level, I discuss different expressions of what I call the politics of (mis)representation in the domains of family, kinship, state, architecture, bureaucracy, patriarchy, or the home. All these are woven together by the category of the house as a total social institution in Soviet and post-Soviet urban Azerbaijan. My aim is to show how an anthropology of the house can be effectively applied to urban postsocialist contexts. It serves well to grasp important domains, processes, and relationships in people's everyday lives that unfold in the context of housing. Finally, my research not only calls for more attention to a rarely considered category in anthropological research but enhances our understanding of contemporary social processes and their relation to past experiences. In this introduction, I will first describe my access to the field which started with seeking accommodation. Second, I provide a general theoretical overview of the concepts that are discussed in the subsequent chapters.

Accessing the Field

During my stay in Baku as a foreign student conducting research on an undergraduate thesis in 2008–09, I spent several months living with the family of Natiq – a student at the local partner university. I had already spent several weeks in Azerbaijan during academic summer schools in the preceding two years and was superficially acquainted with local behavioural codes in public. But only through Natiq's family, who adopted me like a member of their own, was I introduced to private lifeworlds as they unfold behind closed doors. The Qarayevs introduced me to their wider kin, the neighbours in their 1970s housing complex, their friends, and everyday life. They mostly socialised me into my 'host culture' and proper codes of conduct between the genders and people of different age. They also shared their concerns, struggles, and hopes with me.[2] It later turned out that this experience was of outstanding importance because I not only had established a network of close and trusted persons when I returned for my one-year doctoral fieldwork in 2013–14. I also learned about the overall importance and multiple facets of housing that would shape my research interests in the years to come. My host family – the Qarayevs – and most of their relatives, as I learned accidently after some time, were Azeri refugees (qaçqınlar) from Armenia who decided to migrate to their titular nation Azerbaijan in the late 1980s. Like some 160,000 other Azeris, they wanted to escape the increasing ethnic upheavals of that time. In turn, as a consequence of the reviving Armenian-Azerbaijani hostilities, the large Armenian community in Baku (around 180,000 people) returned to Armenia. What was remarkable in that process was that a significant amount of people in both groups engaged in interethnic house exchange and, thus, were able to maintain their dwellings despite displacement (see Huseynova et al. 2008; Roth 2013).

---

[2] All names of my interlocutors are anonymised in order to protect their identities.

A few years later, in the chaotic years of early independence and the outbreak of the Nagorno-Karabakh War (1992–94), my host family moved to Russia for some years. My host-father Asad, together with his elder brother Sultan, started engaging in car-trade business in the city of Khabarovsk near the Chinese border. Actually, it was Sultan who, due to a social network established during his Soviet military service in Khabarovsk, initiated the car-business which was later run jointly by the two brothers. With the money, they supported their parents and younger siblings who were living in Baku. In 1998, they returned to Azerbaijan while Asad's younger brother took over and went to Russia with his family to continue the business. With the money Asad earned, my host family bought the four-room apartment in a Soviet multi-apartment block in the municipality of Qaraçuxur, roughly fifteen kilometres east of Baku's city centre, as shown on the map at the beginning of this book. So it was that my interest in the importance of the house in the Azerbaijani context emerged and was enhanced by the omnipresence of conversations which centred around issues related to housing.

When I returned for PhD fieldwork in autumn 2013, I was married and had a son who had just turned two years old. My family accompanied me for fieldwork. Now, living with a host family in an apartment as before was no option. It would have produced, to our minds, an overcrowded household, and we knew that we would have had troublesome times with the three of us living together in just one room of the family's apartment, as was and still is a common experience for many young families in Azerbaijan. Since I had no intention of risking my own family harmony for the sake of 'going native', other housing options had to be found. I favoured the option of finding accommodation in a courtyard house (həyət evi, pl. həyət evləri). The term həyət evi originally described the traditional form of dwelling in rural areas, in which a central courtyard is surrounded by dwelling spaces for several families of agnates. In urban areas, it had become a common term for various kinds of detached house in distinction from apartment buildings, but they usually also shared the common feature of a courtyard within a walled estate. It is similar to what is described as məhlə or həyət (lit. courtyard/ yard), as a separated yard adjoined by one or more houses (Pfluger-Schindlbeck 2005a: 13). However, for me it was important to follow the path to what others distinctly recognised as həyət evi. This is because only this compound term drew attention to the 'house' and not just the 'yard': although məhlə is used to describe a family group or lineage as well, it is 'primarily a physical space, the courtyard and the land' (Yalçın-Heckmann 2010: 77).

Instead of living in a Soviet apartment building, this, I thought, would enable us to better integrate ourselves into a local neighbourhood. It was not so easy. Finally, as I was running out of time to find suitable accommodation, a friend who knew about my housing quest surprisingly called me with the suggestion to approach his acquaintances in Badamdar, a settlement not too far from the centre, who might have a dwelling to rent out in their *həyət evi*. So, we drove to Badamdar together, more specifically into a neighbourhood colloquially called Bağlar döngəsi.[3] The name literally means 'curve of gardens'. It is a new neighbourhood within the municipality of Baku that became settled only after independence. During the Soviet period any private construction activity was prohibited in the area because of occasional oil drilling nearby and the geologically unstable conditions it produced. In the last twenty years, however, the area became densely built-up with detached houses ranging from average one-storey homes, to better-off middle-class houses, and up to the prestigious villas of the upper class. Over some cups of black tea, the landlord Talıb told me that the said apartment was not available. But he referred to Fikrət – a neighbour down the street who runs a retail shop and was apparently engaged in some renovations for a new apartment. We immediately stopped by the place, entered an appealing courtyard where one of Fikrət's sons was busily tiling the floor of a small three-room apartment in the back of the yard. Within half an hour and some further cups of tea, we agreed with the landlords that I would move in with my family and that all the necessary renovations would be done by our arrival. I was more than relieved to have settled the basic requirement for our stay in Baku.

Our landlords turned out to be a pivotal point for gathering information about what was going on in the neighbourhood. Fikrət was well known and, consequently, the people on our street knew about us, the newcomers from Germany, too. My son joined a local kindergarten, and every day when I brought him there, we were greeted by the men who spent mornings during the warm periods of the year in front of their stores, workshops, taxis, or offices. There were plenty of occasions to bump into spontaneous male gatherings and join their conversations.

While it was no problem to approach men in public as they conducted their daily business, initially it was almost impossible to learn about their lives behind the closed doors and high walls that lined the main street of our neighbourhood. Even after we had spent almost one year living there, many

---

[3] Most of the 'neighbourhoods' recognised and named by Bakuvians as distinct places have no administrative status. They are most likely to be described with use of the term *məhəllə*. The qualities of this term, as well as that for urban administrative districts (raion), will be discussed throughout this work.

neighbouring plots, gardens, and houses, their size and other characteristics, remained unknown to me. Doors and gates were usually kept closed and only in rare moments was it possible to get a glimpse of what lay behind. The different architectures, layouts, and materialities of various urban areas had a clear impact on people's use of public and private spaces (Chapter 5).

After some time, I had successfully established a dense network of friends and acquaintances in my neighbourhood. While I constantly enjoyed the value of hospitality, being invited for eating and drinking together, in some circles at least, I became an active part in the long-term reciprocities and obligations connected to ritual forms of exchange, support, and confirming male friendship. Such occasions ranged from mere lunches among us men, to invitations that were extended to my family, and even to participation in the lavish weddings that have become part of a 'wedding industry' blossoming since the end of the 1990s. At most invitations and feasts, vodka was a loyal companion to the high quantity of food being served to guests, especially among the elder male generation that had grown up during the Soviet days.

Anthropologists long ago acknowledged 'constructive drinking' and the 'importance of drinking in the lives of the people they lived among' (Douglas 1987: 3; see also Manning 2012). The importance of consuming large amounts of alcohol in Caucasian ritual contexts of hospitality is best documented for Georgia (Mars and Altman 1987; Mühlfried 2006). Also, in Azerbaijan, eating and drinking together constitutes an important ritualised framework for men to raise toasts to each other in a show of respect and to establish or maintain social relations. It became an important soft skill to deepen mutual trust with mostly elder males and their 'Soviet' consumption habits. Often, this seemed to be in stark contrast to the younger generation's preference for beer or, as it felt mostly being the case, to refuse the consumption of alcohol altogether. At any rate, I spent most of my time with other males, as that was perceived as the normal code of conduct. Only in very close and familiar settings such as with long-term friends, our landlords and host-families - basically when invitations took place on a family level – did gender separation cease to play a decisive role. However, it sometimes happened nevertheless that I found myself in male company while my wife and son became part of the women's crowd until we finally re-joined as mixed company at the dining table.

Sometimes, people were also very enthusiastic for me to take pictures of them, and I spent a significant amount of time revisiting people in order to distribute pictures. This also consolidated my relationship with many of the people I met. Photographs, generally, turned out to be an important medium in the urban context not only for documenting today's rapidly changing built environment. They also served as mnemonic prompts (Shevchenko 2015). Jointly looking at historical photographs and talking with inhabitants about the past and present of their neighbourhoods were lively happenings that soon attracted more and more people to join in. These circles of people dwelling on nostalgic memories of past times served equally for creating and enhancing social contacts. I was most impressed by this approach when I had archival photographs of places and neighbourhoods. On such occasions, I would soon be surrounded by interested males commenting on the pictures, remembering the old days and details of local history. To sum up, participant observation and other methods of informal character (e.g. simple face-to-face conversations without any technical devices) were usually among the most rewarding in terms of gaining unfiltered opinions on issues of interest. As with most methodological approaches, it is the degree of formality that a research situation constructs in the eyes of the interlocutor which determines the degree of formality in the answers we receive. Beside the everyday use of unstructured interviews, I conducted around eighty structured and semi-structured interviews with architects, lawyers, NGO-workers, real-estate agents, scholars, shopkeepers, current and former state-representatives, as well as with residents from the neighbourhoods under focus.[4] Most of my expert interviews were made accessible through a chain of trustworthy people in a snowball-approach. When I had my first expert interviews, which were often initiated by friends of friends, I received lots of information that I would regard as trustworthy and which allowed me to dig deeper into my matters of interest, predominantly on the informal practices around the issue of housing.

Friends' and acquaintances' mobilisation of their networks in order to support me and my research seemed daily routine for them. In Azerbaijan, generally, networks and personal recommendations of relatives, close

---

[4] Most of my interviews were conducted in Russian. For a foreign researcher, this was accepted as an efficient and consistent approach to interlocutors of various backgrounds and statuses, as it is still the lingua franca in Baku, as in many other capitals of former Soviet republics. Many ethnic Azeris also prefer to speak Russian, while even the 'purest' Azerbaijani includes numerous Russian words and expressions, especially to refer to institutions and experiences of the Soviet period. Language is also a point of local social tensions, particularly with reference to Baku's 'lost cosmopolitanism'. As these have been addressed well by other scholars, including anthropologists, I have not foregrounded them in my work which focuses on experiences that have been largely shared by Bakuvians, regardless of their first or preferred language. It is worth pointing out that even though Russian is often the dominant language, particularly for discussing bureaucratic and legal arrangements, Azerbaijani terms dominate discourses about home and family. Thus both languages work together in the domain of housing. Accordingly, I have only marked local terms as Russian or Azerbaijani when it is not clear from context and yet significant to distinguish them.

friends, and their friends in turn, as well as the ability to mobilise them in effective ways, constitute an indispensable resource in economic, political, and everyday life. When it is about getting a job or access to highly demanded branches of education or a place in a student dormitory, for instance, a positive outcome can be very much dependent on a person's *tapş* or *tapış*. A straightforward translation of this term is difficult. It is not quite 'patronage' because that term tends to suggest that a 'client' depends on a single 'patron', that the patron-client relationship is a socio-economic relationship distinct from relations of kinship or friendship, and that despite his dependence, the client remains personally responsible for his own welfare. Local authors usually explain *tapş* with reference to 'other network-based informal practices such as Soviet *blat*' or the "Chinese *guanxi*"' (Sayfutdinova 2018: 83, emphasis in original). Sayfutdinova explains that 'the word *tapş* is of Azerbaijani origin and comes from the verb *tapşırmaq*, which means to entrust something or somebody into someone else's custody' (ibid., emphasis in original). Although *tapş* shares many features with the Russian concept of *blat* (Ledeneva 1998), a major difference is that, in contrast to the non-hierarchical character of *blat*-relations, *tapş* is mostly associated with differences in hierarchy (see Sayfutdinova 2018: 83). In this context, it means to have someone in a high-ranking or better position than oneself, to whom one is entrusted, and who will give his support. Basically, it involves a person who can effectively recommend and promote people in front of others to make sure that 'things get done'. When people complained about the fact that their sons could not find work, they usually cited their lack of *tapş* as a common explanation. The term *dayı* or *dayday*, in turn, applies to the person who is granting *tapş* to others (in its primary meaning the term *dayı* means 'uncle' or, more precisely, 'mother's brother' in Azerbaijani kinship terminology). In other words, when I have a *dayday*, then I have *tapş*. My own experience with getting access to research contacts, in my understanding, followed that very logic.

While much of my research was rooted in conversations and interviews that focused on people's past experiences of Soviet housing in Baku, I also devoted a significant part of my time to gathering historical data from written accounts. I consulted newspapers but, most importantly, archival documents from the State Archive of the Azerbaijan Republic (ARDA), the Baku Branch of the State Archive (ARDABF), and the State Film and Photo Documents Archive (ARDKFSA).[5] All the archival materials (as well as most newspapers) were exclusively in Russian. Only

---

[5] The current Azerbaijani names of these institutions are, respectively, *Azərbaycan Respublikası Dövlət Arxivi; Azərbaycan Respublikası Dövlət Arxivi, Bakı Filialı; Azərbaycan Respublikası Dövlət Kino-Foto Sənədləri Arxivi.*

from the early 1990s, have official documents shifted to the Azerbaijani language. This historical approach enabled me to reconstruct original material on local housing conditions and the ways it has been officially represented, evaluated, and communicated. Archival documents feature as the main source in the following two chapters.

Kinship, House, and Home in (Post)Socialism

The birth of a son is celebrated as something special in Azerbaijan. The dominance of patriarchal bias in the imagination is reflected in frequent narratives about the priority of male descendants. Often, such expectations are perceived as real social pressure, but they are popularly seen as an ideal, rooted in the cultural tradition and ancient customs in the primordially constructed history of the Azerbaijani nation.

The continuity of the patrilineage is expressed by the tropes of house and hearth in a variety of proverbs: *Mənim oğlum ocağımı yandıracaq, evimin işığımı sönməyə qoymayacaq* ('When my son will light my hearth, then the light of my house will not extinguish') or *Mənim yurd-yuvama sahib olacaq, nəslimi davam etdirlər* ('When there will be a son [lit. owner] in my house, then my family will continue'). Two specific terms that frequently appear in these proverbs are *nəsil* and *ocaq*. The latter meaning 'hearth', is a globally widespread metaphor for the house as it constitutes its very heart (Carsten and Hugh-Jones 1995a, 1995b). The term *nəsil* is applied in a variety of meanings such as family, generation, descendent, or ancestry. But above all, it specifically applies to a person's patrilineal descent group in contrast to other expressions for family such as *ailə* and *qohum*. *Ailə* is usually applied with reference to the nuclear family, that is spouses and children, but in some contexts, it can include other close relatives living in the same household too. *Qohum* (pl. *qohumlar*) means 'relative' in a broader sense and includes all relations by blood or by marriage of both the paternal and the maternal sides (see also Pfluger-Schindlbeck 2005a: 11).

The concept of *nəsil*, however, applies *only* to a person's agnatic kin. It includes all relatives of the paternal line who descend from a common male ancestor remembered four or five generations back in time and whose membership is passed on through the male line (ibid.). Consequently, children, according to customary law, are considered as part of the husband's *nəsil*, but not of the mother's. That *nəsil* appears in these proverbs underscores the specific connections between house and patriline that are different from 'family' and 'relatives'.

It is important to mention that imaginings of the patriline do not necessarily say anything about emotional closeness, support, or the degree of everyday interaction that a nuclear family has with relatives from either side.

As married women have been culturally expected to leave their parental home and move to their husband's household, it has been traditionally the case in rural Azerbaijan that brothers and their families (i.e. the *nəsil* group) lived together in a hamlet. The same kind of residential pattern was widespread in Baku and other cities until the Soviet state's housing programme enabled nuclear families to seek accommodation in a separate apartment.

The *nəsil* is also a concept representing the principle of solidarity within a kin group in social, political, and economic matters. Therefore, the *nəsil* has been described further as a 'solidarity group' (Pfluger-Schindlbeck 2005a: 11–27). In contrast to the concept's normative emphasis on patrilineal descent, in practice, it hardly leads to a permanent support structure but rather constitutes an option which is chosen in specific situations (Pfluger-Schindlbeck 2005b: 337). Since such groups are 'extremely dependent upon the economic success and the social networks of their prominent members, the durability of their solidarity is fragile and could collapse at any time' (ibid.). These descriptions of solidarity groups fit well to housing-related and other economic practices, notions of mutual support, and moral expectations among family and kin (see Chapter 4). Although the urban context differs from the rural context described by the above-cited author, solidarity and economic cooperation within agnatic groups, not exclusively but dominantly, has remained a widespread feature. 'Solidarity among kin' constitutes 'a dominant ideology, prescribing certain generational and gender hierarchies and offering models of support and property exchange alternative to those of civil law and socialist practices' (Yalçın-Heckmann 2010: 163). Its underlying patriarchal ideology has gained a revitalised political importance for the state in the independent era (see Chapter 6). The exclusivity or necessity that such male-centred or patrilineal kin groups had in rural economic contexts, however, was significantly transformed in the Soviet urban housing context. There, mutual support among relatives – whether agnatic or affinal – was critical regarding access to housing, employment, information, and other scarce resources.

If we trace back the genealogy of anthropologists who have written about houses and kinship organisation, one encounters a particularly different approach in socialist and non-socialist scholarly traditions. In the former case, it was Lewis Henry Morgan (1995 [1877]) whose evolutionist ideas were taken further by Marx and Engels who then developed their own teleological model in *The Origin of the Family, Private Property and the State* (Engels 1986 [1884]). Their theory of historical materialism subsumed houses as part of material culture and provided part of the ideological basis of communism. In 1881, Lewis Henry Morgan published his study on

Houses and House-Life of the American Aborigines. The common principle
that runs through Morgan's comparison of house-architecture is its adaption
to 'communism in living' and to the 'law of hospitality' (Morgan 2010:
105). Both these principles bear relevance in an anthropology of housing in
the Soviet Union. An enforced 'communism in living' was nowhere more
prominent than in the Soviet institution of the communal apartment after the
Bolshevik Revolution. However, having not only been a deliberate
implementation of a communist ideology of dwelling, communal living was,
to various degrees in Soviet history, also related to the pragmatic concern of
transforming previous ownership structures and providing accommodation
for the urban proletariat. On the basis of Morgan's model, Victor Buchli
remarked that in evolutionist terms the category of architecture (including
different house forms) 'was inextricably bound up in notions of social
progress [...] but more significantly: moral states of being' (Buchli 2002:
207). The interrelation between socialist ideologies regarding different house
types and associated notions of modernity and morality will be a prominent
topic, especially in Chapter 2 and Chapter 3.

  Morgan's ideas had a sustained influence on Marx and Engels and,
thus, indirectly also on conceptions of Soviet communism. In Western
scholarship, though, a similar wide-ranging influence until the present-day
can be ascribed to Marcel Mauss — another pioneering figure in the
anthropology of the house. In an article on seasonal variations of the Eskimo
(1979), which first appeared in *l'Année Sociologique* (1904/05), he described
the seasonal variations of dwelling forms and interrelated changes in the
social morphology and structure of groups. As a methodological rule, Mauss
posited that 'social life in all its forms – moral, religious, and legal – is
dependent on its material substratum and that it varies with this substratum'
(Mauss 1979: 80). This quote reads as a prototype of his later definition of a
fait social total in his magnum opus *The Gift* where he maintained that 'total
social facts':

> are at once legal, economic, religious, aesthetic, morphological and
> so on. They are legal in that they concern individual and collective
> rights, organized and diffuse morality; they may be entirely
> obligatory, or subject simply to praise or disapproval. They are at
> once political and domestic, being of interest both to classes and to
> clans and families. They are religious; they concern true religion,
> animism, magic and diffuse religious mentality. They are economic,
> for the notions of value, utility, interest, luxury, wealth, acquisition,
> accumulation, consumption and liberal and sumptuous expenditure
> are all present [...] (Mauss 1966 [1925]: 76–77).

If we apply this definition to the house, I can hardly think of another category that fulfils this definition of a total social fact in a more illustrative way. Therefore, it is fair to say that Mauss's early essay on 'Seasonal Variations of the Eskimo' represents the first ethnographic attempt to adopt a holistic approach to the analysis of a society (Mauss 1979: 6). Further, it seems very likely that it was the concept of the house which had a great impact on his influential concept of a total social fact, which he developed on the basis of Durkheim's notion of a 'social fact' (*fait social*). Certainly, the house embodies the total/ holistic character most clearly.

Like the gift, the house serves to reproduce society as a whole. In the post-war period, the Soviet state's housing programme and infrastructural development was publicly represented in terms of materialising visions of modernity for the sake of Soviet citizens (Chapter 2). Housing, as a major focus of urban development, penetrated almost all domains and experiences in people's everyday life. In the context of the centralised Soviet welfare state, only a person's registration at a permanent address (*propiska*) provided official legal access to all kinds of infrastructure. People's mobility, including rural inhabitants' access to larger cities, was much restricted by the propiska. The rights, benefits, and status – but also the restrictions – that were connected to these registrations were so crucial in people's everyday experience and encounters with bureaucratic and state institutions, that only through housing did a person become a proper Soviet citizen (Chapter 3).

Two other prominent French anthropologists left long-lasting footprints in later anthropological studies on houses. Bourdieu's study on the Kabyle house provided the empirical ground for his elaboration of the habitus-concept. For him, the house was a microcosm, a space that reflected hierarchical principles and homologous oppositions between male (exterior) and female (interior) in Kabyle cosmology. These oppositions within the house exist at the same time between the house as a whole and the outside world (Bourdieu 1976 [1972]). As I will describe in Chapter 5, many of these classifications are represented in Azerbaijani ideas of how to conceive of spatial and gendered differences. However, such imagined rigidity in social structures, similar to the spirit of structuralism, must be approached critically; actual realities and practices that can be observed on the ground are often different (see also Vom Bruck 1997; Meneley 2007 [1996]). Among later generations of scholars, Bourdieu's approach to houses arguably proved most influential as it connected concepts like gender, space, the private and public – allowing also for critical inquiry which transgressed disciplinary boundaries.

Through his focus on kinship, however, it was Claude Lévi-Strauss (1982 [1979]) who influenced another strand of anthropologists dealing with the house (e.g. Carsten and Hugh-Jones 1995a; Joyce and Gillespie 2000). Comparing the social organisation of the Kwakiutl with that of noble houses in medieval Europe, Lévi-Strauss introduced the concept of *sociétés à maison*, in which the house becomes institutionalised as a:

> corporate body holding an estate made up of both material and immaterial wealth, which perpetuates itself through the transmission of its name, its goods, and its titles down a real or imaginary line, considered legitimate as long as this continuity can express itself in the language of kinship or of affinity and, most often, of both (Lévi-Strauss 1982 [1979]: 174).

Although constituting a much different context than Lévi-Strauss's example and theoretical argument, it seems almost obligatory to apply the notion of 'house societies' onto the Soviet Union. So far, Lévi-Strauss's concept has received most attention within the anthropology of kinship referring mostly to examples in non-industrialised settings. But the Soviet Union might also be considered a house society. That is, the concept of house society captures the tremendous importance of the housing question for the Soviet state, its republics, and citizens alike. Moreover, the question only pretended to be about a physical structure, but it was equally and more about the social dimensions of living (together), about the importance of family and kinship, and about how these were related to mechanisms of legitimating continuity in dwelling through the transmission of use-rights over time.

In recent debates on kinship, the concept of house societies has earned substantial critique for its evolutionary stance. Normally, the concept is associated with a rigid classification in which it describes a transitional stage from kin-based to class-based society in which members could choose between opposed but interchangeable principles of social organisation (e.g. patri-/ matrilineality, descent/ alliance, etc.). Further critique pointed to its overemphasis on structure and form without sufficient attention towards the content and processes evolving around social relations. However, at the same time, scholars acknowledged that Lévi-Strauss gave attention to the house as a core institution in human life closely linked to marriage and thus stimulating further research on the house's importance in studying social processes (Carsten 2004: 43). But nevertheless, to date such analytic stimulation has remained largely sporadic, thus having also raised claims by anthropologists that the 'investigation of the mutually constitutive nature of house and family ought to be high on anthropology's global research agenda' (Birdwell-Pheasant and Lawrence-Zúñiga 1999: 28). As this book shows, it is this often-stated relationship between the house, the family, and marriage, but also the impact of state power and the emphasis on architectural representation, that is of crucial relevance and everyday importance in Azerbaijani society.

Still, recent anthropological studies have been too rigid in their attempts to revive attention to house societies. With the exception of calling for attention to processual social relations, they have had little concern for modifying the concept to apply to spatial and temporal contexts that are very different from the cases Lévi-Strauss imagined. Recent authors still mostly question whether a specific society can be classified as a house society and whether the original model is applicable (e.g. Carsten and Hugh-Jones 1995b, Gillespie 2000; Hardenberg 2007). Lévi-Strauss's spirit seems to haunt any further engagement with houses in anthropology.

Yet such a neat Lévi-Straussian focus on analytical categories and strictly formulated conceptual limitations does not do justice to the variety of contexts in which houses have a crucial significance and role in people's everyday life and thought – as it is the case in urban Azerbaijan. Instead of dwelling on the minute details of the original concept, I think it is more important to appreciate Lévi-Strauss's insight into the central role of houses in the social construction of kinship and his own impetus 'to take proper interpretative account of them' (see also Howell 1995: 169). It is necessary to also emphasise how the house is an example (as Lévi-Strauss noted) of fetishism in a Marxist sense, and that houses constitute apparently unified alliances between people, so that the house itself appears as a *personne morale*. The house, or home, may be a moral person of this sort in complex urban societies too:

> [The house] through kinship ideology ... upon closer inspection, reveal[s] different economic and political motives for action. As a social and affective unit, the home becomes at once a conduit through which broader political and economic relations are enforced and acted out, a place of domestic retreat and a means through which people engage with kin, community and other local actors (Alexander et al. 2018: 129).

It is *not* Lévi-Strauss's model-like approach to kinship and house-societies in an evolutionist framework, which I find relevant, but rather the potential benefit of his ideas on houses as corporate groups, and the transmission of entitlements through houses, that is fruitful to apply to the context of a socialist urban housing regime.

It might still seem difficult to adapt Lévi-Strauss's notion of *wealth* to this context. After all, Lévi-Strauss held that the house is a 'corporate body holding an estate made up of both material and immaterial wealth'; he was thinking of noble houses in medieval Europe. The Soviet context formally lacked such notions and housing was not considered 'private property' that could be transmitted or inherited to anyone; only co-residents who were officially registered in the same apartment had a claim. Nevertheless, if we insist on adapting his principle argument to the Soviet framework, it might help to fill an important gap in studies on Soviet housing. Patterns of allocation and citizens' rights and duties vis-à-vis the state have been studied, but hardly any study has focused on the equally important dynamics of socio-cultural and moral notions of housing, kinship, gender, and family in the housing regime. I argue that these are important aspects for understanding the local peculiarities of an often-generalised Soviet housing regime from a decisively anthropological perspective.

How then to reconfigure concepts from Lévi-Strauss and Mauss for the Soviet context? The transmission of state-owned housing can be considered 'material wealth' and the 'total' character of the house can be seen in the entitlements connected to Soviet citizens' housing status and residence permit; these latter entitlements can be considered 'immaterial wealth'. According to Soviet law, inheritance of use-rights to any state-owned dwelling was legally based on residence, not kinship (Dragadze 2001 [1988]: 34). However, in practice, family groups were keen to keep and transmit housing resources among family members. This meant that because the law emphasised residence, people turned to a flexible construction of family and kin groups. They enhanced forms of 'relatedness' (Carsten 2000, 2004) to be largely connected to dwellings, rather than to patrilineal descent alone. Soviet housing law 'require[d] one to "cultivate" kin of every category' to prevent housing from falling back to the state's disposal in case of lacking registered co-residents (Dragadze 2001 [1988]: 34). Krisztina Fehérváry, in her monograph on socialist materialities in urban Hungary, similarly argued that 'kinship and property relations [...] mutually constituted each other' as 'state-owned apartments, once allocated, were practically inalienable; they stayed in a family through inheritance and could not be sold', though they could be used for exchange with another state apartment (Fehérváry 2013: 17).

This points to an interesting phenomenon and widespread socialist practice – hoarding – which has been described not only with regard to productive resources in socialist economies (Verdery 1991, 1996) but especially, as this book shows, with regard to housing. In the sphere of bureaucracy and dealing with housing authorities, to cultivate kin guaranteed 'a network of available house and flat dwellers who would allow their kinsman or kinswoman to register with them as a co-resident' (Dragadze 2001 [1988]: 34) – a strategy which was widespread in urban contexts. Citizens could thus make creative use of the propiska system in terms of providing relatives – kin, affines, or others – not only housing (at least on paper) but also necessary rights and statuses to education, employment, and public services (Chapter 3). More generally, kin relations were maintained, confirmed, created, and dissolved on the basis of housing in factual and administrative terms. Though the housing regime was intended to be one in which the state supported the reproduction of society through modern nuclear-family units, the 'house' became a focal point for the corporate dynamics of kinship and family in a much wider sense. In Azerbaijan, the generalised imperative of the Soviet housing regime – to mobilise kin relations for the practical realisation of housing, associated benefits, and their continuity – fell on fertile ground. In their pre-existing socio-cultural meanings, family and house were mutually important for providing family continuity through marriage, for which the house was seen as the prerequisite and symbol at large. The complex, dynamic, and often conflictual processes through which entitlements to the family resource of housing have been negotiated in the Soviet and post-Soviet contexts will be illustrated in Chapter 3 and Chapter 6.

Much more than the 'house', it is the concept of 'home' that has gained increasing popularity among scholars in different disciplines. Most scholars agree that home is a multi-dimensional concept with diverse and ambiguous meanings (Douglas 1991; Mallett 2004; Cieraad 2006a; Lenhard and Samanani 2020). Notably, the English 'home' encompasses a variety of different yet closely related notions: it can refer to the physical structure of a house, to one's place of residence, or a geographical region entailing notions of origin, belonging, and emotional attachment; it also refers to the place of family, to a private space and safe place, or to a symbol of identity. Because of its associated meanings, 'home' is frequently used instead of other terms such as house, family, dwelling, or domestic space precisely to convey something about what these physical spaces mean in social terms. In other words, home 'represents a complex and multi-dimensional amalgam of financial, practical, social, psychological, cultural, politico-economic, and emotional interests to its occupiers' (Fox 2002: 607).

For anthropologists, the seeming lack of terminological accuracy surrounding 'house' and 'home' should not come as a surprise: cross-cultural comparison points to the inclusive, open, and flexible character of the popular house/ home divide. Such a distinction does not apply equally to different cultural and historical contexts. If we focus only the notion of home in its relation to the house, for example, English-speakers would tend to agree that a house obtains the meaning of home through the emotional and social efforts that its inhabitants actively invest into it. The term 'home-making' subsumes a variety of everyday but also ritual processes that accomplish this work to make a house into a home.

Therefore, although anthropologists and others 'have sought diligently to differentiate concepts of "house" and "home", "household" and "family"', we should remember that 'the unity (or mutuality) of these concepts is embedded in many European cultural traditions' too (Birdwell-Pheasant and Lawrence-Zúñiga 1999: 5). Indeed, most anthropologists writing on the home also address the anthropological literature on houses (e.g. Miller 2001). Because home (and house) have so many different meanings 'there can be no standard definition [...], and in [...] every instance these words must be understood as they relate to a particular cultural context' (Low and Chambers 1989: 6). As will become clear, the Azerbaijani case is a perfect example of how such notions of house, home, and family are subsumed by the encompassing category of *ev*.

Finally, when talking about kinship and housing in a post-Soviet context, it is important to remember the ideological underpinnings and broader visions of a communist society that was to be forged in the years following the Bolshevik Revolution. In its first years of existence, the Bolshevik state propagated the creation of collectives and a communal way of life. The 'family' was regarded as a bourgeois and outdated institution (Trudolyubov 2018: 41). The housing and architecture to be planned for a new life according to socialist principles became a crucial part of the state's ideology (Humphrey 2005), and although it was adapted several times, this vision of a new, collective life accompanied the Soviet Union until its very end. Housing became a primary sphere for social engineering and the promotion of *novyi byt* (new everyday life) (Kiaer and Naiman 2006). The communal apartment (*kommunalka*, pl. *kommunalki*) was considered the 'cornerstone' of Soviet civilisation and 'a specifically Soviet form of urban living'. However, at least since Khrushchev's mass housing campaign and the aim to provide every family with a separate apartment, their place in the housing regime ultimately became that of 'a memory of a never implemented utopian communist design' (Boym 1994: 123).[6] Aside from the much-romanticised communal apartment, opinions as to what *novyi byt* meant differed; and the 'kind of housing that was considered appropriate in a socialist society was inevitably informed by people's attitudes towards the family, gender relations, and what form *byt*, or "daily life" should take' (Attwood 2010: 1). The vast size of the country and its social, ethnic, and religious diversity meant that people's attitudes towards family life and gender differed substantially between the republics. Patriarchal biases, for

---

[6] On communal living in Russia during Soviet and post-Soviet times see also the works of the Russian anthropologist Ilya Utekhin (2004, 2015). Together with other scholars he also created the webpage *Communal Living in Russia: A Virtual Museum of Soviet Everyday Life* (http://kommunalka.colgate.edu/index.cfm).

instance, were supposedly stronger in the Central Asian and Caucasian republics, including the Azerbaijani Soviet Socialist Republic (SSR) – the direct predecessor to today's Azerbaijan – than among the Slavic groups. Though the diversity has been declared to exist, few studies have detailed how culturally specific notions of family life, home, home-making, marriage, residence norms, or morals were embedded in housing regimes.

Certainly, the gap between the state's propagated ideology and citizens' everyday experiences generated a constant tension throughout the socialist period. Hence, the oft-heralded emergence of *Homo sovieticus* 'was a product not so much of the revolution as of an acute housing shortage in the rapidly expanding cities' (Trudolyubov 2018: 1). The housing question and widely shared experiences of dwelling literally affected the life of every Soviet citizen: 'Character was formed and careers were made in cramped living conditions, through squabbles and friendships as neighbours battled over square metres of floor space. For millions of people in the USSR, possessing their own home was their ultimate dream' (ibid.).

Yet, again, diversity in implementation marked an otherwise universal tension. The overarching ideological goals were embedded in concerns for developing each of the Union's republics into a common modernity. Especially in the Muslim Soviet republics, the Soviet state articulated a specific need to take measures to overcome the perceived traditional and patriarchal notions of family and gender, as well as the local importance of extended families and kinship as primary focal points of identification, solidarity, and loyalty. The promotion of the nuclear family as the central unit of society and also of women's equality and liberation in economic, political, and everyday life were parts of the Soviet agenda. These constituted a new impulse for the intended modernisation of society that had been started already in pre-Soviet times by Muslim reformers.

Thus we know that the 'original plans for a socialist form of housing were distorted, sometimes almost beyond recognition, by ideological confusion, financial constraints, corruption, ineptness, the banality of daily life [...] and by tacit obstruction on the part of citizens' (Attwood 2010: 1). But we do not know very exactly what happened instead.

Among the dominant debates in post-Soviet scholarship is the question of 'how thoroughly did the Soviet state transform its supposedly conservative Muslim population?' (Liu 2011: 118). Answers to that question have led to a grand dichotomy within Western scholarship on Central Asia that equally applies to the Caucasus. Deniz Kandiyoti (1996) criticised these two major discourses: one group of scholars has emphasised the assimilating effects of Soviet over traditional culture that produced 'cultural convergence', while the second group has insisted that the resilient character of local cultures made for a 'relative lack of penetrative capacity of the Soviet state' (Kandiyoti 1996: 530). As a way to allow explanation in between these extreme positions, I take an intermediate position. Azerbaijan is not explained in terms of either 'colonial onslaught or cultural stasis' (Kandiyoti 1996: 531–32). Rather, I try to give a differentiated account of both developments.

A focus on urban housing allows this approach. As I will show, classifying different types of dwellings as 'modern' or 'traditional' was much embedded in Soviet ideology. How such dwelling types were evaluated in local discourses had an important impact on how inhabitants and whole neighbourhoods became publicly stigmatised and subject to the politics of urban transformation. But still, as it has been argued with regard to the dynamic interplay of Muslim and Soviet identities, either could be mobilised as a positive force in Soviet society. 'Playing simultaneously the roles of the Soviet person (even that of the convinced communist) and of the Muslim more often than not was no contradiction [...], for each of the roles had a space of its own' (Abashin 2014: 181, for Baku see Tohidi 1996).

Housing, Privatisation, and Moral Economies after Socialism

The ideological foundation of socialism is, overall, strongly related to a housing question. It was clear that the increasing number of workers in the urban industries of the mid-nineteenth century were living in increasingly precarious conditions. Hence, in the *Communist Manifesto*, Marx and Engels (2009 [1848]) called for the abolition of (bourgeois) private property. With the Bolshevik Revolution, it was Lenin (2017 [1917]) who called for the 'expropriation of the expropriators', which provided housing for the proletariat in former bourgeois homes (although, as I show in Chapter 3, the practical transformation of ownership in the post-revolutionary years constituted a complicated and ambiguous process).

In fact, there was some disagreement about why workers' living conditions in the mid-nineteenth century were so dismal. Engels did not perceive the unsanitary overcrowded conditions of the proletariat as something particular to industrialisation. Instead, he thought of it as having equally characterised the oppressed classes at all times of history. Industrialisation had rather, so he thought, produced a housing shortage because of the sudden rush of population to cities. Industrialisation had thus increased rents, cramped living conditions, and raised the precarity of workers and the petty bourgeoisie alike (Engels 1872/73).

Either way, pre-revolutionary Baku seemed to fit the general pattern of urbanisation being accompanied by a housing shortage. Due to its important role as the centre of the oil industry in Tsarist Russia since the

1870s, Baku's overall population almost doubled between 1897 and 1913 from about 112,000 to 215,000 inhabitants (Altstadt 1992: 32), of various ethnic and class backgrounds. The oil business was the main driver for the city's growth. It attracted not only international investors, merchants, and administrators, but also peasants from the countryside who sought employment in the oil industry or railroad construction. The latter formed the 'Azerbaijani Turkish proletariat'. They joined an existing 'international' working class of different ethnic backgrounds including Iranian Azerbaijanis, Persians, Tats, Daghestanis, and Volga Tatars, and their labour migration to the new centre of the country's economy 'was the single most dramatic social change of the era' (ibid. 36).

The First World War, but especially the February Revolution and October Revolution of 1917 and the following years of Russian Civil War (1918–22), further exacerbated the precarious living conditions in the city, especially for the workers – despite the existence of the short-lived Azerbaijan Democratic Republic from 1918–20 (for details see Altstadt 1992: 74–107). After the Bolsheviks seized power in Baku in April 1920, as well documented by the archives, the housing question (*zhilishchnyi vopros*) or housing crisis (*zhilishchnyi krizis*) were among the most important for the new government to address – a topic to be dealt with in Chapter 2 and Chapter 3.

With regard to socialist housing, sociologists and political scientists have provided a significant body of literature on legal mechanisms, policies, and inequalities (DiMaio 1974; Barry 1977; Morton 1980; Hegedüs and Tosics 1983; Szelényi 1983; Andrusz 1984, 1990; Bater 1984; Sillince 1990; Hamilton 1993; Brumfield and Ruble 1994; Struyk 1996). Historians have more recently contributed to producing a qualitative picture of housing as it was experienced by citizens and approached by the state (Boym 1994; Obertreis 2004; Semenova 2004; Attwood 2010; Smith 2010; Harris 2013). What is remarkable, however, is that all these studies have been conducted in Soviet Russia or Central and Eastern Europe. Comparable data on the former peripheries of the Caucasus and Central Asia are mostly lacking. Yet it was in these regions that state propaganda insisted on the need for the greatest change.

Accounts of Soviet housing typically focus on Khrushchev's housing programme from 1956 onwards as being characterised by the unexpected paradox of an expansion in citizens' ownership rights. The construction of mass housing stoked citizens' longing for a separate apartment and a family privacy that, in previous decades, had been the privilege of only a few people (Trudolyubov 2018). In the Khrushchev period (1953–64), the 'tenant of an apartment was beginning to look more like an owner' and 'first steps

were taken towards a more secure right of residential ownership'
(Trudolyubov 2018: 150). Mark Smith (2010) showed, however, that the
legal underpinnings for property ownership existed much earlier. Indeed, in
a series of measures between 1917 and 1922, the Bolsheviks abolished
private property in order to hasten the demise of the inherent socio-economic
inequalities associated with capitalism. The property of homeowners in cities
was expropriated and municipalised. But some of this property was returned.
This happened in Baku too: after the general municipalisation of private
homes, quite a substantial share of property was returned to previous owners,
either as a result of official applications or because the dwellings were
deemed unsuitable for re-allocation by the authorities (see Chapter 3).

Despite ideological declarations, Soviet property relations were
complex and the urban housing fund was divided in several tenures. In
simplest terms, property ownership remained possible because private
property (*chastnaia sobstvennost'*) was abolished, but personal property
(*lichnaia sobstvennost'*) was not. It was personal property, 'which allowed a
citizen to own his home, legally, albeit within novel constraints and on the
terms of "socialist morality"' (Smith 2010: 5). Hence, Soviet tenures meant
for residents 'a substantial share of de jure or de facto ownership' which
resulted in the persistence and even flourishing of a citizen's status as an
individual owner (ibid.). In summary, this meant that:

> The Bolsheviks abolished private property in housing [...], with
> serious legal reductions in the status of ownership. Most notably,
> they removed the owner's legal right to extract profit from housing.
> This transformed the economic relationship between individuals—
> and between individuals and their housing. Dwellings now became,
> in legal terms, items only of consumption, with no revenue-raising
> implications. Yet individuals could still own urban housing, and they
> retained limited possibilities for renting parts of it out. The
> consequences of this underpinned the whole housing economy. [...]
> Private property had certainly gone, but individual ownership on a
> major scale remained, even in formal legal terms (Smith 2010: 144).

From an anthropological viewpoint, it is interesting to ask: what does
individual ownership mean in a society that puts such emphasis on family
and kin and perceives housing as a collective resource? This question
appears several times in the book.

It is also important to note that the Soviet state was inconsistent in its
approach to the private construction of dwellings. Private construction was
mostly discouraged by government regulations (concerning for instance the
allocation of building plots, allocation of construction material, credit, etc.);
but sometimes the state supported individual construction because it reduced

the state's responsibility to provide homes for citizens. In rural areas, private construction (on state allocated lots) was the norm throughout the Soviet period. In urban areas, private individual building was especially widespread in the immediate post-war period and continued until a coherent state policy first emerged with Khrushchev's mass housing campaign. Until that time, people often built houses by and for themselves with little interference (Andrusz 1984; Trudolyubov 2018: 146).

Retaining property ownership was not necessarily advantageous during the later Soviet period. The state had a responsibility to maintain and improve the property it owned, and to provide infrastructure for citizens to whom it allocated housing. It had no such responsibility to keep up houses owned as 'personal property'. This means that during post-Soviet privatisation, those who obtained their previously allocated apartments as private property gained a major resource in the new economy. For many urbanites, their privatised house or apartment became the major and sometimes only noteworthy asset and 'the chief source of household wealth' (Zavisca 2012: 1). For others, including the long-term owners of poorly maintained and dilapidated urban dwellings, private property was less an asset than a liability (Alexander 2009: 46). In my assessment, families with privatised apartments had been favoured doubly – first, by being allocated an apartment, and second by solidifying and legalising it as private property. The disadvantages faced by those who did not gain from the privatisation of state apartments are not only in economic but also ideological terms (see Chapter 2).

At the same time, privatisation did not simply produce a category of winning new owners against losing old owners. The Soviet state's housing allocation system had been hierarchically organised and had created spatial inequalities and residential differentiation along occupational group lines (Hamilton 1993). This meant that the 'state's decision to distribute apartments [...] cemented the results of the Soviet hierarchical distribution of accommodation' (Trudolyubov 2018: 167). Some occupations enjoyed more privileges in housing than others. For working-class people, housing usually depended on the size and local importance of their industry. State institutions, universities, and cultural institutions were concentrated in the centre, as was most of the housing stock for their employees. Although having been ideologically framed as a society of equals, housing during Soviet times came to represent the most tangible sphere for the experience and visualisation of social inequalities. For some groups of inhabitants, privatisation and the new housing 'market' therefore marked a continuity of their previous social positions while for others it marked a rupture with their standing in society.

Like elsewhere, in today's Azerbaijan, housing and homeownership is among the major concerns in people's life. It usually constitutes the biggest monetary expense during one's lifetime. During socialism, people had to invest other resources, most importantly time, as waiting for an apartment could take many years. Furthermore, today, homeownership is considered the normal condition of living – having one's own property. Renting is often associated with low socio-economic status. It also has negative ideological associations because the right of private house-owners to sub-let their property, retained under socialism, reflects 'one of the greatest anomalies, from the point of view of Soviet ideology'. It was the 'unplanned and un-coordinated nature of labour movements in a situation of general accommodation shortage' that provided 'a basis for the continued existence of a landlord "stratum"' (Andrusz 1984: 104). The negative associations, however, accrue more to the tenants than to the landlords.

The waiting lists for housing in the Soviet Union stood representatively for 'a complicated socio-political phenomenon' of socialist bureaucracy to which citizens' access or denial 'became a crucial barometer of the relationship between an individual and the state' (Trudolyubov 2018: 160). One important characteristic of socialist planned economies in general was the 'rational distribution' (Konrád and Szelényi 1979) of goods and resources from the centre to state institutions, industries, and citizens which I discuss in Chapter 3. I apply Katherine Verdery's notion of 'allocative power' or 'bureaucratic allocation' in socialist systems which, paired with endemic shortage, led institutions to hoard materials and labour (Verdery 1991). Here, allocative power refers to 'the bureaucracy's *capacity* to allocate' (Verdery 1991: 421, emphasis in original). Though the model refers most clearly to the production of consumption items, hoarding strategies were more widespread. Citizens navigated in and made use of the Soviet housing regime with tacit knowledge of these strategies. With regard to all 'things' that were perceived as scarce resources, citizens, families and state-representatives alike applied strategies to acquire them outside the official allocation system, namely through informal activities on the secondary market.

When looking at how people engaged in housing privatisation and how they have pragmatically approached the new notions of private property, in Baku, people often gave more weight to customary and cultural notions of property than those found in the newly applied privatisation law (see Chapter 6). Patriarchal biases and gendered discrimination within families as well as in state institutions also led to tensions and conflicts during but also after privatisation. This wider process has been described as 'post-Soviet gender ideologies promoting "traditional" gender hierarchies and endorsing the official restoration of male privilege' (Kandiyoti 2007: 602). But is it so simple?

In discussing property and the issue of patriarchy or patriarchal control of property, in the longer-term after privatisation, I ask how different generations cope with such tensions and negotiate their dependencies, rights, and obligations amidst normative power differences such as gender and age. Dealing with such matters, I follow anthropologists who have long been emphasising that in order to grasp the meaning of and social practices around property, it is misleading to stick to legal and economic notions of property alone. Instead, anthropologists deal with the 'embeddedness of property' in regional and social contexts (Hann 1998). Instead of describing the relation between subjects and objects, 'property relations are consequently better seen as social relations between people' (Hann 1998: 4) which are, above all, concerned with 'the distribution of social entitlements' (Hann 1998: 7). Taking the example of housing, I illustrate how such distributional processes in ownership rights have been negotiated after privatisation (see Chapter 6).

With regard to property in general and houses in particular, besides describing it as an asset in the language of market economy, it makes more sense from an anthropological viewpoint to conceive of the house as a base for domestic economy (Gudeman and Rivera 1990) or, what can be broadly defined as 'house economies' (Gudeman and Hann 2015). As I will show in Chapter 4, houses and apartments constitute a base for economic activities, either through their opportunities to allow for employment (e.g. opening a shop), storage, or the possibility to have revenues from renting out. In other cases, apartments as commodities on the market constitute the basis for economic action. Regarding the 'growth of the house [...] through slow accumulation', I will describe how 'savings', or resources more generally:

> are kept as hoards and often put into the house, such as adding a room, a new story, an agricultural plot, or acquiring display items. In developed market economies savings may go toward house improvements for the pleasure they afford, for their display value, or in the hope they will yield a higher sale price of the house (Gudeman 2016: 17).

People's engagement in these house economies, as I describe with my ethnographic cases, corresponds greatly with what anthropologists have described as different kinds of 'transactional orders' (Bloch and Parry 1989). According to Maurice Bloch and Jonathan Parry, the phrase describes 'two related but separate transactional orders: on the one hand transactions concerned with the reproduction of the long-term social or cosmic order; on the other, a "sphere" of short-term transactions concerned with the arena of individual competition' (ibid.: 24). Both orders and their interaction are represented in house-related processes, as will be illustrated by my ethnographic material. There are two cosmic orders to be taken into account: one is the cosmic order that people imagine as being crucial for their cultural identity, the other is the cosmic order of socialist and postsocialist national ideology as understood and represented by the state. I understand people's long-term motivations in the housing sphere as their aspirations to reproduce the social and moral order of the family. The short-term cycle of acquisition and mobilisation of resources, which are oriented towards these long-term motivations, varies with changing social, economic, and political circumstances.

In other words, people use their acquired financial resources for the long-term motivation to provide secure housing for their family and children and to enable the latter to get married and found their own family. The concept of transactional order in its original context was also about challenging existing debates on the difference and suggested distinction between gifts and commodities (e.g. Gregory 1982; Parry and Bloch 1989; Carrier 1995, 2003; Osteen 2002). Bloch and Parry's concept of two transactional orders proposed that 'gifts' and 'commodities' inform and influence each other. Hence, houses embody qualities of both gift and commodity with the former including a whole range of future obligations of the receiving children towards their parents. Further, both dimensions of the house as a gift and a commodity can be transformed several times and switch between being commodity and gift.

Importantly, people's past experiences with Soviet housing and welfare still provide a framework within which citizens structure their economic behaviours and express expectations from the state. Socialist housing constituted a prime example of a 'mixed economy' that integrates all three modes of integration developed by Polanyi (Hann 1992). It entailed reciprocity within and beyond the family in the form of social support. It was a good redistributed (or rather allocated) by the state to its citizens. And it integrated elements of a market (such as being the case with cooperative housing, or on informal paths of the second economy).

In the last part of this section, I will discuss the moral economies of housing in connection to political economy. This connection has been taken up by some anthropologists (Alexander et al. 2018), and even by cultural geographers (Aalbers and Christophers 2014). The concept of 'moral economy' as developed by E. P. Thompson (1971) and James Scott (1976) points to the mutually related struggles between political, economic, social, affective, and moral values and systems at play in 'housing questions'. Following recent authors who aimed at strengthening anthropological research on the 'moral economies of housing', I hold that the concept of moral economy is useful because it helps to link 'popular understandings of social justice, moral obligations, rights and entitlements to persistent structural inequalities' (Alexander et al. 2018: 123).

Among everything else, this book demonstrates processes of social inclusion and exclusion by looking at moral considerations and changing political approaches towards housing in the socialist and postsocialist periods. Housing is one important expression of a social contract between citizens and the state as the former are entitled to material resources, most importantly housing, in return for obligations rendered to the state. However, 'while in the post-war decades, housing was often presented as a right gained through criteria of citizenship and labour, the advent of neoliberalism, financialisation and austerity have redrawn the lines between those who are included and those who are not' (ibid.: 123). I will illustrate and discuss manifold concerns and challenges that people from different backgrounds, age, gender, and status have been coping with in regard to housing (Chapter 4). Questions of morality, solidarity, and support among kin are as relevant as encounters with state representatives at the local, regional, and national levels. It will become clear that multiple 'moral communities' exist. Although it was my experience that people aspired to basically the same moral principles of kin solidarity and cooperation in practice as in public discourse, their everyday acts sometimes followed other patterns than the pronounced cultural and national ideals.

Socialist Legacies, Transformations, and Post-Soviet States

The legacy of the Soviet past comes in a variety of faces. Notwithstanding the manifold social, economic, and political transformations, the imprint of seventy years of socialist experiment are manifold. Most citizens in former Soviet cities, to date, have their homes in socialist pre-fabricated mass housing estates. And even larger housing estates – be it elite gated communities, dull apartment blocks without public spaces, or empty buildings – are being constructed today. In many parts of the post-Soviet world, these estates dominate the cityscapes, even if they are only meant to serve as a backstage for the new futuristic materialities of the urban centres. Perhaps the cityscapes are in direct relation to the strong element of centralisation that still characterises the new governments in the region. Certainly there are some who have proposed that the 'centrally planned nature of the original project affects how it develops in the post-Soviet economy' (Trudolyubov 2018: 203).

In general, the economic, social, and political transformations of former socialist and Soviet states since the early 1990s have been extensively discussed by anthropologists (e.g. Verdery 1996, 2003; Bridger and Pine 1998; Humphrey 1998, 2002; Burawoy and Verdery 1999; Berdahl et al. 2000; Hann 2002, 2006). Altogether, these authors take a critical stance towards popular models and narratives of a unilineal transition from a socialist system towards market economy and liberal democracy. Instead, an anthropological 'focus on the day-to-day realities of postsocialism reveals a much more ambiguous account of the transformation announced with such fanfare by theories of modernization and of market and democratic transition' (Burawoy and Verdery 1999: 6).

Anthropologists working on the Caucasus and Central Asia have written about changes in urban life and imaginations of urban spaces as well as about the reconfigurations of urban landscapes and public places (Alexander et al. 2007; Darieva et al. 2011; Fehlings 2014). Others have thematised the new utopias and futuristic visions that the governments in the oil-rich states of Azerbaijan and Kazakhstan promote by prestigious architectural edifices (Grant 2014; Laszczkowski 2016). With reference to Baku, the American anthropologist Bruce Grant (2014) has described the continuity of the Soviet practice of 'paper architecture' by the Aliyev government. He pointed to the Soviet heritage of architecture and public space as being used by postsocialist regimes for shaping public imaginaries. In other words, Soviet depictions of architectural achievements, planned projects, and yet-to-come utopias of the socialist future were widely circulated by the state. A similar, though technologically updated strategy can be observed in present-day Baku where digital renderings visually represent the country's prosperous future by means of existing, planned, and never-to-be-finished showcase projects. It seems paradoxical that the aspirations of many post-Soviet states to overbuild their socialist urban history and materiality are 'deeply haunted by socialist contexts' (Grant 2014: 505). Similarly, Victor Buchli talked about the supreme significance of architecture in the quest to extend state power and to generate new social structures and moralities (Buchli 1997, 2002).

In these examples, politics is conducted on a symbolic level by the use of architecture and ideology (see Chapter 2). The consensus view focuses on the visual 'spectacle' under creation. In addition to architecture, public events, holiday celebrations, and other performances contribute to a similar politics of projection from the state to its citizen-subject-audience. Writing with reference to Uzbekistan, Laura Adams concluded that '[S]pectacle monopolizes discourse by privileging the definition of truth and reality belonging to the elites and by using technology such as the mass media to create a one-way flow of communication, speech without response' (Adams 2010: 3). With spectacle, a state is promoting its 'domination over the shared meaning of concepts such as heritage and progress' (Adams 2010: 5) with an aim of mobilisation. In Azerbaijan, mass spectacles are also mounted on national holidays, such as the birthday of the former president and 'saviour of the nation' – Heydar Aliyev – or Martyrs' Day on 20 January to commemorate the tragic events of Black January in 1990 when Soviet troops entered Baku and killed more than 130 civilians. Another kind of mass spectacle that the state has been actively engaging in recent years is hosting international mega events as part of its international propaganda and marketing strategy (see Chapter 2).

Monographs on Baku in particular are nevertheless scarce. They have discussed topics like political economy and social transformation (Barrett 2016), the life of Baku intellectuals in the early 1990s (Demirdirek 1993), or the changing life of women in Soviet and post-Soviet Baku (Heyat 2002). In general though, it is the state that has captured the most attention among anthropologists of the Caucasus and Central Asia. In addition to discussion of the state's 'spectacles', research has included the role and perception of the state in the context of legal pluralisms (Voell and Kaliszewska 2015) and the interrelation between people and state through the concept of citizenship (Yalçın-Heckmann 2012; Mühlfried 2014). Other contributions have recently popularised notions of 'affective states' (Militz and Schurr 2016; Laszczkowski and Reeves 2017a). According to these authors '"affective states" [...] cover a range of affects, feelings, and emotions for and about "the state" and its agents, and explore how those contribute to the state's emergence, transformation, endurance, or erosion' (Laszczkowski and Reeves 2017b: 2). Such mobilisation of affective feelings towards the Soviet or post-Soviet Azerbaijani state will also reappear frequently in the following chapters. With regard to the many contemporary states in the region where, during the early 1990s, former Soviet elites established firm and dynastic regimes (Azerbaijan, Kazakhstan, Turkmenistan, Uzbekistan, Tajikistan), it is no surprise that scholars have frequently applied concepts such as neopatrimonialism (Safiyev 2018) or authoritarianism. In the introduction to their book *Ethnographies of the State in Central Asia: Performing Politics*, the editors rightly mark that the frequently applied term 'authoritarian' can only act as a shorthand to describe these regimes. It is only through 'intimate explorations of how the state is experienced and produced in everyday encounters' that we can 'provide insights into the nature of contemporary authoritarianism' (Rasanayagam et al. 2014: 5). In my book, I hope to contribute insights on experiencing authoritarianism with special reference to the state's role in Baku's urban remaking and public representation.

In all the above-described contexts, state ideologies have played an unabated role in shaping state-citizen relations – a characteristic that has not changed amidst so many other aspects of transformation. As other anthropologists, I use the term 'ideology' not in the Marxist pejorative sense of mere propaganda or false consciousness. Rather, ideologies are 'systemically structured processes and [...] experienced social relations through which human subjectivities are constituted and through which humans act upon the world' (Verdery 1995: 9). In other words, ideologies are 'beliefs or ideas materialized in action' (ibid.). In my understanding, such a definition includes, but also goes beyond, Geertz's approach to ideology as a 'cultural system', (i.e. a system of symbolic meaning) (Geertz 1973: 193–233). We can comparatively approach emic narratives of kinship, state, nation, society, culture, or modernity within the analytic framework of ideologies. From an anthropological perspective, and coming back to the role of affections, ideologies are able to endow these very concepts with efficacious collective emotions. 'Ideology bridges the emotional gap between things as they are and as one would have them be' (Geertz 1973: 205) – an attestation which seems nowhere more suitable than in the Soviet context. As such, ideological thought is emotionally charged and a crucial component in state-citizen relations. It is not by surprise that political anthropologists working on Central Asia have recently come up with concepts of the spectacular and affective state, as explained above. And houses, as buildings, have been there all along: after all Soviet ideology encompassed questions of infrastructure and architecture, and state officials believed in the transformative effect of building, both literally and figuratively, towards a new socialist way of life (Humphrey 2005).

Politics of (Mis)Representation

On a broader level, this book is concerned with the politics of (mis)representation as it has unfolded in the Soviet and more recent history of Azerbaijan's capital city, Baku. An immediate term that comes to mind and which has also been used by some of my informants to describe recent regional development is 'Potemkin villages' (Ru. *Potemkinskie derevni*). This popular metaphor captures the ambiguities and the tensions between official public representation and the everyday realities that unfold behind the façade politics in many post-Soviet capitals. Today, this expression has gained universal popularity and is widely used to describe 'something that appears elaborate and impressive but in actual fact lacks substance'[7] or 'an impressive facade or show designed to hide an undesirable fact or

---

[7] http://www.thefreedictionary.com/Potemkin+village (last accessed on 25.01.2017).

condition'.[8] The term's historical origin refers to how Prince Grigorii Potemkin, a Russian military leader and favourite of Catherine the Great, supposedly used façade villages to fool the Tsarina and her delegation when they visited the newly conquered lands of Crimea in 1787. Although having been deconstructed as a myth, an exaggerated allegation disseminated by the Saxon envoy Georg von Helbig (Panchenko 1999; Montefiore 2001: 380), this 'narrative of duplicitous stagecraft' has been 'so enduring [that] it has persisted to the present day' (David-Fox 2012: 20). In other words, it conveys central images about the relationship between state representatives of different hierarchies, the relation between and mutual perception of domestic elites and foreign delegates, and between rulers and the ruled. Another essential component in the narrative is the active interaction between people and architecture, whether real or fake, and its power to create factual realities. I argue that transposing the Potemkin narrative into post-Soviet urban contexts allows us to approach recent developments in the region from an alternative angle. Hence, I develop the concept of the *Potemkin city* to highlight the relevance of the Potemkin myth within urban contexts, the specific role which cities play as showcases for national and international promotion, and the heuristic value for research within and beyond post-Soviet space. What I want to make clear from the outset, in taking the example of Azerbaijan, is that I do not mean this term or any other in the derogative political senses in which they are so often used. Baku is no more a 'Potemkin' city than Moscow, Berlin, Washington, or London. The politics of (mis)representation discussed in this book – *Potemkin city, façade politics, papereality, pərdə*, and *pokazukha* – are locally and historically contextualised phenomena that arguably have permeated daily social, economic, and political interactions in all times and at all places, sometimes more, sometimes less obvious. They are, so to say, the basics of what we call diplomacy. And more generally, of politics. In German, such political stagecraft is referred to as 'Protokollstrecke'; the term is especially well known to people who lived in the former GDR where it referred concretely to the official routes taken by domestic and international politicians and that served as deliberate showcases (and to conceal shortcomings of the system) (Wolle 1998: 163). In other words, it refers to the universal political performance of self-representation at one's best. What makes the difference in each case, however, is the degree to which the representation matches the represented reality.

With regard to the Soviet state, historian Michael David-Fox (2012) has elaborately described such techniques and their underlying historical,

---

[8] https://www.merriam-webster.com/dictionary/Potemkin%20village (last accessed on 25.01.2017).

ideological, and political relevance as the 'Potemkin Village Dilemma' that characterised the early Soviet state's elaborate methods of *kul'tpokaz* (cultural show). This dilemma was real in that 'it exposed the Soviet urge to plan, limit, and control what visitors did and saw' while the latter where well aware of and only expected to be presented 'Potemkin villages' (David-Fox 2012: 126). Western diplomats and prominent supporters of the Soviet experiment were one important audience for the 'show', especially in the 1920s and 1930s, but David-Fox also cautioned that 'model sites of socialism' were not 'built solely to dupe foreigners'; they were also of critical 'importance for the push to transform the […] population' (David-Fox 2012: 8). Hence, I will show that present techniques of national representation are significantly rooted in Soviet ideology and politics towards urban development and modernisation, which were largely embedded in sophisticated techniques of *kul'tpokaz* – of showing-off 'culture'.

Scholars who deal with urban transformations and state politics in post-Soviet space sporadically refer to the Potemkin village metaphor (Allina-Pisano 2008; Heathershaw 2014: 29; Laszczkowski 2014: 166, 168). However, a number of accounts on Central Asia and the Caucasus have discussed similar dynamics under a variety of different notions. That of the 'spectacle', as discussed above, has been one of the more pronounced. Yet I still prefer the concept of the Potemkin city.

To me, this term still seems best for conveying the balance of local and universal qualities at play in Azerbaijan's and Baku's politics of performance. Moreover, it should call to attention not only the arts of distraction, but also of indulgence. The term itself was coined by the Austrian architect and publicist Adolf Loos (1870–1933) who harshly polemicised against the lavish architecture, ornamentation, and decadent lifestyle in the city of Vienna around the *fin-de-siècle*. In his brief article 'Die Potemkin'sche Stadt' (the Potemkin City), which was originally published in 1898, Loos criticised the palace-like architecture and ornamentation of apartment buildings in Vienna of that time as an expression of false and pretentious human existence.

While refraining, again, from any kind of similar moral judgement, I think that the concept serves as a useful category to approach the façade politics throughout the Soviet Union and not only in Baku. As David-Fox also insisted about Soviet *kul'tpokaz*, this is and was 'an elaborate, top-down political stagecraft' and its ability to convince both foreign and domestic observers, whatever their degree of scepticism, is linked to the fact that it is 'lavishly enacted on a regular basis' (David-Fox 2012: 8).

Hence, in Chapter 2, I argue that Baku's present urban development and Azerbaijan's representational strategy provide an illustrative example of a Potemkin city. I shall emphasise the prevalence of a two-fold process that decision-makers apply in a strategic way for elevating the city's (and ergo the nation's) image to the world, to its own citizens, and also to political superiors. On the one hand, urban landscapes are boosted by the construction and renewal of architectural showcases and model sites that represent a modern, prosperous, and sovereign nation. On the other hand, we can observe an active strategy of concealment regarding those unfavourable spaces that do not match the government's envisaged vision of the national future. Today, this concealment happens at various levels: visually it is achieved through the extensive use of walls along major traffic routes, as well as by the superficial application of new façades to publicly exposed buildings, without actually renovating them. This also hides the increasing socio-spatial inequalities that have exacerbated in recent years. The Potemkin city is part of a wider *façade politics* that characterise not only political interaction and processes of representation but also penetrate citizens' interactions with the state, their everyday lives, codes of conduct, and private spheres. Ultimately, this book describes different aspects of such façade politics in the context of people's housing experiences by using ethnographic, oral, and historical accounts. Thereby, I aim at contributing to existing literature on urban transformation in postsocialist contexts.

Surprisingly, there have been few attempts among urban anthropologists to approach recent processes with a broader comparative focus on spatial and historical commonalities and continuities. But the post-Soviet states' and citizens' long-standing embeddedness in a centralised Soviet ideological, political, and bureaucratic system with its institutionalised and sophisticated politics of representation, I think, sets an important basis for comparative studies to follow. The concepts of the Potemkin city and façade politics can provide such a framework for a systematic and critical comparison of the recent material, social, and political transformations in post-Soviet urban spaces. This will enable a better understanding of the social and political dynamics behind the façade of an aspiring Caucasian metropolis and beyond.

Other material façades and politics of representation that have been of crucial importance in the Soviet housing regime and processes of allocation, are well described by David Dery's concept of papereality (Dery 1998) which I use as an analytical tool in Chapter 3. According to Dery, 'organizations create and maintain [...] "papereality", defined as a world of symbols, or written representations, that take precedence over the things and events represented' (Dery 1998: 678). I maintain that papereality constituted the very basis for the state's management of housing allocation and the planned economy in general. However, I argue that there were several paperealities existent as written representations which, in many cases, were constantly modified and reinterpreted by state representatives in the bureaucratic hierarchy as an outcome of their formal and informal interactions with citizens. Not only bureaucrats but every economic institution in the socialist centrally-planned economy manipulated realities by means of reports, tables, and paperwork in order to increase their 'allocative power' (Verdery 1991).

Shifting the attention on façade politics from the level of the state to everyday performances of impression management (Goffman 1959) and interaction among family members, neighbours and society in general, I then discuss the emic Azerbaijani notion of *pərdə* (see Chapter 5). *Pərdə* means curtain in the strict sense and constitutes an indispensable domestic object without which a home is considered incomplete. In a metaphorical sense, though, the term has profound social and moral implications which is best captured by the Azerbaijani phrase of *pərdə saxlamaq*, meaning 'maintaining' or 'protecting' the curtain, meaning one's personal and family privacy but also respecting others' privacy, intimacy, and secrets. Analogous to properly setting up the window curtains, which is about the skilful physical and visual protection of private space and affairs from the public, *pərdə saxlamaq* stands for similar skills and requirements to master instances of social interaction between people of different gender, age, and status according to prevalent social expectations within a local community or society at large. On a broader level, the concept of *pərdə saxlamaq* refers to protecting a person's, a family's, or another social group's honour – 'to save face' – in many other socio-cultural contexts. While 'maintaining the curtain' emphasises the collectively shared moral value to keep private family matters within the house, the same practice is applicable on the state level when governmental actors promote the Azerbaijani nation while concealing and hiding social, institutional, and legal deficits. As Michael Herzfeld has argued, 'state ideologies and the rhetoric of everyday social life are revealingly similar' (Herzfeld 2005: 2) – a phrase that applies well to the Azerbaijan case. If in small-scale interactions *pərdə* aims at maintaining the intimacy of the house (see Chapter 5), we can see many examples of how this serves a similar purpose on the national level (see Chapter 2). Most importantly, it represents a technique of 'cultural intimacy' which describes 'the recognition of those aspects of a cultural identity that are considered a source of external embarrassment but that nevertheless provide insiders with their assurance of common sociality' (Herzfeld 2005: 3).

The Potemkin metaphors, paper architecture, papereality, and *pərdə* do all 'describe gaps between external appearances and underlying realities' (Pisano 2018: 278). There was another expression, known across the former Soviet Union, which also appeared in local discourses during my research: *pokazukha*. Derived from the Russian word *pokaz*, which means 'display', 'presentation', or 'show', it was a slang and derogatory term 'signifying the wool pulled over someone's eyes' (David-Fox 2012: 99). Yet anthropologists have provided more nuanced accounts of the term's meanings and use in daily social interaction, which underscores its close relation to cultural intimacy. *Pokazukha*, they found, 'constitutes the main pattern of public behavior [...]. The Russian word pokazukha refers to putting on a false show to cover up the actual state of affairs. It is a strategy to manipulate the impressions and opinions of strangers' (Sántha and Safonova 2011: 75). In their account, the authors describe the collective effort of a village community in Buryatia, in staging the vibrant life and use of the local House of Culture during the visit of a commission from the capital city.

The usually dominant feature of the House of Culture is its abandoned condition. Rather than offering an endless and diverse array of cultural activities and entertainment, the building serves as an informal marketplace for women selling imported cosmetics from China. But with the arrival of the commission, 'people pull together in an attempt to conduct *pokazukha*, to create the illusion that these organizations actually function effectively and are free of serious problems or defects, when in fact nothing functions properly or according to the plan' (ibid.: 75–76). *Pokazukha* presentations were actually widespread in the regional state-funded institutions, which means that the commission was probably not deeply deceived (ibid.: 92). But the authors suggest that this may not matter: 'The pokazukha show is appreciated by the bureaucratic institutions of the state, because the stable image of a culture and community gives the impression of controllability' (Sántha and Safonova 2011: 93). It seems that, even when there is no one left to fool, maintaining curtains, projecting spectacles, making paper plans, and building façades is still important.

Such insight into the interaction between the state, local state institutions, and citizens in housing-related issues is critical (Chapter 3). However, if we transpose these performative and interactional insights into other social, political, and national contexts beyond the bureaucratic one, it will deepen our understanding of postsocialist societies, and not only those.

Chapter 2
Staging the Capital: Infrastructure, Modernisation, and the Potemkin City

First-time visitors to Azerbaijan's capital Baku are often stunned by the recently constructed and impressive architectural landscapes of the city along the main artery from the airport to the city centre. Having passed by monumental edifices and landmarks such as the Olympic Stadium, the twisted SOCAR Tower, the SOFAZ Tower[9], the Heydar Aliyev Centre, or the Port Baku Mall, one approaches the central districts at the shore of the Caspian Sea – an area that is made up of architectural ensembles of past and present model sites. The most prominent example is the walled İçəri Şəhər (lit. Inner City, but more commonly referred to as the Old or Medieval City) including Maiden Tower (Qız Qalası), the city's traditional landmark, surrounded by a ring of architectural gems from the oil boom of the late nineteenth century – all of them lavishly refurbished in recent years. These historical showcases, now meant to display the Azerbaijani nation's proud history, have been joined by newly built and futuristic-looking landmarks designed by foreign, internationally-renowned architects. They signal a new modernity and bright future for Azerbaijan as a prosperous, oil-rich, independent nation. Furthermore, the architecture of those new edifices similarly represents aspects and symbols of the country's cultural tradition. Most noteworthy along the Baku Bay are the Azerbaijan Carpet Museum (Azərbaycan Milli Xalça Muzeyi) in the shape of a furled carpet and the International Mugham Center (Beynəlxalq Muğam Mərkəzi) based on the shape of the tar – a string instrument being used in the country's traditional *muğam* music. Further to mention is National Flag Square (Dövlət Bayrağı Meydanı) prominently exposing the national flag with measurements of 70 by 35 metres from a 162-metre-high flagpole – the world's tallest flagpole until Dushanbe, Tajikistan erected a taller one. Adjacent to National Flag

---

[9] The two towers bear the names of the State Oil Company of the Azerbaijan Republic and the State Oil Fund of the Republic of Azerbaijan.

Square is Baku Crystal Hall (Bakı Kristal Zalı), built for hosting the 2012 Eurovision Song Contest. The view uphill towards the city's topological amphitheatre with its three natural terraces is dominated by the Flame Towers (Alov Qülləri). These three flame-shaped skyscrapers were inaugurated in 2013 and have become the city's most important landmark as they symbolise Azerbaijan's etymological identity as the 'Land of Fire'. At night, the towers are illuminated by LED-lights that animate flames or a waving national flag. In general, most of the prominent sites in the centre including parks, monuments, government buildings, and even residential buildings along the main roads are lavishly illuminated to present all the renovated façades of downtown Baku in a most favourable light.

Infrastructural developments and the implementation of prestigious architecture have been part of a wider construction boom – strongly pushed through the authoritarian government's political and economic entanglements. The state's flourishing oil sector has helped to pay for the tremendous transformations in Baku's urban landscape since the early 2000s. Simultaneously, such remaking has been accompanied by the large-scale demolition of pre-Soviet residential neighbourhoods. In public discourse such demolition is usually legitimated with reference to these areas' deficient infrastructure and dilapidated housing conditions. In light of such urban remaking, citizens' housing security and property rights do not count much against the government's ambitious transformation of cityspace (see also Grant 2014: 508).

These processes are part of a longer-term strategy that the government aims to implement that will promote Azerbaijan as an economically prosperous and sovereign state after seventy years of Soviet domination. The capital serves as the material embodiment of the country's modernisation and has become, increasingly, the stage for international mega-events. These events also serve as a political and cultural expression of the country's ambivalent foreign politics, as Azerbaijan is attached to Western states as well as to Russia (Ismayilov 2019). Image-makers emphasise values such as democracy, tolerance, diversity, and openness, as well as reliability as an economic and political partner. This national image is boosted by hosting international sport and culture events such as the Eurovision Song Contest in 2012, the first edition of the European Olympic Games in 2015, and the Formula One Grand Prix of Europe in June 2016 which has, since then, been held annually as the Formula One Azerbaijan Grand Prix. The importance of such a pro-Western national agenda in terms of domestic and foreign policy is well captured in a speech by President Ilham Aliyev at a meeting of the Organising Committee of the European Olympic Games in February 2013 (see also Roth 2019: 54):

Over the recent years, Azerbaijan has managed to assert itself
globally as a dynamic, modern and strong country. [...] The city
infrastructure is being modernised. Baku is one of the most beautiful
cities in the world today. It is noted for its beauty, historical
appearance, and modernity. Additional measures will be taken to
develop the urban infrastructure. We will continue to develop Baku
to make it even more beautiful.[10]

Seen from a different angle, most local intellectuals I met have criticised the
city's material transformation and the state's effort in creating a 'Dubai on
the Caspian'. They see that the effort to make Baku into a 'global city'
involves spending vast amounts of oil revenues on infrastructural projects,
but that there is no solid development plan to ensure that it is successful. To
a great extent, Baku's renovation serves the economic interests of decision-
makers (i.e. government officials and business elites) with little concern for
others (Valiyev 2013, 2014). The increasing power and authoritarian rule of
President Ilham Aliyev, who took over the presidency from his father
Heydar Aliyev in 2003, has resulted in the absence of an open civil society
and starkly contrasts with the country's official pro-Western promotion
strategy. Like public demonstrations in general, protests against the
demolition of residential areas or corrupt practices among political elites are
rare as people run the risk of being jailed for often fictitious accusations –
this happens regularly to human rights activists and opposition members.

US-anthropologist Bruce Grant illustrated that Baku's urban
development symbolically reflects more than just the 'showcasing [of] the
face of a brave new world' for international recognition (Grant 2014: 502). It
has also been seen as a result of the 'government's invocation of a certain
material strategy to exorcise the [Soviet] past and to compete on a world
stage' (ibid. 505). Building on Aihwa Ong's concept of 'hyperbuilding'
(Ong 2011), he argued that Baku is an example for the remaking of
authoritarian rule by a kind of discursive 'domination-through-surplus', but
it also follows a Soviet logic. 'Surplus' is expressed in at least three ways
(Grant 2014: 506–507): first, the financial surplus generated through the oil
sector is being directed to the remaking of Baku's urban centre; second, the
creation and restructuring of additional downtown areas involves a mass
eviction of thousands of inhabitants in Soviet and pre-Soviet residential
buildings; and third, there is a vast increase and dissemination of analogue
and digital illustrations in public space that depict images of future
constructions. This third surplus of plans and images very much resembles

---

[10] Ilham Aliyev chaired the first meeting of the Organizing Committee of the European
Olympic Games due to be held in Baku in 2015. http://en.president.az/articles/7175. Last
accessed 21 December 2016.

the 'paper architecture' of Soviet days – 'chronicles of the built and unbuilt that circulate in ways separate from actually existing structures' (ibid. 507). This draws attention to the resilience of former Soviet approaches to architecture and urban planning, even as part of the postsocialist utopia. Grant's analysis foregrounds socialist continuity, but I want to point, as well, to the changes within that continuity. Hyperbuilding also serves to obscure the dominant issue of housing in the everyday life of urban residents amidst the state's modernisation programme. And though architecture still points to the future, the shape of utopia and those whom it is intended to benefit have changed.

Azerbaijan's capital is far from being a unique case for the promotion of capital cities in former Soviet states, however, not all of them can draw on comparable economic resources and foreign investment. Similar developments have been documented for Georgia (Salukvadze and Golubchikov 2016), Armenia (Fehlings 2014), Turkmenistan (Koch 2015) and Kazakhstan (Buchli 2007; Bissenova 2014; Laszczkowski 2016). The 'spectacular urbanization' (Koch and Valiyev 2015) of Baku and other post-Soviet cities is not only a strategy to attract global attention and reputation. Towards the nation's citizens, it further serves the strengthening of national identities, the allocation of public funds for private interests, as well as a legitimation of the political status quo attached to large-scale urban transformation (Broudehoux 2007; Koch and Valiyev 2015; Müller 2015; Müller and Pickles 2015; Makarychev and Yatsyk 2016).

This chapter provides a general overview of the city's urban development in Soviet and present times with a special focus on infrastructure and housing. As part of my wider argument, I shall discuss the tension between the official representation of Baku as a modern city on the one hand and its impact on residential areas in the 'urban backstage' (Amin 2014) on the other. In particular, I focus on a neighbourhood locally known as Sovetski which is located in Baku's administrative district of Yasamal. My aim is to demonstrate how Soviet state ideologies and approaches of representing urban development and a modern society are applied in the present, though embedded in a completely different global context. For many inhabitants, memories towards socialism are very much alive and provide a template against which present developments are interpreted. As others have concisely summarised, there is a certain risk for scholars 'to lose sight of the still largely regnant Soviet cosmological frames that long lent, and still lend, so much meaning to so many' (Grant 2001: 333).

The Baku case points to the material and immaterial legacies of the socialist infrastructure regime and how they relate to current 'neoliberal' developments in the country (see also Roth 2019). I argue that the present government's techniques of promoting infrastructural renewal in the context of urban transformation as a symbol for national progress and modernisation shows much resemblance to the Soviet state's 'infrastructural ideology' and creation of a socialist utopia. Despite apparent continuities in the deployment of these techniques, however, there is a marked shift in how modernity and progress is shaped by the state. Of crucial significance is the abandonment of social welfare: in the Soviet narrative, the promised utopia constantly pointed to a near future without a housing shortage and strongly emphasised the benefits of infrastructure for the sake of its citizens. Today's emphasis, however, as echoed by the president's quote in the chapter's beginning, has shifted towards a generalised beauty, prosperity, and modernity. There is no named benefactor for the representational and impression management of Baku as the 'pearl of the Caspian'. Since the end of socialism, housing and other infrastructure increasingly transformed from a legal right of citizens into the most salient factor for accelerated social exclusion and spatial inequalities (Roth 2019: 58). In order to better understand the general developments in post-Soviet cities, I here propose to consider the subtle continuities and adaptations of Soviet approaches.

Façades, Sovetski, and the 'Other Baku'

We begin with a close look at the neighbourhood called Sovetski. From the mid-nineteenth century until the present, this neighbourhood has been 'typical' of many in Baku. It is typical in its architecture; it is also typical in how it persistently defies the city's planned image.

Sovetski is located close to, though invisible from, Azerbaijan Avenue. Azerbaijan Avenue is one of the main roads in the city centre; its side streets lead uphill to Sovetski. The street is an important connector between landmarks and various tourist sites such as İçəri Şəhər, Fountains Square (Fəvvarələr Meydanı), Winter Park (Qış parkı), and museums and national monuments. It is lined with multi-storey residential buildings from socialist times. As with most other buildings in publicly exposed inner-city areas, their façades have been renovated recently by applying the eclectic and historicist style of Baku's architecture in the late nineteenth and early twentieth century – at the peak of the country's first oil boom. Altogether, these buildings constitute a visual border to the hillside area located behind which also includes the Sovetski neighbourhood in the upper part. Architecturally, the buildings are connected with each other beyond the small streets that lead uphill and which can be accessed through the archways commonly built in major Soviet cities during Stalinist times. The architectural ensemble of buildings enhances the impression of a spatial division between the metropolitan frontstage along the main road and the urban backstage uphill.

Plate 1. Frontside view of residential buildings along Shaumian Street (later Gusi Gadzhiev Street and since 2008 Azerbaijan Avenue) before 1940.

By the time of my fieldwork, Sovetski was estimated to have around 50,000–60,000 inhabitants. Its lower part is marked by solid, good quality residential buildings from Tsarist times that later provided home to important national artists, writers, and composers during the Soviet era. The upper part consists of badly maintained small dwellings set-out around courtyards. These are predominantly occupied by multi-generational extended families, and are considered the hallmark of the area. The dwellings' chaotic appearance is mainly a result of continuous informal extensions to the original structures at times of marriage and other enlargements of the households. Plans for demolishing the neighbourhood have long existed but state-led 'gentrification by demolition' (Valiyev and Wallwork 2019) only began in 2014.

Plate 2. View over parts of Sovetski from uphill in February 2014 including the recently renovated Taza Pir Mosque. From left to right at the middle of the picture one can see the long row of residential buildings along Azerbaijan Avenue. The background marks a striking contrast with its numerous post-Soviet highrises.

Any precise delineation of the neighbourhood is difficult because its boundaries have shifted with state-led reconstruction activities during and after the Soviet period. The neighbourhood emerged in the second half of the nineteenth century as Baku developed rapidly from a small fortified port town with a predominately Muslim population into a booming centre of the global oil industry and the fastest growing city in Tsarist Russia (Swietochowski and Collins 1999: 32). The first oil boom, starting in the 1870s, resulted in an unprecedented rise in construction as immigration swelled with workers coming from other parts of Tsarist Russia, European investors, and unskilled Muslim workers from the countryside and nearby Persia.[11]

During my research, one interlocutor described early Sovetski, known then as Nagornaia, as 'some kind of semi-criminal favela' (a label that, by referring to a low-income slum neighbourhood that we know from the Brazilian context, already points to the negative perception shared by many

---

[11] For further details on Baku's history, socio-economic, and urban development in the nineteenth and twentieth centuries see Henry 1905; Fatullaev 1963; Swietochowski 1985; Altstadt 1992; Ashurbeili 1992; Fatullaev-Figarov 1998; Auch 2004; Rumyantsev 2008; Guliyeva 2011; Huseynova 2015.

locals). He told me its history: as the population exploded, a significant share of the low-income Azeri population was placed on the hillside north-west of the Old City (İçəri Şəhər). As indicated by its colloquial name, Nagornaia (Ru. hillside), the area was inappropriate for any substantial housing construction, and before the Soviets, no serious investments were made. When the Soviets came, they changed the neighbourhood's name and made plans to replace the squalid huts in later decades. But, he said, nothing was changed and in the late Soviet period Sovetski continued to be neglected by city officials.[12] Furthermore, in light of socialist modernisation discourse, inhabitants of this and other historical and centrally-located quarters who were predominantly Azerbaijani-speaking have been depicted frequently as the self-proclaimed guardians of their neighbourhood (məhəllə) as well as of traditional customs (adət) and honour (namus).

By the time the Bolsheviks took power in Baku, low-rise dwellings like those still in Sovetski dominated the city. In 1923, 88 per cent of Baku's built space was occupied by one- or two-storey buildings (Efendizadeh 1971: 3). In addition to low-rise neighbourhoods, there were also barracks for workers and soldiers. The remaining 12 per cent of multi-storey buildings included the homes of economic elites constructed during the city's first oil-boom in the late nineteenth century. After the nationalisation and municipalisation of bourgeois property, they became subject to the so-called policy of uplotnenie (densification),[13] in which the urban poor were housed in spacious apartments usually by allocating one family per room. Although forging a higher lodging density per dwelling, this meant an improvement of living conditions for many workers who had been accommodated previously in barracks. The former owners of the large apartments suffered more, as they were usually allocated only a single room within their former house.

The Bolsheviks' early vision of building a new society was dogged by the realities of serious problems in the quality of housing and infrastructure that were inherited from Tsarist times. Reports and correspondence between authorities that are lodged in the archives frequently testified to the severe 'housing crisis' and unsanitary conditions in the city. For instance, in 1925, the Bakgorispolkom (Baku City Executive Committee) reported to the Zaknarkomfin (Transcaucasian Commissariat of Finance) that, due to the

---

[12] Fuad Akhundov, personal communication 18 November 2014.

[13] I have used a translation that resonates with English terms from urban planning. Other scholars have preferred terms that foreground the interrelations between domains of Soviet planning related to agriculture, work schedules, living spaces, and urban planning: consolidation (Fitzpatrick 1999); condensation/packing in (Humphrey 2005); compression (Attwood 2010).

unsanitary conditions of dwellings and courtyards, their extreme population density (up to 600 inhabitants per hectare) and extraordinary construction density (65 per cent of the overall yard space), there was a high rate of disease and mortality in the city.[14] Photographs give a vivid impression of the low-rise-settlements on the hillside that spread well beyond the territory of later Sovetski.

Plate 3. Dwellings to be demolished on the hillside area in the 1930s.

The neighbourhood's known history is bound up with views of it now too. People commented on Sovetski frequently, and it seemed impossible to enter the neighbourhood without commenting on it. The place demanded commentary, opinion, and emotional response.

During my fieldwork, I occasionally joined Murad, a friend whom I first met in 2008/2009, on his weekly visits to a hamam (public bath/ bath house) in the colloquially named neighbourhood of Kubinka. Kubinka is an inner-city neighbourhood that emerged in pre-socialist times; it is comparable to close-by Sovetski with regard to its small and often dilapidated dwellings. It also has a bad reputation. It was the site of Baku's black-market during socialism, and like Sovetski, it is said to be characterised by a proliferation of petty crime and narcotics trafficking. After the hamam, we got into Murad's car and headed towards his apartment. Our route took us from downtown to the hillside. When we turned off the main road into one of the narrow streets that crosscut Sovetski,

---

[14] 'V Zaknarkomfin' (undated document from 1925); ARDA, f.1933, op.1, d.306, l.8.

connecting the lower downtown with the uphill area, differences in traffic infrastructure and housing conditions were recognisable immediately. The narrow, steep, and bumpy street was flanked on both sides with old dwellings in rather bad condition. Their architecture appeared protective and inward-oriented. Houses were standing neatly side-by-side, and walls, closed gates, and doors concealed the inner courtyards from the view of outsiders. The basic rectangular blocks of streets were corrugated by narrow blind lanes that led further inside the neighbourhood.

Plate 4. Partial view of the hillside area with the typical courtyard houses, undated.

Murad drove his Mercedes steadily up the road until we reached the end of a long chain of cars, jammed at Nariman Narimanov Avenue. This street, called Sovetskaia Ulitsa (Soviet Street) from 1929–91 had given the neighbourhood its colloquial designation. Murad started complaining heavily about the traffic that had become a serious problem in the connecting streets between the lower and upper sides of the hill. This led to further statements on the inferior quality of housing and the neighbourhood in general:

> It is a bad place to live. You see all those old and dilapidated dwellings? They are not nice to look at. What should people think about us who visit our country? It is good that our government finally took steps to demolish the neighbourhood. Such plans have already existed in Soviet times but were never realised. I mean, it is not good for people to live like that, is it? Everything is chaotic and dirty.

Murad's view resembled what I regularly heard from Bakuvians, and sometimes occasionally from dwellers in the neighbourhood. I visited the neighbourhood frequently during fieldwork and had even lived there for some months during an earlier visit. Other eyes might see positive qualities in the neighbourhood: the privacy of the dwellings and courtyards, the human scale of the buildings, and the historic buildings themselves. However, public discourse has focused on reproducing a negative image of this and similar neighbourhoods since Soviet times. It is striking, too, that people regularly associate the kind and quality of these dwellings with certain groups of inhabitants. They are invariably 'undesirable' social types: if not 'criminal', then at least 'traditional' or 'poor'.

Plate 5. Street view in Sovetski in August 2014.

Plate 6. A narrow lane in Sovetski in August 2014.

Despite ideological assertions that the Soviet Union was a society of equals, housing was taken as a proxy of socio-economic background and status in the urban social hierarchy even during socialism. 'Housing classes' were recognisable in many Soviet cities (Hegedüs and Tosics 1983; see also Roth 2019: 61). While processual and dynamic approaches towards houses among anthropologists have rightly pointed to the interrelation of people, buildings, and ideas (Carsten and Hugh-Jones 1995b), the mutual impacts between the social and symbolic meanings of architecture produce some enduring hierarchies too. In the Soviet context, there was 'a definite pronounced intention of the state to make use of the materiality of dwelling to produce new social forms and moral values' (Humphrey 2005: 39–40). While the state's original intention was often deflected in practice, the plan itself contributed to a widely shared 'ranking of urban dwellings according to desirability, from the unheated wooden shack, through the barracks, the hostel, the shared flat in an old house, to the separate flat in an apartment block' (ibid. 45). As a consequence, material perceptions were transposed into social hierarchies between groups of urban inhabitants.

In local literature, as well as in daily conversation I had with people, references were often made accordingly to the mentality (*mentalitet*) of social groups that were implicitly associated with the specific kind of housing they inhabited. While Murad was driving the car slowly uphill, he reproduced such public discourse for Sovetski too:

> It is a dangerous neighbourhood with its own unwritten laws. In general, mostly Azeri people have been living here. They are very conservative and highly value traditional customs and moral codes. Honour (*namus*) has always played a more important role than in other parts of the city. In contrast to Baku proper, many people here do not speak Russian at all. They have mostly been *chushki* (derogatory term for rural people) who in the past migrated from the countryside.

Just passing a middle-aged man with hat and beard, Murad made a derogatory gesture and said: 'Look! Such are the people I'm talking about.' Murad's lumping together of the neighbourhood's inhabitants has clearly been biased by a long-standing public discourse among local intellectuals on the demise of the city's international and cosmopolitan character (Grant 2010). In official discourse, Sovetski – like other pre-socialist neighbourhoods (e.g. Kubinka) and regions that emerged as squatter settlements of rural Azeri migrants in the 1960s and 1970s (e.g. Dağlı, Xutor, or Papanın) – has been represented continuously in public as a place of stagnation. Indeed, many of the families in Sovetski have been living there for several generations – at least this was the case with most inhabitants to whom I talked. But, one should raise questions about what such continuity means in social and political terms.

Official statistics about movements into and out of the neighbourhood are not available (as demographic data is processed on the district level). However, discussions with informants reveal that people have sought to move out. What is said, is that if financial means allowed them to do so, many long-term residents who did not acquire a new apartment elsewhere in Soviet days left the neighbourhood after independence. In turn, migrants from the countryside or others in search of relatively affordable prices for accommodation in central Baku moved here.

Social continuity is therefore somewhat discontinuous. Inhabitants' perception of their neighbourhood is also ambiguous. To most long-term inhabitants I talked to, the emotional attachment to their houses and neighbourhood, and the value of dense networks of extended kin and long family friendships were frequently emphasised. On the other hand, people also expressed resentment for not having been given apartments during socialism. Aydın, a local inhabitant in his sixties described the situation as follows:

> Mostly, male inhabitants of the neighbourhood remained here. Take me, for example. I have five brothers and three sisters. My sisters left the house after marriage and moved to their husbands' while my brothers and I stayed here in our father's house. Due to the small size of the dwellings, we built a second storey when someone got married and strived to live together somehow. Despite the small size of our living space, we brothers have divided it up among ourselves. It happened only rarely that there were problems with the housing authorities. Most issues could be solved with bribes (Ru. *vziatki*, Az. *rüşvət*) to make the authorities turn a blind eye. Today, due to the difficult economic situation, there is no possibility to buy a separate apartment somewhere else. If there is a small plot of land, then everyone builds it up further. What should you do, if there isn't any possibility for buying something else?

Whereas Aydın emphasised the lack of financial resources for moving into a less crowded dwelling, Baxtyar, another of my interlocutors, commented resignedly that his house was built in 1890 by his great-grandfather and that it had been home to their whole (extended) family. He himself was living here in the fourth generation. He said, 'already when I was a child, everyone said that the house is soon going to be demolished and that we will be given an apartment. This was in the 1960s. But nothing ever happened'.

The Baku-born sociologist Sergey Rumyantsev has referred to neighbourhoods like Sovetski as 'the other Baku' (Ru. *drugoi Baku*) because they stand in a stark ideological contrast to the city's public image as a cosmopolitan, multi-ethnic centre of Russian-speaking urbanites (2008: 248). Historically, the neighbourhoods of the other Baku were mostly inhabited by Muslim people and ethnic Azeris, and were referred to by locals as *məhəllə*.[15] As indicated above, there are many multi-generational families inhabiting these neighbourhoods, but there are also always newcomers. Today, as in many past waves, the newcomers are predominantly from rural areas. They also include internally displaced people from Azerbaijan's

---

[15] The term is Arabic in origin, but has entered most if not all societies in the sphere of later Islamic influence. Generally, Bakuvians apply the term in its neutral, technical meaning of 'neighbourhood' or 'settlement', but it is used in some contexts as an evaluative term. As in the case of the above-mentioned neighbourhoods, the term ascribes a traditional lifestyle to the place, further suggesting that it has its own rules, is dangerous to enter for any male stranger, and is often violent and strongly resistant to any state authority. Inhabitants themselves describe it as an island of traditional values where people still behave respectfully to each other and highly acknowledge 'traditional' principles of power, seniority, and gender.

territorial conflict with neighbouring Armenia over the Nagorno-Karabakh region since the late 1980s that led to a war between both countries in 1992–94. The neighbourhood has been mostly attractive to low-income groups due to the relatively cheap dwellings in a central location.

Such urban divisions of space as modern and progressive or traditional and backward were characteristic for other capitals and major cities across Soviet Central Asia and the Caucasus. For instance, the city of Osh in southern Kyrgyzstan has been described as a *Tale of Two Cities* (Liu 2007) due to its ethnic heterogeneity and contrasting lifeworlds. The long-standing divide between a 'traditional Central Asian' and 'modern Soviet sector [...]' captures the coexisting presence of divergent orientations and aspirations within the city' (ibid. 66). As in Baku, people in Osh share such notions of a spatial division along the ethnic, occupational, and economic backgrounds of its citizens (ibid.). The Uzbek capital of Tashkent provides another example of a second life beyond the façade of egalitarian multi-ethnic coexistence. Tashkent 'was not just a dual Russian/ Uzbek urban area; it was also divided between the modern Soviet centre and the rest of the city, which was replete with dirty shantytowns, distant suburban areas, poor transportation systems, and filthy water' (Stronski 2010: 209). In Baku, such a divide has even characterised the very central region dominated by urban Soviet materiality and cultured lifestyles with its ideological counterparts being hidden – at least metaphorically speaking – in the backyards of Soviet modernisation. Contrasting this modernity, media reports in recent years still represent Sovetski (not without a glimpse of nostalgia due to its then-planned demolition) as a 'bastion of tradition'.[16]

To summarise, rather than describing a solely geographical region, Sovetski further represents an imagined space. This 'other Baku' is an uncivilised, traditional, and criminal inner-city space. Its qualities are perceived against a strong Soviet-era vision for urban modernisation, infrastructure, architecture, and lifestyle. The self-made traditional courtyard houses (*həyət evləri*) of Sovetski have marked a stark visual and symbolic contrast to the mass housing to be planned and built by state authorities and urban planners.

This material contrast was well observable from the window in Murad's living room. After we had slowly crossed Sovetski, we finally reached Nariman Narimanov Avenue. It was only few minutes more until we reached Murad's home – an apartment which was located on the thirteenth-

---

[16] See, for example, F. Mahmudbeyli and V. Alibayli, 'There Goes the Neighborhood: In Construction-Crazy Baku, another Old District Faces the Wrecking Ball'. *Transitions Online: Regional Intelligence* 4 June 2014. http://www.tol.org/client/article/24329-there-goes-the-neighborhood.html. Last accessed 12 November 2014.

storey of a postsocialist high-rise. It was located right amidst the upper part of Sovetski. From his living room, I could see the many low-storey dwellings with their courtyards being squeezed-in between postsocialist mass housing estates.

Plate 7. View from Murad's living room on Sovetski's upper part bounded by post-Soviet residential highrises and with the Flame Towers and the TV Tower in the background (top left).

The view was instructive. Like the frequent assertion of Sovetski's social stability and stagnation, the insistence that it has never been developed bears scrutiny. The low dwellings visible from Murad's apartment have not yet been swallowed by new construction projects, as happened to many others during the 1990s and 2000s. Indeed, historical sources testify that many dwellings on the hillside have been demolished for reconstruction projects in several waves since the 1930s and long after the Second World War. This included the restructuring of streets, squares, and the urban layout, the extension of the tramway system, as well as the construction of multi-storey housing.

Urban Development and Visions of Socialism before and after the Second World War

The period between the 1930s and 1950s was a time of intensive remaking of the central districts, including the hillside area. Not only were major traffic lines and central streets in downtown renovated. The exploitation of new urban space on the hillside plateau in the 1950s included the construction of a variety of public institutions, including the Academy of Sciences, the Polytechnical Institute (now Azerbaijan Technical University), and associated residential housing. The construction extended the city's limits. Eventually, the historic area of Salaxanı, about 1.5 kilometres north-west of Sovetski, saw the construction of one of Baku's first *mikroraiony*[17] on an area measuring 23 hectares (see Aliyeva 1979: 69). This meant that far from being an area 'neglected' by development, Sovetski and other hillside neighbourhoods stood in the middle of the path between 'old' and 'new' Baku.

Within this process, significant parts of Sovetski and the hillside area were equally transformed, not least because the neighbourhood connected downtown with the newly planned hillside plateau. All in all, around 50 hectares of 'old residential areas were demolished to provide for the enlargement of main roads and the clear spaces needed for squares and new buildings in the centre', as well as to provide for 'new and improved residential homes' (Efendizadeh 2012: 59). This also included a large-scale reconstruction of Sovetski Street, the extension of the tram line, the construction of squares, and therefore, the demolition of low-storey dwellings.

---

[17] A micro-district (Ru. *mikroraion*, pl. *mikroraiony*) refers to the Soviet concept of a usually large residential area that contains all kinds of public services and infrastructure for the inhabitants and which has been constructed since the 1960s by the use of standardised and industrialised panel production, mostly at the fringes of cities. Micro-districts have come to stand emblematically for the Soviet architecture of living and residential construction. Despite their size and intended range of services, they do not normally acquire the administrative status of *raion*, but remain subordinate to a city district.

Plate 8. Demolition of houses due to the reconstruction of Sovetski Street in the 1940s.

While continuous (re)construction of the central and adjacent areas took place from the 1930s, largely based on the master plans of 1927, 1932, and 1937, it was mostly after the Second World War that the proposed architectural ensembles and main compositional elements in the city's layout (i.e. main streets, squares, and landmarks) were realised (Efendizadeh 2012: 34–57). The implementation of the architectural and infrastructural plans was further characterised by 'a widely felt desire to impart a message of triumph in all [...] monumental and ceremonial forms (ibid. 57). The spatial extension of the city into its peripheries, as well as the transformation of already existing urban landscapes with 'monumental and ceremonial forms', reflects a common strategy of political regimes, namely the (re)signification of space and time. As Katherine Verdery pointedly stated, 'among the most common ways in which political regimes mark space are by placing particular statues in particular places and by renaming landmarks such as streets, public squares, and buildings. These provide contour to landscapes, socializing them and saturating them with specific political values: they *signify* space in specific ways' (1999: 39–40, emphasis in original). Baku's Soviet and post-Soviet regimes have followed suit.

    Baku's post-war construction boom was publicly promoted as a great achievement in providing masses of citizens with modern infrastructure and housing. The Soviets lauded their mass housing as a 'Soviet' achievement, but similar programmes (and paternalistic attitudes) were adopted by many Western European states at the time. 'In light of a [housing] shortage that was enhanced by the destruction of the Second World War, state-subsidised mass housing came to be universally accepted as the most efficient answer to the challenges posed by social plight: it became synonymous with modernization' (Urban 2012: 13). The political importance of the Soviet Union's large-scale housing programme developed after Stalin's death until which priority was given to developing the industry. Housing was important, but hardly the main focus of Soviet construction and building works. It was the new First Secretary, Nikita Khrushchev, who raised the profile of housing as he proclaimed the advent of de-Stalinisation in his 'Secret Speech' at the 20th Congress of the Communist Party in 1956. Under the slogan 'to every family its own apartment', Khrushchev took direct aim at the post-war housing crisis that had been intensified because large-scale industrialisation and the collectivisation of agricultural land had resulted in a sharp increase of urban populations. As Khrushchev declared optimistically in 1957: 'We know that we have an acute shortage of housing [...]. The program for the development of housing in the USSR [...] sets the task of insuring a considerable increase in available houses, with the aim of ending the housing shortage in the next 10 to 12 years' (*Izvestia Moscow*, 7 November 1957, p. 3, cited in Barry 1969: 1).

Stalinist housing architecture was further criticised as being too bourgeois, ornate, and expensive, and as having been allocated mostly to privileged groups within society. Khrushchev's policy meant a significant shift toward a functional, minimalist, and economical form of mass housing. This new period of industrialised mass housing construction and planning of huge *mikroraiony* from the 1960s onwards marked a new step in housing policy and implementation all over the Soviet Union.[18] In Baku, as I will show below, this new direction was enthusiastically embraced by public media.

Khrushchev-era construction continued the basic pattern set in the 1930s and 1950s. That is, large-scale projects rarely involved the destruction of existing built areas, but focused mostly on undeveloped areas of free space on the city's margins. Salaxanı was a favourite for development, as were five micro-districts built in the city's far north-west (Aliyeva 1979: 69).

---

[18] Such post-war development of mass housing was not unique for the Soviet Union but something typical in most Western European countries. It gained important impulses from modernist architecture of the early twentieth century. Hence, for design and planning of Khrushchev-era mass housing 'Soviet architects drew from both domestic and international sources, such as the 1920s Soviet constructivism and contemporary mass housing programs in other countries' (Harris 2015: 181).

During the 1970s and 1980s, the locus for mass housing in Baku shifted towards the eastern parts of the city, including four planning districts – 8th Kilometre, Akhmedli, Byul'-Byul' and Zykh – that provided housing for around 400,000 inhabitants (Aliyeva 1979: 70; Efendizadeh 2012: 147).

Even as new micro-districts presented an efficient solution for mass housing, many socialist cities also struggled with questions on whether and how to transform their densely built inner-city areas. These remained overcrowded and characterised by dilapidated low-rise dwellings. In Baku, for instance, the city authorities enquired in 1965 on possible solutions for the 'reconstruction of old buildings in the central parts of Baku'.[19]

In Baku, authorities struggled with the limited space produced by the city's topology as well as by the vast facilities of the oil industry which encircled the city. Other Soviet cities did not seem to face such acute limitations. Baku also seemed to have an exceptional density and spread of old houses; these were said to account for 80–85 per cent of the city's territory. In the old parts of Baku, they still made up around 2 million square metres of living space, characterised by difficult sanitary and hygienic conditions and inhabited by more than 300,000 people. In terms of their composition, layout, and physical conditions, these dwellings were reported as very much insufficient for meeting Baku's needs for work organisation and everyday life. Some 400,000 square metres of housing were being constructed in central Baku every year, but planners estimated that by 1970, there would be no more free space available for construction. There was not much time to confront the 'dilemma': either it would be necessary to build more housing in suburbs far distant from the centre, or it would be necessary to systematically reconstruct the old housing stock in the centre. While the latter option would include much higher costs to adapt necessary infrastructures, the city planning authorities found it the 'indisputable' option. The question arises in the mind of the reader on why this option was favoured despite the relatively higher costs?

Since the early 1950s, the development of Baku's centre has proceeded apace. Old houses were demolished to make space for new transport infrastructure and residential buildings. This seemingly never-ending need (or demand, to use an economic term) for convenient mass housing in the centre was further fuelled by privileged institutions and their employees. It seems evident in the light of my interviews with older people that, similar to today, the new housing construction in the centre benefitted already privileged groups, such as Party-functionaries, scientists, artists, and

---

[19] The information in the subsequent paragraph is based on the following document: *Spravka rekonstruktsii staroi zastroiki tsentral'noi chasti goroda Baku* (1965); ARDABF, f.10, op.1, d.174, ll.6–11.

white-collar employees. The former inhabitants whose houses had been demolished for new construction were compensated with dwellings outside the limited and highly appreciated domains of the central areas.

It was not impossible for non-elites to stake a claim to housing in the centre. In 1977, M. Mukhtarov lost his house to demolition for a new construction in the city's centre. Mukhtarov lived with his wife and daughter. As compensation, they were granted a three-room apartment of 38.6 square metres of living space.[20] It was located in the recently constructed *mikroraion* of Akhmedli, some fifteen kilometres away from the centre. Mukhtarov refused the compensation, and emphasised to the authorities his need for an apartment in the city's central region. Since no appropriate place was available, Mukhtarov and his family found temporary accommodation with relatives and acquaintances. Finally, the authorities offered a central two-room apartment of 29 square metres, and the family agreed.[21] The case shows that, for reasons of locality, especially long-term Baku residents sometimes denied the state-heralded modernity of mass housing in the newly developed micro-districts in favour of a smaller but centrally located dwelling.

How were these large-scale urban transformations in Baku represented in official state discourse? After the Second World War, the newspaper *Bakinskii Rabochii* (The Baku Worker) was the medium of the Central Committee of the Communist Party of Azerbaijan. On the front page of a 1957 issue, appeared a lead article titled, '*Baku stroitsia*' (Baku under Construction). It is accompanied by a photograph depicting a nearly finished, large residential housing block still partly scaffolded, with trolleybuses passing by on fresh streets lined with newly planted trees and greenery. The article opens by stating that such new buildings have become many in Azerbaijan's capital today. What was 'the city's periphery until not long ago has now been noticeably transformed. New construction sites are spreading limitless on the hillside plateau and new houses on Gusi Gadzhiev Street [today Azerbaijan Avenue] are making it look completely different to the [once] dark street of one-storey [houses]'. The article further mentions that in the post-war years 'workers in the capital city of oil' have received 700,000 square metres of living space. As one can assume that most readers were far from able to make sense of such quantitative assessments (on which basically the whole Soviet planned economy was based on), the author

---

[20] The given area refers only to 'living space' (*zhilaia ploshchad'*), and excludes the area of the kitchen, bathroom, and corridor). Overall 'apartment space' (*obshchaia ploshchad'*) would have been larger.

[21] *O pereselenii zhil'tsov v sviazi so snosom,* 29 November 1978; ARDABF, f.23, op.1, d.1681, l.71.

himself answers that 'No doubt! This is much, at the same time it is not [much] because today's housing problem in our city is very intricate'.[22]

Just two weeks before, the same newspaper propagated the upcoming elections of the local Soviets and published an article on 'getting acquainted with voters in their new homes'. The journalist had interviewed several working class people: a female customs official, a foreman at Stalinneft (the Stalin Oil Trust, part of the state oil company), an oil engineer, a boatswain from Kaspnefteflot (the Caspian Oil Field Fleet), and a driver who had recently received new apartments. The overall image presented is a promotion of and glorification of the city authorities' successful housing policy. Three photographs depict a new five-storey apartment block and happy faces of new dwellers. The caption under the picture with a smiling father who is sitting at the living room table and surrounded by his two sons and two daughters, says 'Wholeheartedly, we thank the Soviet authorities for our bright life!' In the text it further explains that this is Iaver Rzaev, working as a driver, who welcomes the journalists of *Bakinskii Rabochii* with the words 'What a pleasant coincidence! Together with our daughter we just finished a letter to your editors because we want to express our appreciation for your care of the working man'. Further, the newspaper printed excerpts of the said letter:

> My family and I constantly feel that great care [*bol'shaia zabota*] for the Soviet Man that surrounds us. Six of my children are going to school; our health is guarded by attentive and empathetic doctors. The other day we moved into this beautiful and comfortable apartment [...] and we are deeply grateful to the Party and the government for our bright and joyful life. [...] thanks, from a simple worker![23]

Another example from the newspaper *Stroitel'* (Builder) refers to the Seven-Year Plan which was adopted in early 1959 and presents its expected achievements in the most favourable and glorifying light.[24] Under the headline 'Our capital is getting more beautiful!' it says:

> Thanks to the care [*zabota*] of the Party and Government, with every day the capital of Soviet Azerbaijan – Baku – is getting more beautiful. In front of our eyes new residential housing and factories, schools, cinemas, and hospitals are growing. Squares are being

---

[22] 'Baku stroitsia'. *Bakinskii Rabochii*, 2 March 1957, p. 1.

[23] 'Poznakomimsia s izbirateliami novogo doma', *Bakinskii Rabochii*, 14 February 1957, p. 3.

[24] The tradition of the Five-Year Plan (*Piatiletnii Plan*) for all-union economic planning experienced a one-time extension to a Seven-Year Plan (*Semiletnii Plan*, 1959–65) which was adopted at the 21st Congress of the Communist Party with the expectation to better cope with the Soviet Union's economic challenges.

developed and main roads constructed. A city in the forest of new buildings. At the end of the Seven-Year Plan our city will be even better. Several billions of Roubles will be invested into the housing, communal, and socio-cultural development of Baku. [...] Almost 500,000 square metres of living space will be built at the expense of workers and employees with the support of state loans. Altogether, the Bakuvians will receive around 3.5 million square metres of living space. Thanks to this, the housing problem in Baku can be considered as being solved.[25]

This optimistic medial promotion of a near future in which the housing problem would be solved by state construction and also by stimulating citizens' individual housing construction with the help of state loans hardly materialised. As time went by, the housing problem continued to be among the most pressing of challenges for the city authorities. Despite the constant housing construction, the city was far from able to provide separate apartments for all its citizens.

In the 1980s, newspaper articles unabatedly heralded the utopian vision of a socialist society and modern housing for all Bakuvians. The year 1986 had special significance for Soviet Baku as it constituted the adoption of the city's last master plan (titled *Baku 2005*) that projected its future development for the upcoming twenty years. Hence, newspapers widely disseminated the vision of the development to which the state and urban planners aspired in words and images (see also Roth 2019: 60). An extensive double page article, entitled 'A look into the future: the master plan of Baku's development constitutes a new stage in the development of Azerbaijan's capital' depicts drawings and miniatures of planned model sites, high-rises, and residential estates.[26] Those visual renderings are supported by several subheadings like 'an apartment for every family', 'a maximum of comfort for Bakuvians', or 'fast, convenient, and comfortable transportation'. The text explains that the whole city infrastructure (water, heating, light, canalisation) will be further developed and, since the Party aimed at solving the housing problem with '243,000 convenient apartments' being built by the year 2000, every family would finally obtain its own separate apartment. Around one month later, Feizulla Guliev, architect and leading author of the new master plan wrote in an article entitled, 'The year when hopes come true: thinking of 1987':

---

[25] 'Khorosheet nashi stolitsa!' *Stroitel'*, 20 June 1959, p. 2.

[26] 'Vzgliad v budushchee: general'nyi plan razvitiia Baku – novyi etap v razvitii stolitsu Azerbaidzhana'. Baku, 28 November 1986, pp. 2–3.

> For us architects, the upcoming year is a special one. The
> implementation of the new Baku master plan begins – this grandiose,
> sophisticated construction programme for the upcoming twenty
> years. [...] The care for people penetrates every part of the new
> master plan. Be it residential construction, cultural and everyday
> services, development of urban transport, the organisation of
> people's leisure, environmental protection, or communal provision.
> [...] The planning of four high-rise residential buildings at Sovetski
> Street has already started.[27]

When comparing the above examples on the official state discourse on
modernisation between the 1950s and 1980s, some characteristics are worth
mentioning. Generally, it was the development of urban infrastructure at
large and, closely connected to it, the provision of modern housing for the
citizens of Baku that appeared on the centre stage. It was the Party and the
government who were praised for the care and welfare shown towards the
Soviet people. Continuously, it seemed that the bright utopian future of
realising the ideal society and providing every family with a separate
apartment was becoming true almost tomorrow.

But more than the new urban materiality, the leap forward made by
Soviet state and society was reported as being embodied and represented in
the lives of the people, Baku's citizens, the ordinary workers. Infrastructure
and housing was said to have changed the lives of ordinary citizens (along
with education and medicine), and the latter were always heard to express
gratitude and indebtedness to the Party. Is that how these developments were
perceived and experienced by people? How and in which aspects did the
endless construction and allocation of housing affect citizens' everyday
lives?

In contrast to the voices of Sovetski inhabitants above who never
received their expected state housing, the following paragraphs show that
public perception in general was rather ambivalent and personal biases
differed between those who received and those who did not.

Azər, who will be introduced in more detail in Chapter 4, was born in
Baku in 1962. Initially, he and his parents had been living at his paternal
grandparents' home until his father received a separate apartment in 1969.
The family's new apartment was not newly built, but was in a 'modern'
building from 1929. Like his grandparents' place, the new apartment was
located in the neighbourhood known colloquially by older Bakuvians as
Armenikend in today's Nəsimi Rayon.[28] It is an Azeri name which means

---

[27] 'God sbyvshikhsia nadezhd: mysliami v 1987'. *Baku*, 31 December 1986, p. 2.

[28] Nəsimi Rayon is the current Azerbaijani name for one of Baku's 11 administrative districts
(rayon/-lar). In most other instances, I have used a transliteration of the equivalent Russian

'Armenian village' and refers to the majority of Armenians who settled in the area before the Bolshevik Revolution. Then, it marked the city's periphery, and it had been a site for one of the earliest of Soviet construction projects. In the late 1920s, the young state constructed a workers' settlement named Shaumian after the Armenian Bolshevik revolutionary who was one of the major figures leading the revolution in the South Caucasus (and who was arrested and executed by counter-revolutionaries in 1918). The three- and four-storey buildings are famous examples of the Soviet constructivist style. Like other workers' settlements built in those days, Shaumian was intended to provide healthy living conditions, and it can be considered one of the best examples for modern housing in early Soviet Baku. Basically, the planning and construction of the settlement, with all its public services and infrastructure like childcare institutions, schools, and shops reflected the state's ambitions to create the framework for a cultured way of life according to socialist principles.

From 1969 until the late 1980s, Azər lived in Shaumian with his parents and younger brother. They had a two-room apartment in a four-storey building. The whole housing complex had 25 entrances, almost 200 flats and around 800 inhabitants. Still, there was not enough housing. He recalled:

> These housing blocks were densely populated at the time. I remember from my childhood, that people were even dwelling in the basement rooms. That is also why Khrushchev started the housing programme. Because there were so many people who were accommodated in basements who had to be resettled somehow. But there was just not enough housing available. Imagine, there were 25 entrances in our block, each with a cellar where people made their dwelling. Practically, people lived underground. Then, after Heydar Aliyev became First Secretary of the Communist Party of Azerbaijan in 1969, he built the housing district of Akhmedli in 1974–76.
>
> These were nine-storey buildings – *Leningradski proekt* – decent quality![29] And within one year all people who lived in basements were the first to receive new apartments there. *Everyone* got an

---

term (raion/-y), from which the Azerbaijani term developed, to refer to both the city's districts and the country's 59 administrative regions. Although Russian and Azerbaijani use only one term to designate inner-urban and sub-national administrative divisions, I have generally used 'district' for Baku's administrative sub-divisions and 'region' for Azerbaijan's sub-divisions.

[29] In contrast to the Khrushchevka and Stalinka whose names derive from a specific era, *Kievski (proekt)*, *Minski (proekt)*, and *Leningradski (proekt)* are named after the cities in which they were first projected (see also Roth 2019: 68, endnote 6). Among these three, the Leningradski was mostly said by my informants to be of the best quality due to its large balcony, convenient floor space, and other convenient features.

apartment! All people were employed – there were practically no
unemployed – everyone was registered in a waiting list for
apartments. All my classmates, whose families lived in these cellars,
all of them moved there.

Azər mentioned some time later, that there had been a previous allocation of
an apartment to the family. When he was still going to kindergarten and his
brother was not yet born, the family moved briefly from his paternal
grandparents' place into a four-room apartment in 8th Kilometre. This
neighbourhood had started to be developed in the late 1960s (see Aliyeva
1979: 70), but it did not satisfy Azər's family. Azər commented on the
desert-like impression of the place. 'There was nothing there at all back then.
There was only one bus and one train going there. No other infrastructure –
they only built houses and roads'. As his father was employed 'in town' (*v
gorode*), the distance from home to work was too long and made the
organisation of daily tasks a challenge. His father spent a lot of daily time
commuting to work. Also, Azər had to be taken a long way to kindergarten
every day, as the public infrastructure in the new district had not been built.
And no one was yet thinking of a metro, which only existed in the centre.
So, his father decided to exchange the apartment with a smaller two-room
one closer to his workplace and parents. 'This was in 1969', Azər
remembers, 'I was seven years old and was in my first schoolyear'.

Azər's story, like Mukhtarov's, shows some of the reality behind the
triumphantly presented paper architecture in the newspapers. The press
encompassed a variety of representational forms, – photographs, drawings,
or architectural models – and usually presented depictions of both the
already materialised and yet-to-be materialised structures. They visually
sped-up, even erased, the months and years that were to elapse between
initial construction and full liveability. But these were critical months and
years in the lives of human families, and many sought other housing
solutions to the much-touted new apartments. 'Overcrowding' was
preferable if it came with relations of care, reasonable transportation, and
access to social services.

At the level of neighbourhoods, the authorities found it difficult to act
on problems that required something other than new construction. Parts of
Sovetski had been subjected to modernisation and became part of newly
constructed model sites, but the remaining parts were further pushed into the
background of public attention. Even in the mid-1970s, the executive power
of October District (today Yasamal District) approached the central Baku
authorities for 'urgent support' in modernising the infrastructure to
counteract the catastrophic hygienic conditions on the hillside. The
submitted document stated that, despite significant improvements in housing

and infrastructure within the district, sanitary conditions in the pre-revolutionary neighbourhoods were far from current standards. The out-dated canalisation system did not provide the capacity required for the increasing output of sewage water by local households. Hence, frequent gushes occurred and dirty water streamed down the steep terrain into the adjacent city centre, thus causing anti-sanitary conditions throughout the affected streets especially after heavy rainfalls.[30]

Generally, numerous internal letters, reports, and complaints from the archives testify to severe problems between administrative branches and government institutions with regard to unclear responsibilities, unmet achievements, delays, and the misallocation of financial or material resources, especially in the sphere of infrastructure and housing construction (see Chapter 3).

Baku, like other Soviet cities, was governed by a City Council of Workers' Deputies (Gorodskoi [Baku] Sovet Deputatov Trudiashchikhsia) – the Baksovet. This council elected various executive committees, including the Bakgorispolkom[31] (Baku's City Executive Committee), which features throughout this work. A city was divided administratively by district (*raion*), each of which had its own Sovet and local executive committee (*raiispolkom*). The *raiispolkom* or *ispolkom* – both short for *raionnyi ispolnitel'nyi komitet* – was the highest authority on the district level and was subordinate to the Bakgorispolkom. The dual structure of Party and administration, combined with the division of city-wide and district-level governance, meant multiple possibilities for collaboration and for conflict between housing-related projects, directives, policies, and offices.

And whereas official media frequently propagated the state's efforts and achievements of modernisation, such successes in everyday realities were, naturally, much more heterogeneous, spatially different, and could not be enjoyed equally by all members of society (when thinking about the divergent quality of infrastructure and accommodations in new Soviet neighbourhoods compared to the older ones like Sovetski).

This offers a glimpse behind the façade of bureaucratic institutions and official representation pointing to the tensions of resource allocation and hierarchies between central and regional authorities as well as to the lack of priority for neighbourhoods located in the urban backyard of the city's showcasing areas. In other words, the ideal and generalised representation of the city's modernisation and urban development faced particular constraints in those spaces that did not fit the Soviet ideology of social progress.

---

[30] *Predsedateliiu Bakgorispolkoma*, 16 June 1976; ARDABF, f.23, op.1, d.340, ll. 11–14.

[31] The abbreviation stands for Bakinskii Gorodskoi Ispolnitel'nyi Komitet. The general term for a city executive in any city was *gorispolkom*.

    In the next section I discuss the state's shifted notions of urban
development and modernisation in contemporary Baku. A recurring topic
that has been mentioned by my interlocutors is the concept of *zabota*, the
care and welfare offered by the state to its citizens. Like *zabota* in Baku, the
general welfare policy in socialist countries constituted the very basis and
main principle for urban development across the Eastern Bloc until 1991.
Similar aspirations were followed by Western European states in the
aftermath of the Second World War, but were slowly removed from their
political agendas from the early 1970s (Urban 2012: 3). The end of socialism
and the resulting privatisation of industries, urban infrastructures, and
housing, to different degrees, meant an erosion of state welfare in favour of
neoliberal market models. At the same time, this meant redrawing the lines
of social inclusion and exclusion for urban citizens in the era of
independence, especially when housing had so long been considered an
expression of a social contract between citizens and the state (Alexander et
al. 2018: 123). In Azerbaijan today, national progress and images of
modernity are still playing a prominent role in state propaganda. However,
the meanings of progress and modernity have changed tremendously, as I
will argue in the next section. At the same time, Soviet approaches and
techniques of ideology-making and its dissemination have remained well
alive under the new regime.

Remaking the City in the New Millennium

Since my first visit to Baku in 2007, I was struck during subsequent research
trips by the pace of urban transformation. Not only were new buildings and
landmarks mushrooming across the central areas and accompanied by
digitalised versions of Soviet paper architecture. An important element was
also the provision of Soviet buildings with new façades. Soviet residential
buildings, for instance, obtained a new appearance. Locals, even architects,
were critical of the renovations because new elements had been merely
added on top of the old structures. Sometimes the original building was just
encased in new walls that left a significant amount of space between the
original and new structure, creating dark corridors in front of people's
windows. Sometimes the windows even ceased to match with the new
cladding (for a similar description, see Grant 2014: 509). I first noticed this
kind of 'renovation' when I walked by Azerbaijan Technical University on
an April morning in 2014. The always impressive building boasted a new
façade. As I got closer to the building, I noticed that the new façade was
merely imposed on the original structure – the original showed through at
the flank sides of the building that faced the minor side streets, and the old
and new position of windows did not match. When I later talked to an

architect friend, he recounted his own surprise at this kind of renovation. Then, with a slight sense of resignation, he explained that 'such an act simply reflects the conditions in our country – the lack of respect for the people, the lack of democracy, lacking professionalism of the architect and the customer's knowledge. Tell me – is that ever possible in a normal country?'

It seems that the superficial renovations were further motivated by the approach of the European Olympic Games, to be held in summer 2015. Once again, construction projects repeated the dominant material contrasts of the urban fabric. The demolition of some 4,500 pre-socialist dwellings within the Sovetski region was finally approved for demolition by the city council. Then, the Sovetski restructuring plan was to be carried out in several waves and was to affect around 10,000 dwellings, in an area of around fifty hectares that provided homes for 50,000– 60,000 people.[32]

Nor was Sovetski alone among the 'old' neighbourhoods to be targeted. Its demolition stood in continuation with an urban beautification plan that started in 2009 with the demolition of the nearby Jewish Quarter for renewal of streets and traffic infrastructure as well as the construction of Winter Park as part of a large greenery project in the downtown area. The city administration planned the creation of a large cohesive inner-city park comparable to Central Park in New York. The pace of urban transformation gained an important impetus with the preparations for a series of mega events that started with the Eurovision Song Contest in May 2012 and which all resulted in the large-scale eviction of local residents accompanied by regular violation of property rights, lack of transparency, and inappropriate compensation.[33]

During one of my visits in the neighbourhood in 2013–14, I noticed that state representatives had already started to mark houses which would be demolished by spraying numbers on their doors. Many people complained that the state had already started to prepare for demolition before negotiations with the city officials concerning the amount of financial compensation had started – thereby creating a *fait accompli*. In personal conversations, inhabitants made frequent comments about their dissatisfaction with the government's insufficient financial compensation. In early 2014, the standard amount set by the authorities was 1,500 AZN per square metre of living space. This was equivalent to around 1,900 USD.

---

[32] 'There goes the Neighborhood', op. cit.

[33] Sultanova, S. 'Giving up their Homes for a Song: With Police at the Ready, Baku Evicts Families and Razes Residences to Make Way for Eurovision'. *Transitions Online: Regional Intelligence*, 7 March 2012. Available online, https://www.tol.org/client/article/23033-giving-up-their-homes-for-a-song.html. Last accessed 14 November 2015.

Over time, the amount in AZN has not changed, but following the currency crisis in 2015, its value was only about 880 USD by 2018.[34] Even in 2014, the rate of standard compensation was much lower than the regular market value of 4,000 AZN per square metre in the area.[35] Though suburban housing was cheaper per square metre, it was also typically larger than the pre-socialist dwellings which measured in the range of ten to thirty square metres. Soon-to-be-former inhabitants of Sovetski were unlikely to be able to purchase replacement housing anywhere in Baku with their compensations.

In early spring 2014, I attended the single noteworthy demonstration of around 1,000 local inhabitants who claimed higher compensations for their houses. However, this one-time gathering remained unsuccessful. Although city authorities had promised to meet that day with representatives of the neighbourhood for further negotiations, they did not show up. Instead, there were hundreds of policemen who were subjected to mostly older female inhabitants' loud expression of their indignation. Some other older female participants were holding up photographs of the former and current presidents. They hoped for the personal protection and support from the latter; many people were convinced that he would not approve the compensation policy of the Baku city officials if he knew about their methods. In a similar way, it was reported that the citizens' plans to hold weekly demonstrations would result in their voices reaching the president 'of whose social justice and attention to the needs of citizens they had no doubt'.[36] For them, the president represented a sacrosanct and caring father and powerful representative of the nation who only needed to be informed to act on their behalf.

People's opinions were strong and they voiced a real sense of distress. One male inhabitant in his mid-fifties even suggested that the current political situation was worse than that of Stalin's days. Referring to a diffuse local narrative on Stalin which is hard to verify historically, he lamented: 'Throughout the Soviet period, Sovetski maintained its own laws. It was a state within the state. Even Stalin once said that, "where Sovetskaia Ulitsa starts – Soviet power ends." But now in the era of independence, our neighbourhood fades from existence. [This is] something in which the Soviet government never succeeded'.

---

[34] The Azerbaijani New Manat (ANM) was introduced as the national currency in 2006.

[35] 'There Goes the Neighborhood', op. cit.

[36] 'A Tripartite Meeting on Resettlement of Residents of "Sovetskaya" – Central Sections of Baku to be Held Today'. *ABC.az*, 18 February 2014. http://abc.az/eng/news/79485.html. Last accessed 27 February 2014.

Yet the defence of Sovetski and other pre-socialist neighbourhoods seems usually limited to those who live there. The value of the buildings and the neighbourhoods have precisely to do with the fact that they are 'home', not just physical structures for human habitation, but social places that provide for many of their inhabitants' needs better than any other conceivable habitats. An inhabitant of a neighbouring socialist-era residential building in Sovetski upheld the government's plan of demolition: 'We will soon host the European Olympic Games and many visitors from other countries will come here. Can we really show them this unfavourable part of the city? Of course not!'

This neighbour's statement, like so many from the government, diverges in an important way from those of Soviet times. *Zabota* is no longer a motivation for reconstruction. The only motivation is related to appearance and impression:

> Development of the transport system and road infrastructure of Baku is among the priority directions of the state policy. [...] The government also takes important steps to upgrade the image of Baku by removing and replacing unsuitable buildings that hinder the development and deteriorate appearance of the city. One of these plans implies restoring Sovetski area, which is a home to aged and ugly buildings. The improvement of the area along with improving living conditions of residents residing here are the priority project for modern Baku appearance.[37]

The mention of 'improving living conditions' seems gratuitous and unsubstantiated either rhetorically or pragmatically. Other demolitions in the recent past have shown that compensation is rarely adequate to secure a replacement dwelling. The state media occasionally reports about dislocated families who have been given new apartments as compensation[38] but these are rather isolated and deliberate state promotions that distract attention from the lack of a serious and appropriate compensation scheme.

In their protests, affected inhabitants insisted 'We do not need money, we want our house!'[39] However, even the inhabitants of Sovetski seem

[37] Nazarli, A. 'Major Infrastructure Projects Reshaping Baku'. *Azer News*, 11 August 2017. https://www.pressreader.com/azerbaijan/azer-news/20170811. Last accessed 19 October 2018.

[38] 'New Apartments Given to 111 Families who Had Small Houses in Baku's Sovetsky'. *Kaspi Online*, 13 June 2016. http://kaspi.az/en/new-apartments-given-to-111-families-who-had-small-houses-in-bakus-sovetsky/. Last accessed 14 June 2019.

[39] 'Zhil'tsy novostroiki na «Sovetskoi» ne soglasny s vyseleniem: «Gde my eshche naidem dom s takimi usloviiami?»'. *1News.az*, 16 February 2017. http://www.1news.az/news/zhil-cy-novostroyki-na-sovetskoy-ne-soglasny-s-vyseleniem-gde-my-esche-naydem-dom-s-takimi-usloviyami---foto. Last accessed 28 June 2019.

willing to give up their 'homes', if they could at least get a 'house' in return. Many older people nostalgically referred to Soviet times when inhabitants were compensated for their old houses with equivalent or more spacious homes. Some even added jokingly that for decades they had been waiting in vain for the Soviet government to make their house subject to demolition in order to receive a new apartment —as if it were an officially recognised path within the state's scheme of housing allocation. Now the demolition has come, but without the offer of a new apartment.

Now that the city officials have finally taken measures for modernising the area, the inhabitants face a precarious future related to their housing and socio-economic conditions. One wonders if earlier solutions of 'overcrowding', a kind of deliberate 'down-sizing' in order to maintain other 'living conditions' will be the solution now too. An older woman who shares her small dwelling with her divorced daughter and grandchild told me:

> Here, at Sovetski Street, there were also many such small houses in the past. During the time of reconstruction, the state built five-storey residential buildings and relocated the dwellers of the demolished houses. We want the same: apartments in new buildings. I do not claim much! I'd be satisfied with one room, for me, my daughter and my granddaughter.

Some five years after Sovetski faced its first demolitions of 2014, most parts of Baku's Central Park (Mərkəzi Park), designed by an Austrian architect on 20 hectares, had been completed. The park contains two cafés, nine fountains, seven playgrounds, and an underground parking lot.[40] The whole park complex will still take some time to be completed fully, however digital renderings and numerous photographs during different stages of the construction process well document the actual proceedings and the architect's vision of the final outcome.[41] One of the striking elements of the 'paper architecture' surrounding the park's completion is the reintroduction of some elements of *zabota*. Numerous photographs have appeared of the president and his wife, visiting the opening of an adjacent garden, surrounded by 'residents'. The accompanying captions indicate that the couple is meeting with residents to 'familiarize [...] themselves with the problems of citizens'.[42] It remains unclear what kind of residents are referred

---

[40] 'President Ilham Aliyev Attends Opening of Garden outside Tazapir Mosque and Central Park Built along Fizuli Street'. *Report News Agency*, 23 May 2019. https://report.az/en/ domestic-politics/president-attends-opening-of-garden-and-central-park/. Last accessed 28 June 2019.

[41] See https://www.skyscrapercity.com/showthread.php?t=1943654. Last accessed 28 June 2019.

[42] 'President Ilham Aliyev attends opening', op. cit.

to, but we can assume that (as it is the usual practice when the president shows up in public) nothing has been left to chance. The 'problems' to be shared with him will have almost certainly been carefully orchestrated and hermetically sealed in advance.

Nevertheless, it is unclear whether *zabota* can be reintroduced, or whether it has been lost in a bygone era. In one of my meetings with a senior official at the State Committee for Urban Planning and Architecture (Azərbaycan Respublikası Dövlət Şəhərsalma və Arxitektura Komitəsi) who has been dealing with issues of urban planning since Soviet times, the official revealed his rather ambivalent opinion towards recent developments in the city. Referring to the former President Heydar Aliyev and his time as First Secretary of the Communist Party of Azerbaijan (1969–82), he emphasised the care policy (*politika zaboty*) of those days:

> It was our major duty to provide people who were living under unfavourable conditions with adequate and healthy dwellings. At the same time, the old dwellings were demolished with the support of the district offices which created special departments for that purpose. But today, dealing similarly and effectively with such issues in a well organised and structured manner is not part of a market economy.

Besides this shift in the state's care policy, he also refers to the Committee's reorganisation in 2006 by a presidential decree that he criticised as a compartmentalisation of previous responsibilities, with, for instance, the transfer of important previous functions to the Ministry of Emergency Situation (Azərbaycan Respublikası Fövqəladə Hallar Nazirliyi). In his view, the reorganisation negatively affected the proper regulation, coordination, and effective implementation of successful urban planning and resulted in the recruitment of partly unqualified personnel on the level of ministries and local executive authorities.

The official's perspective was instructive. On the one hand, he made a clear representation of the ideology underlying the state's provision of housing as *zabota*. He was convinced of the merits of the past ideology and had internalised the professional responsibility that it entailed for a specialist like himself. In his telling, the once propagated care policy was still a civilising mission through urban planning, and it still clearly reflected the paternalistic stance of a welfare state that aimed to raise its citizens according to socialist values. But, for him, it still made sense, still had value, and was still clearly navigable as a system from both sides of the bureaucratic desk – the citizen in need of housing and the official able to allocate it – could see through to a common solution. From this perspective my informant denied that he could understand the view or needs of citizens now that the 'market' is the arbiter of housing allocations. Let me illustrate:

Referring to the construction of Winter Park and the preceding housing demolition, he stated 'Many inhabitants lived under inhumane conditions but still did not want to leave the place. Others, in contrast, were even demanding to be relocated sooner rather than later'. Linking this concrete case to the general approach towards urban planning, he continued:

> The kind of accommodation has always constituted the main factor for the health and reproduction of society. Where you have decent housing, there you also have normal reproduction of society and healthy citizens. When a person lives in a favourable environment under good conditions, he will always look healthy. If, let's say, a young specialist is given a one-room apartment of 20 square metres and he marries subsequently [with his wife moving into his apartment], then he cannot get onto the waiting list for a bigger apartment. But if they become parents of a first child, a second child, then life in a one-room apartment is impossible. These are not healthy living conditions. Therefore, I assert that the health of a nation and the reproduction of society all depend on housing. But today in the era of market economy, housing has turned into a business.

Here, he seemed to describe, in ideological terms, something like the real situations and decisions described above by informants negotiating the housing system of the 1960s and 1970s. Today's housing situation with its large-scale demolition of residential areas, the uncertain character of residents' ownership rights in the face of urban development, and the constant decrease in affordable apartments for average citizens has led to a nostalgic memory of the Soviet Union's housing policy and welfare measures among many.

Conclusion

I started this chapter with observations on the large-scale remaking of Baku in terms of architecture, infrastructural development, and the government's attempts to present the country as a modern, prosperous nation towards the international community and to its own citizens. Then, I shifted attention towards the neighbourhood of Sovetski as a representative case for the city's 'urban backyard' that sharply contrasts with the official narratives of Baku as a modern city. By focusing on this region, I discussed past and present dynamics of how infrastructure, architecture, and housing have become main drivers for state-induced modernisation. They embody visions of socialist and postsocialist futures by their very materiality. They also serve as agents for the utopias and visions of the ruling elites. 'Paper architecture', the visual portrayals of existing and imagined materialities, that the Soviet state used to constantly remind citizens of the endpoint of the road to modernity has remained an important medium after Azerbaijan's independence. I have argued that this technique, having adopted newly available technologies of visual dissemination, has experienced a new heyday under the authoritarian Azerbaijani government. At the same time, the current paper architecture is embedded in a different notion of modernity and infrastructural ideology than what was upheld in Soviet times. While in the past it aimed at improving the living standards for the whole society, the postsocialist emphasis is on impression management. Infrastructure, hence, ceased to be a measure for reducing social inequalities in terms of its once inclusive and integrative function for urban inhabitants, but instead accelerated social exclusion of disadvantaged groups in the city. But although most aspects of the Soviet welfare state's care policy have disappeared in the independent era, many people's past experiences and nostalgic memories still provide a vivid framework for evaluating their present livelihoods as well as their hopes and expectations towards the state.

Chapter 3
The Soviet Housing Regime Reconsidered: Bureaucracy, Informality, and Papereality

This chapter addresses the role of bureaucracy in the Soviet housing regimes and deals with people's interactions with state authorities, their efforts, concerns, struggles and strategies in the process of obtaining proper housing. Besides giving a general overview on the mechanisms and challenges of the state's allocation practices, this chapter will provide answers to the following questions: how can we explain housing inequalities, bureaucratic flaws, and spatial peculiarities within Baku's urban society through the lens of housing? What was it like to apply for an apartment and what were the official criteria for eligibility? Which strategies did citizens apply to bypass official norms? What was the role of housing officials in this process, and how did they cope with the different expectations they had to face from superiors, their kin, and local communities? How did officials, the state, and the media deal with violations of rules at different levels of the administration hierarchy?

By following these questions, my argument in this chapter follows three themes. The first concerns the 'allocative power' of state institutions, hoarding at all levels of society and the production of chronic housing shortages, and informal strategies on the part of citizens to obtain housing. The second is about papereality and the use of numbers and other documented measurements in decisions related to housing allocation. The third is about the blurring of agency.

The anthropologist Katherine Verdery has relabelled the principle of 'rational distribution' said to characterise socialist economic systems as 'allocative power' or 'bureaucratic allocation' (Verdery 1991: 421, with reference to Konrád and Szelényi 1979). She did so in order to call attention to shortage and bureaucratic allocation as two key elements in 'actually existing' socialist planned economies. As a response to central planning that usually overstated productive capacities, she noted, firms and institutions applied strategies to hoard materials and labour so that they could deploy them when it counted most (Verdery 1991: 422). One such strategy would be to deliberately slow down output numbers or lower the quality of performance, like the Baku City Executive Committee accused the housing construction sector of doing in the 1950s (see below). With the bar lowered, firms could 'over'-perform by performing normally when necessary; they could also demand additional resources from the state or intermediary institutions, claiming that a 'lack' of these resources was hindering performance. Hoarding for later allocation was also widespread among families and networks of extended kin.

The Soviet state's constant rhetoric of a housing crisis and shortage should point our attention to housing as a key example of how the Soviet economy worked. Certainly, this rhetoric had a great impact on citizens' perception of housing: a constitutional right that was also a scarce resource. If we approach housing further as 'owned' not by an individual, but rather by families, we can further expect hoarding and allocation to be central elements of people's relations to housing.

What we know is that as a reaction to systemic shortage, people applied various strategies to acquire goods outside the official system in the informal or second economy (Verdery 1991: 432). The second economy played an essential role, for instance, in acquiring building materials. People could also deliberately bend the official system of allocation to its limits or apply various informal strategies to obtain housing. As housing was always in short supply, informality and the practice of *blat*, 'the use of personal networks and informal contacts to obtain goods and services in short supply and to find a way around formal procedures' (Ledeneva 1998: 1) was applied frequently in the allocation of dwellings. Having kin, friends, and acquaintances in neighbourhood, municipal or higher-levels of state institutions could have significant impact on the waiting time and the quality of an allocated apartment.

Hence, I seek to show here through informant accounts and archival documents, that allocative power, which increased with 'the bureaucracy's *capacity* to allocate' (Verdery 1991: 421), was not only important with regard to distributing the means of production among state firms. It also played a significant role in the allocation of some means of social reproduction, like housing. All of the economic strategies, formal and informal, that have been documented with respect to the production and procurement of consumer goods appeared in the quest for housing too. My examples in this chapter show also that such allocative power could be gained as quickly as it could be lost – as in those cases where state representatives and their beneficiaries were dismissed from office or otherwise sanctioned.

Second, in the book's broader context of representation and façade politics, I will demonstrate the primary importance for and reliance of the Soviet housing authorities on written paper and measurable numbers in decisions about allocation and the interaction between bureaucratic institutions. A central concept here is 'papereality' (Dery 1998) which was originally applied to the context of learning in bureaucratic organisation generally. The author contended that 'organizations create and maintain [...] "papereality", defined as a world of symbols, or written representations, that take precedence over the things and events represented' (ibid.: 678). As will become clear, this was also the case in the Soviet housing sector. Fulfilling the criteria for getting a place on the housing waiting list was based on valid registration and available living space per capita – quantitative assessments that only partially reflected the qualitative experience of dwelling for many households. Further, such 'representational reality created through paperwork necessarily simplifies, and at times even obscures, the lived, experienced everyday interactions between state representatives and citizens/ subjects [...]' (Endres 2018: 38). Housing officials had to create and also report on their activities and achievements through formal criteria and quantitative measurements: so many square metres allocated, so many registered persons, and so on. (If a person registered, then was allocated, then refused, then re-registered – as indicated in the previous chapter – the full chain of activities was disaggregated and alienated from the individual). The result was a tension between paper and non-paper realities.

Furthermore, I argue that it is worthwhile to conceive of paperealities in the plural as written representations at times became modified and reinterpreted on their path through institutional hierarchies. As examples in the chapter will show, authorities had the power to make exceptions and advocate a usually non-eligible case to higher authorities who would cross-check the appropriateness of changes in the papereality.

Finally, against the often-implied assumption that the Soviet state functioned smoothly between and within the state's housing-related bodies, a consideration of its housing politics demonstrates that there were not infrequently conflicts between the multiple levels of state institutions regarding blurred responsibilities, duties, and quality of performance. Furthermore, a similarly blurred picture arises when looking at the endemic multiplicity of roles among state representatives as they were also embedded in social and moral networks inside local communities – especially in the many neighbourhoods with individual construction where dense social networks and neighbourhoods were characteristic. As elsewhere in the world, state representatives worked rarely, and inconsistently, as robots that were programmed to decide applications only in strict accordance to official rules. Instead, cases were also decided on grounds of moral consideration towards the level of neediness and/ or vulnerability of the applicants.

I address these three themes of allocation, papereality, and conflict through three sections. In the first section, I describe the early Bolshevik state's attempts to transform previous ownership structures and the abolition of private property. The example of Baku demonstrates that this was far from a straightforward process but, instead, was characterised by conflicts between local, regional, and all-Soviet economic state institutions. Furthermore, I maintain that early Soviet housing policy of the 1920s constituted a basic cornerstone for old and new social inequalities that further exacerbated social differences during the large-scale housing construction programmes after the Second World War. Early housing policy, in its aftermath, turned out to disadvantage those citizens who regained their property due to the government's particular demunicipalisation policy or those who generally maintained their property due to its 'unsuitability' for public interests. This policy not only allowed the state to sort out unattractive housing stock but, simultaneously, passed on responsibilities for maintenance to the owners. This strongly contributed to the ideological ascription of inferior status to private housing and to those who inhabited them and led to a resilient hierarchical representation and evaluation of social space and housing, as described in Chapter 2.

Next, I will introduce the reader to Soviet housing norms, regulations, and practices as well as to the basic principles that decided citizens' eligibility for a new apartment – the *sanitary norm* and the *propiska*. By describing the importance of waiting lists, apartment size, registration, and housing authorities' power in the allocation process, I show how state representatives, especially on the neighbourhood and municipal levels, leveraged their power to allocate housing across the range of activities on which they held responsibility and authority. Similarly, citizens deployed a variety of legal loopholes and informal strategies to raise their chances to achieve an apartment or to improve existing housing conditions.

On the basis of public media and archival material the final section discusses the city's challenge and approaches to cope with administrational shortcomings in waiting lists and the allocation process. Many of these activities involved conflicts with housing officials at the lower end of the administrative hierarchy, namely those state representatives who had closest contact to the dwellers and the neighbourhood. At times, these intermediaries between citizens and the state lived in the neighbourhoods themselves, and were personally embedded in state hierarchies and private networks at the same time. Stephen Kotkin has stated that 'The authorities were well aware that control over the allocation of living space afforded them considerable power, which they exercised energetically' (1995: 163). While he was referring to such power as being exercised by authorities over citizens, my material shows that such power could equally be used against the state in favour of supporting one's private network. Hence, I will also demonstrate how these 'local state actors struggle with structural constraints and their discretionary powers while being embedded in many other relations within the local community that involve different sets of norms' (Thelen et al. 2014: 8). Hence, in many situations, loyalties were handled rather flexibly and attained an ambivalent character.

The Housing Question and Transformation of Property after the Revolution

After the Bolshevik Revolution, the housing sector, like all other nationalised sectors of the economy, became subject to large-scale reconstruction. The transformation of ownership structures together with the process of building up the new state and society was far from straightforward. Instead, there were administrative challenges, unclear responsibilities between state institutions, and conflicts over resource allocation. In the years after the establishment of the Azerbaijani SSR on 28 April 1920, the housing situation for Baku workers, inherited from Tsarist times was reportedly disastrous. Protocols of the Baku City Executive Committee give an idea of how officials perceived and represented the housing issue: due to the recovering oil industry and national economy, the housing question had exacerbated so much that if new residential construction did not start immediately, then the city would face very shortly a national disaster (*narodnoe bedstvie*) due to overcrowding.[43] In the same year, the Baku Soviet (Baksovet) wrote complaint letters to the Central Committee in Moscow about the lack of adequate housing for Baku workers.[44] It accused the Moscow authorities of not taking measures to counteract the 'miserable conditions of the urban economy' (Baberowski 2003: 376). The Baksovet emphasised the 'catastrophic decay' of the housing economy resulting in an average living space of only four to five square metres per person. There were specific problems too: school buildings were occupied by Red Army soldiers; more than ten workers often shared a single room in a city apartment.

---

[43] Untitled protocol from a session of the *Bakgorispolkom* sometime between May 1924 and October 1924; ARDA, f.1933, op.1, d.209, l.230.

[44] The Central Committee was the highest body within the Communist Party structure – its members elected the members of the Politburo, which was the Party's executive committee and centre of power.

Daily life and housing conditions in Baku were reported to outstrip the misery of every other aspect in Soviet everyday reality (ibid. 377). Other archival records stated that, for instance, that the average per capita living space was 40 per cent below the minimum hygienic requirement.[45] The poorest parts of the population were facing even more precarious conditions with an average space of merely two to three square metres per person, often in basement dwellings. Another challenge, besides the constantly increasing population, was that the Bolsheviks had appropriated too much of the existing housing stock for public institutions like clubs, libraries, and army barracks. This occupied space, it was criticised, would be enough to provide 7,000 people with housing. Another factor described was the catastrophic decline in the rents which tenants were supposed to pay to the municipalities. The cost of rent was set too low to maintain the local housing economy. As a result, proper renovation and maintenance of the housing stock was made impossible for those institutions in charge.

Similar problems were reported for private homeowners. The political climate and the revolution meant a sharp suspension of private construction and a serious reduction of renovation activities until, finally, houses became uninhabitable. Thus, dwellers even abandoned their property, especially in the city's peripheral regions. Finally, a further obstacle was created by the official decree On the Construction Law which obliged people to transfer their ownership rights over recently constructed dwellings into the city's property fund (*sobstvennost' goroda*) after a defined period of time. Consequently, this was reported to have discouraged any engagement in further individual construction.

Another problem arose in a shortage of resources for individual construction that were to be provided by the administration. The local Soviets lacked necessary resources and were not supported by the higher state institutions. On that ground, several measures were suggested to react on the stated problems and to counteract the housing crisis. Most importantly, the Baku City Executive Committee insisted on obliging industrial, economic, and other corporate institutions, particularly Azneft (the state oil company created after the Bolshevik Revolution), to engage in housing construction for the majority of workers who were accommodated in overcrowded hostels.

The urgent demands by the Baksovet to pass on housing responsibilities primarily to Azneft point to a deeper conflict between the Baksovet and local industry. After 1920, Azneft became primarily a supplier

---

[45] All information in this paragraph is based on the following archival document: *Predlozheniia kommunkhoza: priniatie prezidiumom Baksoveta o zhilishchnom krizise* (1924); ARDA, f.1933, op.1, d.205, ll.233–234.

of products to Moscow and did not pay taxes to the local government (Baberowski 2003: 376). Back in those days, it neither contributed to the development of Baku's urban infrastructure nor to the education of desperately needed skilled labourers (in contrast to the pre-revolutionary period). Instead, skilled labourers were sent from the centre to the periphery to save money for their education and to foist off responsibility for infrastructural development and education on the local government (ibid.). As a result, the Baksovet criticised Azneft for generating profit without participating in financing communal services (ibid.). With regard to the provision of housing construction, activities improved between 1923 and 1932. During this time Azneft provided for 46 per cent of all new housing in the city and its surroundings, while the Baksovet contributed 18 per cent and oversaw the private sector (of self-built houses) which amounted to 12 per cent of new housing stock (the rest was provided by other urban industries and institutions).[46] With only few exceptions of architecturally sophisticated residential areas (e.g. Armenikend, Mamed''iarov, or Montin), most housing construction in Baku during that time consisted of low-storey buildings for the masses of workers. These examples from the 1920s reflect the institutional struggles over unclear responsibilities, duties, and organisational questions which apparently improved partly in the case of housing construction in Baku (although deficiencies in the housing construction sector was a constant issue). In later decades, discussions seemed to shift more towards the (non-)fulfilment and deliberate manipulation of plan quotas.

Concerning the Fifth Five-Year Plan (1951–55), for instance, the chairman of the Bakgorispolkom reported to the State Planning Committee of the USSR about the insufficient performance (only about 65 per cent had been accomplished) and increasing difficulties of fulfilling the plan.[47] He put blame on the country's ministries and institutions which continuously decreased their construction activities year after year. The lack of

---

[46] *Spravka o nalichii i sostoianii zhilogo fonda i ob"eme kapital'nogo stroitel'stva zhilykh zdanii v g. Baku i v uezdakh (raionakh) Azerbaidzhanskoi SSR za 1922-1932 gg.* (1959); ARDA, f.411, op.38, d.166, ll.76–90.

According to A. S. Aliyeva (1979: 66), the construction activities by *Azneft* in that period created or extended settlements such as *Binəqədi* (for 8,000 persons), *Yeni Suraxanı* (12,000), *Binə* (5,000), *Lökbətən* (15,000) or *Stepan Razin* (today *Bakıxanov*, for 25,000). Today, *Binəqədi* is an administrative district within Baku, while the other settlements are counted as municipalities.

[47] The State Planning Committee was referred to as Gosplan, an abbreviation for the literally translated *Gosudarstvennyi planovyi komitet.* Letter from 1956 in response to *Gosplan's* enquiry to the *Bakgorispolkom* about the plan performance in the housing construction sector in the years 1951–55; ARDA, f.411, op.38, d.148, ll. 82–86.

achievements, he stated, 'are the results of insufficient attention from the side of ministries and departments to meet the aims in the housing construction sector'. He also criticised the unsatisfactory work of the contractor organisations, especially of the Azerbaijani SSR's Ministry for Urban and Rural Construction. As he further stated, the unsatisfactory quality was also connected to deficiencies in the whole production chain for building materials. All in all, he concluded, there was no organisation in the construction sector which performed according to the requirements. They all significantly slowed down the construction speed and lowered the quality of their performance.

Having seized power another major challenge for Bolshevik authorities was managing the transformation of existing ownership structures. With the municipalisation of the city's housing stock, ownership of local properties was transferred to the municipal authorities (i.e. to the districts' *ispolkom*). Based on the Decree on the Abolition of the Private Ownership of Urban Real Estates from 20 August 1918, the Bolsheviks nationalised and municipalised the urban housing stock shortly after having established the Azerbaijani SSR on 28 April 1920.

The difference between nationalised and municipalised housing is based on the official distinctions between types of housing tenures which were applied throughout the USSR's existence. Housing within the state sector was divided into municipalised and nationalised housing. Municipalised housing was that owned by the local Soviets of each district. In the early Soviet period, the local Soviets were primarily responsible for the expropriation of property from its former owners and then controlled the redistribution of it. Nationalised housing (usually referred to as the departmental fund), included housing belonging to and run by 'state institutions, enterprises, organisations, trade unions and other co-operative bodies' (Andrusz 1984: 27).

Two categories of housing remained that were neither municipalised nor nationalised, hence outside the state sector: the house-building cooperatives, and the private sector. The cooperative sector played a significant role only in the years after the Second World War. In the Bolshevik period, housing cooperatives became subject to antipathies within the Party due to their semi-autonomous status and attraction for the privileged section of society (ibid.: 38). Finally, there was the private sector of individual construction or, 'the tenure of personal property' (Smith 2010: 89). The private sector played a prominent role in most Soviet cities, even though this role was publicly downplayed for ideological reasons. As in Baku, the private sector provided a buffer for the state against the constant pressure to produce sufficient residential units.

Shortly after the Bolsheviks' wholesale expropriation, a large share of housing property was returned to the previous owners. Some authors have described the measures of denationalisation and demunicipalisation in the 1920s as 'the cornerstone of Soviet urban housing policies' during the New Economic Policy (NEP) of 1921–28 (DiMaio 1974: 12). Based on the decree On Reviewing Lists of Municipalised Houses by Communal Sections from 8 August 1921, the local Soviets received the order to review their municipalised housing stock within a period of two months. The decree 'was a call to the entire population, especially to former house owners, to help repair and save existing residential buildings' (ibid.). After approval by the People's Commissariat of Internal Affairs (NKVD), houses could then be returned to their former owners because of their small size or 'unsuitability to public needs' (ibid.). The state was completely overburdened by the requirements of providing necessary repairs and maintenance to the entirety of its recently acquired housing stock and therefore had a great interest in returning such responsibilities to the former homeowners (Obertreis 2004: 77). Baku archives contain numerous applications from the early 1920s for the restoration of property rights through demunicipalisation. By March 1922, Baku officials had received around 7,000 applications for demunicipalisation and around 5,300 houses had been returned to their former owners.[48] Compared to other cities, this was a relatively high amount. In Saint Petersburg, officials at first followed a model of transferring a life-long use-right to former owners —a plan which had not been envisaged by the central authorities in Moscow. After adapting the union-wide demunicipalisation policy, Saint Petersburg's city administration had received only 2,749 applications and approved 1,385 by August 1927 (ibid.: 88). Thus, we can summarise that, on a general level, officials and decision-makers were unclear about how to properly organise and administer the private housing sector and 'the implementation of the process as well as the difference between municipalised and nationalised housing remained often unclear to the authorities in charge' (ibid.: 78). What is also important to note is that a relatively large proportion of the private housing stock in Baku had never been municipalised in the first place. The campaign only affected dwellings with an estimated pre-war value of more than 30,000 Rubles. According to the Archive of the Central Bank of Russia, this would have been in the range of 15,000 USD at the time. As a result, in 1927, only 38 per cent of overall square metres of living space were at the Baksovet's disposal – a share that, after all, reached 69 per cent in 1933 as homeowners transferred ownership to the municipalities.[49]

---

[48] *Spravka o nalichii i sostoianii zhilogo fonda;* ARDA, f.411, op.38, d.166, l.76.

[49] *Spravka o nalichii i sostoianii zhilogo fonda;* ARDA, f.411, op.38, d.166, l.80.

The expropriations and returns of property points to the often-contradictory processes in the transformation of economic, institutional, and administrative relations during the early Soviet years. Alongside the effort to implement structures based on the vision of a communist society came the demand for pragmatism. The greater market-orientation of the NEP was meant to make this possible, but it also conflicted with directives and procedures given during the hardship years of revolution.

Through demunicipalisation, the state redirected responsibility for the property that was to become its least attractive and least viable as housing stock. Over the long-term, citizens who maintained or who were given back their status as private owners, found themselves in a structurally disadvantaged position. Whereas initially the continuity of private ownership seemed attractive, private owners could foresee neither the relatively high costs of maintaining their property nor the chronic shortages of building materials. During the privatisation-campaign of the 1990s, again, they were disadvantaged because the value of their houses – by now old and badly-maintained – was significantly below that of the privatised socialist apartments.

Mechanisms of Housing Allocation: Waiting Lists, the Sanitary Norm, and the Propiska

With Khrushchev's housing campaign, citizens developed a new kind of awareness for the scarce good of housing which was promised overnight to every family. Such political prioritisation of providing citizens with separate apartments was later legally codified. Article 44 of the Constitution of the USSR, adopted in 1977, says that 'citizens of the USSR have the right to housing' and that this right, *inter alia* is ensured by 'fair distribution under public control of living space'.[50] However, 'fair distribution' was not defined in the constitution, and the people retained the right for themselves to judge whether or not the distributional system was fair. To a large degree, one's perception of fairness depended on whether or not one belonged to the group of new 'homeowners'.

When applying for an apartment, the first step was to get on a waiting list. This constituted the primary obstacle to obtaining housing. Colloquially, the waiting list for housing was called *ochered'* while in official documents it was referred to as *kvartirnyi uchet*. The waiting list, 'which anybody who lived in the USSR remembers only too well, [...] proved to be less a

---

[50] For the Russian version see:http://constitution.garant.ru/history/ussr-rsfsr/1977/red_1977/ 5478732/ chapter/7/#block_700. Last accessed 23 April 2015.

pioneering communist institution than a complicated socio-political phenomenon' because '[g]etting a place on the waiting list or being excluded from it become a crucial barometer of the relationship between an individual and the state' (Trudolyubov 2018: 160). To get one's name on the list, people had to meet specific requirements – most definitive were those concerning one's right to live in Baku (i.e. that one's propiska was issued to a Baku address) and the size of one's current dwelling (i.e. that it did not meet the sanitary norm). But before registering, one also had to decide on which list to register. There were two types: waiting lists connected to the workplace or, for citizens unable to work (such as pensioners, invalids, or single mothers with many children), the waiting list at the local housing office (ZhEK). Because almost everyone was employed, most people were expected to register on the waiting list of the employing institution. The system was sufficiently complex, however, that the best procedure was rarely clear in advance and people remained very much dependent on the housing authorities. These authorities, being integrated in a chain of bureaucratic hierarchies, could exercise enormous influence on the outcome of each and every case.

ZhEK (Zhilishchno-Ekspluatatsionnaia Kontora), the Housing Management Office, constituted the most local level institution dealing with all housing-related matters. Established in 1959 to rationalise and improve the organisation and administration of the state-housing stock (Andrusz 1984: 57; see also DiMaio 1974: 155–174; Reid 2011), it was the primary nexus between citizens and the executive committees with regard to housing applications, maintenance, supervision, and control. The ZhEKs were subordinate to the regional executive committee (*raiispolkom*). They were tasked to preserve and manage the housing stock; to properly conduct the housing economy; to implement routine and major renovations of buildings; to smoothly provision service, equipment, and the maintenance of residential houses and private homes for good sanitary conditions; to ensure the careful treatment of apartments and houses by tenants; and to improve the living conditions of residents. The ZhEKs were also responsible for keeping a detailed record of each person's place of residence and other personal data. Clearly the duty of registering citizens made the ZhEKs 'an instrument of central government and surveillance, subjection and control' (Reid 2011: 162), but they were meant to serve the citizens' interests.

Each ZhEK was headed by a director who was approved by the executive committee of the local Soviet. And the ZhEKs were meant to carry out all their economic and organisational duties in close contact with the public housing committee and the assets of residents' houses (see Prokhorov 1972: 217). However, as I will show below, ZhEK-employees also followed their own interests and could use their position to favour people in their close networks. The quality of a ZhEK's performance differed from district to district, and even from office to office, but in general 'it was notorious for its corruption and inefficiency' (Reid 2011: 160).

Regardless of whether people applied for the waiting list at their workplace or at the local ZhEK, all lists were cross-checked and approved by the *raiispolkom*. Successful applicants received a confirmation letter that contained information on the size of the presently inhabited room or dwelling as well as on the number of people in the applicant's household and their degree of kinship to the applicant. When a person was granted an apartment (or rather a family, since a single person had almost no chance of getting on the list), he or she would receive the so-called *order*, an almost sacred document which marked the allocation of an apartment. A family could wait several years, sometimes more than a decade, to receive the *order*. Some groups of citizens enjoyed privileged access to waiting lists and additional housing space, basically 'those most favoured by Soviet society in other ways as well' (Barry 1977: 7). This included 'responsible workers' such as high-rank Party-officials, Heroes of the Soviet Union, Heroes of Socialist Labour, high-rank military members, professors, scientists, and members of the various unions of creative artists (ibid.). Among the underprivileged were the 'urban poor' (Morton 1984: 75) – suburbanites, migrants who were officially restricted from moving into the city centre, workers living in dormitories or barracks, as well as those inhabiting dwellings in pre-socialist *məhǎlləs* like Sovetski.

There were two major criteria for any access to the waiting lists and to urban housing in general. These 'two most powerful routine administrative tools' (Smith 2010: 159) to exercise control over housing allocation and tenancy rights were the sanitary norm and the propiska. The sanitary norm (*sanitarnaia norma*) stipulated the minimum living space per capita. A family was eligible to move into a bigger apartment when the available square metres per capita were below the sanitary norm. The propiska, or residence permit, confirmed a person's legal right to dwell in a specific urban area. Both these mechanisms were closely connected and frequently manipulated by citizens. The more people who held propiskas for a particular dwelling, the less space there was per capita. Hence, the better were the chances of receiving additional living space. For instance, the main tenants of an apartment might register family members to their apartment, even when the individuals did not live there (see below). But there were limits: the request to issue a propiska could be denied if the sanitary norm of the apartment would be violated by the extra tenant.

The whole process was based on counting people and space, in quantifiable terms, which were translated into official documents. In order to somehow manage, organise, and institutionalise itself, the Soviet state, like any other, was based on a bureaucratic apparatus which can only work well and effectively on the basis of numbers, statistics, and 'paper'. Although such a reductionist, simplifying, and generalising approach made the situation manageable, it also resulted in a distorted view of everyday housing conditions and inequalities. Government reports carried information on the quantitative assessments, 'average' housing conditions, and statistical figures about existing or to-be-built square metres of living space. They never told much about the inner workings of the system, or why it never seemed possible to resolve – or overcome – the housing 'crisis'. By use of additional sources, the following sections provide a more accessible view on citizens' experiences and interaction with state representatives and the decision-making processes of the latter.

The sanitary norm described the amount of per capita living space that was guaranteed by Soviet law to people residing in cities and urban settlements (Barry 1977: 2). However, this norm was far from uniform and the amount differed between the Union republics and also changed over time. For instance, in 1926, a union-wide sanitary norm of nine square metres of living space (*zhilaia ploshchad'*) per capita was set (Andrusz 1984: 20). But the republics could set their own higher norms, and Georgia and Azerbaijan set it at twelve square metres (Barry 1977: 7). In practice, the threshold served not as a minimum but as a maximum, as authorities limited the allocation of 'excess' housing space. Housing applications in the Baku archives from the mid-1970s to the mid-1980s, for instance, show that people were usually rejected when the per capita living space of their current housing exceeded five square metres. Thus, though they were legally entitled to twelve, they could not become eligible until they lived in less than five.

The propiska system has been the focus of lively discussion. In addition to its relevance for a person's eligibility for urban housing, it regularly triggered conversations on the wider issue of society's cleavage between city and countryside. The propiska constituted 'a shadow area of Soviet law whose rules are largely unpublished or published for restricted use' (Barry 1977: 12). It served as a control mechanism to restrict migration into cities and to regulate people's general mobility (Matthews 1993: 27; Höjdestrand 2009: 22; Attwood 2010: 215) and, more specifically, to prevent 'migrants from integrating themselves into distributional networks in restricted cities' (Buckley 1995: 896). The propiska 'was the stamp in the internal passport with which local housing administrations registered Soviet citizens at their home address. It was an absolute legal requirement, which was incidentally checked during unrelated bureaucratic processes, from starting a job to getting married' (Smith 2010: 160).

The propiska system was created in 1932 alongside a new passport system that aimed towards restricting people's mass immigration to large cities due to rural mass famine and expanding urban industrialisation (Höjdestrand 2009: 22). Long afterwards, the propiska granted and restricted access to all kinds of public services and infrastructure. For those who wanted to access the capital cities to enhance their future perspectives, getting a propiska was the primary obstacle. As one of my informants explained to me:

> A propiska was absolutely needed. If a person from the countryside came to Baku in order to inscribe for higher education, then he was automatically granted a propiska. Or if the person was a close relative, one would forward a written application to the authorities who, then, usually granted a *propiska* [if the sanitary norm per capita allowed for it]. The government did not have capabilities to construct large amounts of housing but in connection with the urbanisation process many people came here for their studies, for work, and for building up a livelihood. In those days, this was a common characteristic of urbanisation that led to a large housing problem within the city. Therefore, the state applied such a rule – without a propiska you could not obtain urban housing, hence, you had to live in the countryside. Simultaneously, that practice artificially slowed down the process of urbanisation.[51]

The lack of a propiska did not necessarily prevent rural migrants from moving to the cities. Instead, people found ways to negotiate and arrange themselves with the district authorities.

When a person wanted to apply for any housing list, one requirement was to prove residence in Baku for at least five years. Young specialists who had studied at an institution of higher education for the standard period of five years would have resided and become registered usually in student dormitories of the respective institutions. Apart from them, only a very limited amount of people, usually with special qualifications, could be invited to move to the city by a higher organisation, ministry, or department as well as by the decision of a Party committee or by the Cabinet of Ministers. This, at some level, was perceived as dividing citizens into two major groups, urban and rural dwellers.

---

[51] Expert interview on 11 December 2013.

Among those who had been allocated housing, a frequent practice carefully regulated by law (Barry 1977: 19) was apartment exchange – a feature of the Soviet housing system that was famously described in Yuri Trifonov's satirical novel *The Exchange* (*Obmen*), published in 1969. Primarily, getting to live closer to one's relatives but also changes in household size due to birth or death of its members were usual reasons for exchange. Equally widespread were exchanges after divorce when former couples sought to exchange their apartment for two smaller ones. Old age could serve as a reason for families with pensioners to exchange a fifth-storey apartment for one on the ground level. Often, exchange was additionally motivated by spatial-locational considerations in order to live in closer distance to the workplace or to family members who needed care. Both housing exchange between and within cities were common.

One case from my ethnography illustrates some important aspects of this process: Rahib Gözəlov, a 77-year-old man with a small retail shop in our neighbourhood lived with his Russian wife, his second son, and the son's family what had been a three-room Khrushchevka-apartment[52] until they had divided it in two and made a separate entrance for each unit. At the age of 21, Rahib had moved to the Russian city of Volgograd where he worked as an ambulance driver and got to know his future wife. After their son and first daughter were born, they applied to a housing cooperative and received their own apartment in the early 1970s. Generally, cooperative housing constituted an alternative to the much longer waiting lists for state housing and gave dwellers the right not only to exchange but also to sell the apartment. Cooperative housing was also of better quality than in the state housing sector. A member paid 40 per cent of the apartment's price in advance. After moving in, dwellers continued to make monthly payments until the dwelling was finally paid off. First established in 1924, cooperative housing was abolished by Stalin in 1937, and then reintroduced in 1962 (Andrusz 1984: 83; 2002: 135).

In 1975 the Gözəlovs decided to give up their cooperative apartment and moved to Baku 'via' apartment exchange to be physically closer to Rahib's relatives. He explained how:

> During one of my visits to Baku, I made an announcement in the journal *Birzha*. After a person had read my ad, his wife came to Volgograd to see my apartment. In turn, I did not look personally at

---

[52] The Khrushchevka is the still widespread term for mass residential housing introduced by Khrushchev in the mid-1950s and constructed during his political leadership. Mostly built with standardised panel elements, they allowed construction at a high pace and a focus on functionality. Hence, this also meant sacrifices in quality for which they later became perceived as inferior compared to most residential construction before and after.

their apartment in Baku. Since my brother was living in Baku, I asked him to inspect it on my behalf. He liked the place and I finally decided to exchange my three-room apartment. Then I returned to Baku.

After having managed the necessary paperwork and several visits to the housing authorities, a more or less equal apartment exchange like this was usually approved. Every larger city had a Bureau of Housing Exchange (an agency of the Department of Registration and Allocation of Housing) with offices in each urban district. They accepted advertisements for the regularly published *Bulletin* and they had a card file with exchange-seeking citizens (Morton 1980: 245).[53] Additionally, in Baku as elsewhere there was also a 'lively open-air "stock market" trading rooms and flats [...] just outside the central exchange bureau's office' (ibid. 246). Sometimes, these practices led to labyrinthine apartment exchanges involving several families in several cities (see also Morton 1980: 239).

At times, however, it was not enough to rely on the stipulated institutional rules for urban registration, housing requests, or exchange. Social networks were an important means for gaining required information and support at various points. Members of a privileged group or institution could almost be sure of a positive outcome, regardless of how complex the operation – if only because they benefitted from the advocacy of people with influence. In one case, for instance, a 39-year-old female chief inspector of a polytechnic succeeded in exchanging her apartment, not with another individual tenant, but with the *ispolkom*. She received crucial support from her director who wrote a letter to the chairman of Baksovet. The main reason to apply for apartment exchange was the distance of the original apartment to her daughter's school. Over a full two pages, the director described the 'serious burden' experienced by the family, and then detailed a convenient solution in which the *ispolkom* would act as the other party in the exchange process. It should be further pointed out that the applicant had already identified the apartment of her choice: it was a recently vacated apartment in the communal housing fund. (That she had picked out an apartment testifies to significant work she had undertaken, presumably through social networks; that she got the one she wanted testifies, again, to her relative privilege). The director closed his letter by referring to the attractiveness of the exchange for

---

[53] Besides placing their advertisements on public noticeboards, individuals could also advertise in the mentioned bulletin 'issued monthly which [was] devoted solely to house exchanges (*Byulleten' po obmenu zhiloi ploschchadi*)' (Andrusz 1984: 213).

the *ispolkom* because the applicant would give a three-room apartment for a two-room one.[54]

As I pointed out in the introduction, the widespread application of informal arrangements – in Soviet as well as in present-day Baku – was characterised to a high degree by what is locally known as *taps* and which is largely dependent on personal connections to a *dayday* – a powerful supporter in economic, bureaucratic, and administrational issues. As I will show in a later section of the paper, some people were creative and skilful in using personal networks and kin relations for housing issues – although this has always been a risky undertaking for everyone involved.

The following decisions on applicants' approval or rejection to the housing list shall demonstrate, that besides simply sticking to official rules, authorities often acknowledged other criteria important in individual cases. Also important is that housing norms were sufficiently vague (Barry 1977: 24), and this ambiguity provided further fertile ground for bending official rules in favour of private interests – for applicants as well as for housing authorities especially on the local level institutions. The following archival material documents all belong to *fond* 23 which is assigned to the *ispolkom* of the former October District (since 1992 Yasamal District). In the first example, I translate the document close to the original structure and formulatii in order to give the reader an impression of the language used. Later, I describe the cases in my own words to prevent stereotypical formulations.

> Sadykhova Mekhpara Agaguseyn kyzy,[55] family composition two people (herself, son), registered and residing in a dwelling of the local Soviet at the following address: [...], living space 18 square metres. Sadykhova M.A. is a widow of a fallen war-veteran and, connected to this, she approached the *ispolkom* with the request to accept her for the housing list. On common grounds, Sadykhova cannot be accepted for the housing list because the surplus of living space is 8 square metres. However, considering the occupied living space located in an old housing stock with limited public services and the fact that two people of different sex are living in one single room, the *ispolkom* considers an exceptional acceptance on the housing list as possible [...].[56]

---

[54] Untitled letter to the chairman of Bak*sovet*, 9 December 1990; ARDABF, f.16, op.1, d.4035, ll.63–64.

[55] The document notes the woman's family name, personal name, and patronym in feminised form (daughter of Agaguseyn).

[56] *O priniatii na kvartirnyi uchet* (22 February 1985); ARDABF, f.23, op.1, d.2252, l.37.

The document shows – not only how the minimum sanitary norm (5 square metres per person) was used as a maximum – but also that housing authorities had the power to bend official rules and to make exceptional decisions in favour of the applicant. Furthermore, in this case, the authorities mentioned to forward their decision to the Bakgorispolkom which should finally decide about the decision's legitimacy. I encountered many similar exceptions in which decisions were based on whether household members of different sex had to share one single room. Other reasons in the above example that are taken to justify an exception include belonging to a privileged group (e.g. war veterans and their widows), the aged housing stock, and limited public services. Interestingly, while official papers put emphasis primarily on numbers and square metres of available living space, people I talked to almost exclusively put much more emphasis on the number of rooms related to household compositions and questions of gender. This suggests that the latter criteria gained additional weight in the decision-making process of housing administrators. Arguments about care-arrangements and children's schooling, as seen in the previous case and in Chapter 2, also mattered.

In most cases, official data diverged from the actual living situation in a house. The practices to create maximally favourable conditions on paper were an open secret among citizens, housing officials, and administrative bodies. Whether the secret was kept, and the curtain maintained, at least in socially dense neighbourhoods, was dependent on the quality of social relations. There was no clear distinction between state and citizens in this regard; administrators within the housing system acknowledged it as common practice:

> There were certain components in the propiska system which one could make use of. Let's consider for instance my personal case. Initially, I, my wife, and a relative of mine received a three-room apartment. Later, after the birth of my two daughters, we were five people registered there. My kids grew up, my elder daughter married and moved to her husband's. In order to receive a bigger apartment for five people, I did not cancel her name from the list although she was already living elsewhere. We went to the *raiispolkom* and explained that in our family we are five people and that a three-room apartment is too small. We asked for a bigger one – that is how we got it. Formally, she was registered with us despite the factual situation. This was common practice everywhere; Russian families acted like this as did the Azeri ones – everyone did it.

Only by such practices one can one make sense of a case in a housing list from 1978 in which 19 people (the applicant, his wife, their three children, his father and mother, three sisters, three brothers, one brother-in-law, and five nephews) shared an apartment of 47 square metres.[57] This makes less than 2.5 square metres overall living space per person – the number of registered persons probably raised questions to every state representative who looked at the application about phantom registrations, additional though undocumented living space, or how such a people-space ratio could work in practice.

A strategy that had been useful at one point in an individual's or family's life could cause problems later. Discrepancies between the address listed on one's propiska and one's actual dwelling constituted such a case, but housing authorities could and would sometimes negotiate the outcome of exceptional cases in the claimant's favour. In general, propiska and work were inseparable, as suggested by the common phrase, '*propiski net, raboty net – raboty net, propiski net*', which means 'no propiska, no job – no job, no propiska' (Höjdestrand 2009: 23). Still, the housing system might help one around the Catch-22, as happened not once, but twice, for M. Zarbaliev:

> The citizen Zarbaliev, M. [...] is residing at the following address without propiska: [...]. However, he is legally registered at the dormitory N° 43 [...] because it was necessary for him to find work in order to support his four children. His first child [son's name], born on 15 February 1953 and not registered anywhere, consequently cannot obtain a registration certificate from the military commissariat. His other children are underage and also live at the above stated address without propiska. Considering the fact that citizen Zarbaliev [...] actually is not living in the dormitory he was consequently discharged [lost his propiska there]. Though, in order to work, he requires a proof of residence, which he could not submit and was therefore dismissed from work. [...] Currently, he approached the *ispolkom* to apply for a propiska for himself and his four children at the address where he is actually residing since 1964 [...]. The request [...] is granted and the passport department of the October District shall be instructed to register [the applicant] with his four children at the following address [...].[58]

Similar double-bind situations were quite common, motivating widespread jokes and criticism of the Kafkaesque character of Soviet bureaucracy.

M. Zarbaliev's actions would have been anticipated, perhaps even recommended, by the housing authorities. For newcomers to the city, it was common way to first move into a hostel or dormitory in order to get the (temporary) propiska which was required to find employment. Equally

---

[57] *O priniatii na edinyi kvartirnyi uchet* (11 August 1978); ARDABF, f.23, op.1, d.1663, l.42.

[58] *O propiske gr. Zarbalieva M.* (27 July 1971); ARDABF, f.23, op.1, d.1009, l.19.

common would have been for a newly hired worker to be offered a place in the employers' hostel. Such hostels, however, were often unsuitable for families, and after obtaining a propiska linked to a hostel, a worker was likely to arrange a private room for his family (Andrusz 1984: 104). Like Zarbaliev, who kept his old propiska for seven years (from 1964 until the above application in 1971), many hesitated to undertake the procedures that would normalise their registrations. On the basis of other archival material, historical accounts by people I interviewed, as well as observations on the contemporary housing situation, it is clear that people often hesitated to engage in bureaucratic matters unless and until it was absolutely necessary. In the above case, that point was reached when Zarbaliev's eldest son had to register for military service. It is striking that other authorities, in the education and medical systems, had passed over the anomalies in the children's registrations – but a certain laxity concerning the registration of children was widespread in the Soviet Union (see Matthews 1993: 44).

Such hesitation was not necessarily motivated by long-term strategy, as some of the earlier examples of apartment allocation and exchange might be construed. Sometimes it was due to the fact that many people were not so familiar with the peculiarities of the urban housing regime. Navigating housing, like any other bureaucratic sphere, required competencies that were gained by experience and by actively seeking out the necessary information. Indeed, even in the postsocialist period, it became clear from personal conversations, that many of my informants privatised their apartments quite late and then only because they wanted to sell the apartment or because they needed collateral to obtain credit. For many, privatisation was just perceived as a cumbersome journey into the jungle of bureaucracy without any real benefits. In the beginning, at least, they perceived their rights as tenants in a state-owned dwelling as very similar to those of private owners. The slight difference, in their eyes, was that private owners had the right to sell their house, but until people had the intention to sell, this difference did not matter.

In contrast to citizens' alleged powerlessness in the official propiska system, individuals were also able to influence, negotiate, and manipulate the process within the system's boundaries. Cynthia Buckley, for instance, wrote about 'the myth of managed migration' and claimed that the Soviet propiska system actually 'exerted only a slight influence on aggregate urbanization patterns and migration flows' (Buckley 1995: 896). The myth lasted even as data disproved it: Henry Morton (1980) accounted for the strategies and loopholes that people applied to bypass official regulations. With regard to the propiska system he stated that, 'like many other controls in Soviet society, [it] is in the good Russian tradition – beatable, and housing bureaucrats frequently deal with phantom figures' because 'many people living in large cities do not live at their place of registration' (Morton 1980: 242). Most importantly, it seems that phantom registrations were often deliberately used in order to obtain better housing, or simply hoarded because it was valuable: 'Like any scarce commodity, housing is hoarded. Why give up something valuable when it can be put to good use for exchange [...], for rental, and, most importantly, as a legacy for one's children' (ibid.). Thus, in the long-term 'most families sought to enlarge and improve their housing resources' which were rather perceived by citizens as being owned by a family and not by any individual (Roberts et al. 2000: 86). In order to hoard such a resource, the propiska was the elementary requirement because the use-right of a dwelling could be transferred to or inherited only by registered co-residents. As I explained in the introduction, it is in that very sense that the house in Soviet urban contexts was transformed into a corporate body, a moral or legal person in Lévi-Straussian terms. This process was strongly enhanced by the administrational and political framework of the Soviet housing regime.

The acquisition, exchange, and maintenance of property, however, also engendered cooperative relations along broader social networks. To show the degree to which obtaining housing for one person or family might draw on solidarities between colleagues, neighbours, and strangers, it is useful to consider fictitious marriage, queue jumping, squatting, and unauthorised construction.

According to Morton (1980), fictitious marriage and jumping the queue were among the most regularly applied informal strategies for obtaining (better) urban housing. Fictitious marriage (*fiktivnyi brak*) was one way for people to get access to the cities. It was 'a quick route out of the provinces' if one could find 'a marriageable resident with a *propiska*' (Morton 1980: 249). A female lawyer verified that this had been practised in Baku too:

> Fictitious marriage was a widespread method to improve housing and to access the city. If a person lacked the possibility to obtain housing through official ways, then he or she would seek alternative ways, particularly by entering a fictitious marriage. But in some cases, state authorities paid occasional visits to homes in order to check whether the family lived together on the basis of a fictitious or decent marriage. It was a regular reason for court trials since such arrangements were strictly forbidden. However, despite prohibition, people engaged in the matter and were even paying money for that.

But, in the case of Azerbaijan, she explained, such a strategy was primarily applied by middle-aged people. These were people who had been married 'properly' before, founded a family, and then gotten divorced. In such cases, a fictitious marriage was not likely to cause problems in the romantic, sexual, or domestic life of either party and could be treated as a purely contractual relation.

From the state's perspective, the problem of fictitious marriages cannot be underestimated. An archival document of the October District's *raiispolkom* from 1991 states that an increase in fictitious marriage for obtaining housing had become such a pressing issue that the Baksovet passed a decree to counteract the illegal acquisition of housing by means of fictitious marriage. According to that decision, the legal right to housing space through marriage expires if the husband/ wife/ tenant *moves out* within six years after registration of the marriage.[59]

Jumping the housing queue in order to shorten the waiting periods was another widespread practice and usually involved bribes and good contacts (Morton 1980: 250). Yet it seems rare that bribing alone could move one more than a few spaces up in the queue. Beyond the individual level, such practice was reportedly applied on a collective and institutional level, too, as I was told by one of my informants:

> For instance, if a person knew that he was next on the housing list, then he could approach the responsible person in the *raiispolkom* and say, 'I know that in this month you will be allocated five apartments from the municipal housing fond. I ask you to allocate one of those apartments to institution XY in which I work'. Since the person would be first on the list of his institution, he would be the one to receive the said apartment. Thus, by paying a certain amount of money one could accelerate the process.

Thus successful queue jumping also required certain kinds of information – such as how many apartments were coming up – but it was also useful to know the hierarchy of allocation among firms. Of course, a particularly skilful chairman might negotiate a better rank for his firm in the allocations of the authorities:

> Every organisation had a different yet unwritten priority for receiving apartments. In Baku we had an air-conditioner factory which was producing for the whole Soviet Union and which was given more priority to housing allocation than let's say a small bread-producing factory. Much was also dependent on the head of an enterprise. If it was a respected, dignified, and punchy personality, he was able to negotiate more apartments at the *raiispolkom* by arguing that he has many employees, a much too long waiting list,

---

[59] *Rasporiazhenie* No. 05/35 (1 March 1991); ARDABF, f.23, op.1, d.2835, l.40.

and so on. He would further approach his employees and tell them to collect money to have, let's say, altogether 10,000 Rubles, that he then would forward to the responsible housing official. Consequently, such a person could negotiate more housing units for his workers, who, having contributed to the pot, would receive their apartments faster than usual.[60]

In contrast to fictitious marriages and queue jumping, which have been often mentioned in the literature on Soviet Russia, cases of house squatting are far less discussed. There are some famous cases: the historian Steven Harris (2013), for example, began his monograph on mass housing and everyday life after Stalin with an account on 131 construction workers who, in 1956 together with their families, had squatted in twenty apartments of the state housing project which they just had completed in Moscow. For three days they resisted the police's attempts to remove them, after which the documentation of their exploits disappeared. In Baku, squatting occurred primarily in the city's low-rise neighbourhoods (like Sovetski) among larger families who dwelled under cramped conditions. An internal document of the October District's *raiispolkom* from 1978, for example, noted that eight families in Sovetski, each consisting of six to nineteen members and officially inhabiting one or two rooms from the municipal housing fund, had squatted in the adjacent rooms and apartments of their buildings after the former tenants had moved out.[61] In some cases, the 'squatters' had been living under such illegal conditions for twenty years. Presumably, the situation could persist for so long because the apartments taken over by the squatters were not in condition to be re-allocated. It was only in November 1978 that the *ispolkom* legalised these cases without any sanctions due to the lapse of time.[62]

Finally, one widespread strategy to access housing in urban areas was through the unauthorised construction of additional rooms, balconies, and other structures.[63] Though technically of a different order than fictitious

---

[60] Ibid.

[61] The example with 19 people having shared one room of 10 square metres is again telling with regard to people's propiska politics. In addition to the main tenant, there was registered: his father, mother, 2 brothers, sister, 2 daughters-in-law, 10 nephews, and son-in-law. The combination is an unlikely one, as one notices that certain people are missing: the tenant's wife, two sons, one daughter, and the spouses of his brothers and sister are not registered.

[62] *O predostavlenii zhilploshchadi grazhdanam iz osvobozhdennogo zhilogo fonda* (29 November 1978); ARDABF, f.23, op.1, d.1681; ll.76–77.

[63] The term for these constructions, *samovol'noe stroenie*, conveys a certain ambiguity about whether they were 'prohibited' or simply 'not authorised' by the authorities, as *samovol'noe* can be translated as 'self-willed' (i.e. self-authorised). Usually, it is applied in contexts where authorisation is required.

marriage, queue jumping, and squatting, unauthorised construction nevertheless concerned the authorities. An enquiry by the Bakgorispolkom gives an idea about such activities in the October District in the first half of the 1970s. On 1 January 1971, the Bakgorispolkom started an initiative on the 'prevention of unauthorised construction [...] of living rooms, kitchens, shower rooms, garages etc.' – activities that were reported to 'intensify with every year' and because of which the district Soviets were instructed to investigate on the issue. The available reports do not explain why the construction bothered the authorities, but it is clear it could not be tolerated. In 1973 alone, 80 unauthorised houses were demolished in October District, of which 30 had been built recently between 1968 and 1971. Further, 39 garages and 80 glazed balconies were torn down. Also, ten drivers who were illegally transporting construction material were arrested.[64]

Why does the problem of illegal construction, alongside other violations connected to housing, seem so prominent in the October District compared to other Baku regions? Reasons are several and include the relatively large amount of densely populated courtyard houses with their inward-oriented architecture – this facilitated informal arrangements. Newer districts did not have the same issues with allocation as in the overcrowded inner-city districts. There it was not only more difficult to engage unauthorised construction, but also less necessary (with exceptions being the installation of balcony windows in order to increase living space). It was more difficult because the spatial planning of mass housing estates and *mikroraiony* was characterised by open spaces and more extensive building would have been more noticeable. It was less necessary to undertake 'repairs' because newly-built state housing was in good condition and was maintained by the state.

So far, I mostly dealt with the informal strategies employed by citizens in their efforts to obtain housing. Next I consider how officials in direct contact with housing claimants and their neighbourhoods, enacted multiple roles and positions along different levels of loyalty. Importantly, because the strategies for obtaining housing were an open secret, housing authorities were institutionally and individually susceptible to criticism and public censure.

---

[64] *O khode vypolneniia Bakgorispolkoma za No.62/1147 ot 01.02.74g. O khode vypolneniia ispolkomami Nasiminskogo, Narimanovskogo, Oktiabr'skogo, im. 26 bak. komissarov resheniia BGI No.40/704 ot 03.03.76g. O grubykh narusheniiakh zemel'nogo zakonodatel'stva v gorode i merakh po ikh ustraneniiu v svete postanovleniia BK KP Azerbaidzhana ot 8 iiulia 1973 g.* (4 September 1976); ARDABF, f.23, op.1, d.1337, ll. 5–11.

Ambiguous Loyalties: Informal Practices among Local State Representatives

On 23 November 1971, the newspaper *Baku Worker* published a full-page article on irregularities and violations by housing authorities in the registration and allocation practices in October District.[65] As a reaction to 'numerous letters of complaint by journal readers', the journal was coming to the end of a one-year long investigation on registration and housing allocation practices in the district. The findings might be guessed from the sections above, but when 'exposed' they were deemed 'serious shortcomings'. The journalists reported that their exposé had caught the attention immediately of the Party and that it had instructed the Bakgorispolkom to take appropriate steps.

The publication thus presented both the shortcomings that had been uncovered and the city's administrative efforts to overcome them. After the intervention by the Party organs, the administrative practice of the district's *ispolkom* was reported to have improved significantly. According to A. Akhundov, deputy chairman of the Bakgorispolkom, many of those in serious need had received new housing. However, a closer look by the investigative journalists revealed that those who were allocated housing by the *ispolkom* were much farther down on the list than many others who actually should have had priority. The people who had received apartments were inscribed in double-digit and even three-digit positions of the list. Consequently, the article raised a central question: 'Was this a random mistake or was it pointing rather to fundamentally incorrect practices in the priority order?' The flaws were illustrated with some concrete examples: An enquiry at the registration office revealed that one person on the waiting list was not even residing in Azerbaijan. Obviously, said the paper, employees of the *ispolkom* had ignored that the applicant did not or could not provide the necessary propiska. Concerns were also raised about those who had been by-passed. These included Z. Chafarova, a single mother of four children living in a moist and small cellar-room, and T. Abdulzade, who, since the death of his wife, was a single father of young children, and living under acutely dangerous conditions. The newspaper article not only criticised the October District's housing allocation system but more generally questioned its overall organisation and competence in dealing with the public interest. This critique referred to the inefficient municipal measures taken after heavy rains in autumn 1968:

---

[65] Y. Ivanov and M. Sukhov, 'Komu byt' novosolom. O praktike ucheta i raspredeleniia zhil'ia v Oktiabr'skom Raione'. *Bakinskii Rabochii*, 23 December 1971.

Whereas in other city districts, affected people were supported
without haste and flaws, here, because of the carelessness of the
district's leadership, the commission responsible for dealing with the
issue set not one common but seven (!) independent lists for people
in need of resettlement, who were designated rather by subjective
than real assessments.

The *ispolkom's* listing strategy was problematic, indeed. Each list recorded
the affected persons not according to their level of neediness, but only
according to the order in which their apartments had been inspected. This
meant that all assessments had to be made more or less as an exceptional
case on its own merits. The authors also noticed that the *newly* composed
staff of the *ispolkom* (which suggests that the former staff had been replaced,
at least partly) was searching for a way out of the current situation and was
choosing candidates for new housing 'extremely carefully'.

At the same time, the authors acknowledged that the weaknesses in
housing allocation needed serious and continuous support by other officials
and the members of the *ispolkom*. That this was not yet the case was
illustrated by the fact that the housing commission (*zhilishchnaia komissiia*)
had been unable to start their work. Out of its eleven members only four had
taken up their work and the assemblies had so far been attended by only four
to five people. That is why proper decisions on whom to take on the housing
lists could not be implemented. The article ends by summarising the regional
specifics and challenges of the October District:

Many of the problems which have still to be solved by the *ispolkom*
are linked to the territorial peculiarities of the October District, one
of the oldest regions in Baku with still many old houses. The
difficulties are objective and it is obvious that the district needs
strong support by municipal organisations. But by virtue of the given
circumstances, the *ispolkom* must do everything to overcome the still
existing deficiencies in and violations of housing lists and housing
allocation as soon as possible.

I encountered this newspaper article in an archival folder of October
District's *ispolkom*. The article had been discussed in internal
correspondence between administrative institutions, which allowed further
embedding of the article.[66] Another document conveys the district
authorities' internal reaction and decisions in reaction to the newspaper
article five days after its publication. The document starts by noting with
approval that the published article 'basically reveals shortcomings in this

---

[66] *Reshenie No. 17 ispolkoma Oktiab''skogo raionnogo Soveta deputatov trudiashchikhsia o
stat'e opublikovannoi v gazete 'Bakinskii rabochii' ot 23/XII-71g. 'Komu byt' novosolom'* (28
December 1971); ARDABF, f.23, op.1, d.1077, ll. 2–4.

matter correctly'. It then refers to a meeting of the *raiispolkom* on 17 December in which the inquiry of the journalists had been already the subject of discussion. At this very meeting, decisions directed towards the elimination of the shortcomings mentioned in the article were taken:

> The majority of families mentioned in the newspaper article – those in acute need – have been provided already with housing space. On the basis of decision N° 16 from 17 December 1971, the deputy chairman of the *ispolkom*, comrade Mustafaeva, together with the housing commission, were mandated to check the housing conditions of those citizens mentioned in the article [...] as not having received housing yet. For a generalisation of all materials as well as for compiling lists of the citizens affected according to the level of their needs, the *ispolkom* considers it indispensable to set up a commission with the participation of chairmen from public organisations.

It is further noted that this commission 'has begun already its work by enquiring the issue of housing lists and allocation practices of residential space among enterprises, institutions, and organisations'. The investigation shall be finished within roughly two months by 1 March 1972. Finally, 'in order to eliminate substantially the serious shortcomings revealed in the article', the *ispolkom* decided on eleven statements and measures of which I briefly want to mention the most relevant ones.

The deputy chairman of the *ispolkom* is instructed to supervise and control the implementation of decision No. 16. The members of the responsible housing commission are then listed according to name, profession, and the institution they represent. Among its fifteen members, six are women. The names suggest a mixed ethnic background of the commission's members with the majority of nine Azeri, four Russians, and one Ukrainian and Armenian respectively. By 1 March, the commission should forward the lists with those citizens eligible for apartments to the *ispolkom* for final discussion and approval. The commission was said to largely consist of members with no experience and knowledge about registration and allocation processes. Therefore, the deputy chairman of the *ispolkom* and the chairman of the responsible department are instructed 'to conduct a training seminar for the chairs of the housing commission [...] on the issue of registering for and distribute housing in accordance with the existing laws'.

Another important factor in the state institutions' performance of housing allocation is, again, the responsibility of superiors for the performance and mistakes of their employees. Thus, the head of the department for housing registration and distribution is obliged 'to eliminate immediately any shortcomings in his department and to strengthen control on its inspectors' activities' as well as 'to make up a plan for measures to improve the performance of the department'. The *ispolkom* is additionally assigned 'to provide practical assistance'. Finally, the measures are directed to the lowest institutions of the regional ZhEKs, whose performances have to be improved as well, with special reference to submitting all necessary documents and information to the department which concern registrations and distributions of apartments.

The above material points to several issues that are important for a better understanding of the internal dynamics of Baku's late Soviet housing regime – at least with regard to October District and comparable cases in other Soviet cities. Furthermore, housing officials' often inadequate knowledge and competency regarding the complex sphere of housing rules and their implementation is also reflected in documents that sanctioned misconduct among the ZhEKs of October District. (The documents mention, as well, the probability that certain state employees have been recruited on the basis of social relations and not for their individual qualifications or skills). Also, effective mechanisms of mutual check, control, and independent judgement on housing matters between responsible state institutions were absent or weakly performed. Finally, the late Soviet Union enabled distinct ways for negotiating citizens' rights through the Soviet institution of writing letters of complaint to administrative bodies in Baku and even Moscow (see also Chapter 6), or to a newspaper. Such letters could trigger 'investigation'. Such complaints via registered mail constituted 'a powerful weapon' among citizens and state bodies alike as they had to 'be adequately registered, dispatched, and counted at the end of a review period' (Dery 1998: 679).

In the remaining section I discuss the district's management, or rather, key aspects that were widely and publicly regarded as mismanagement. There were numerous actions by state employees that were considered a violation of administrative norms. Some misused their position and proved to be more loyal towards their own kin and social environment than to the state. In the sphere of housing, this is most evident for employees of those institutions which functioned as intermediates between citizens and the *ispolkom* – the ZhEKs. Besides deliberate informal practices, conflicts also arose out of a lack of transparency, familiarity, and knowledge about housing laws among state-representatives and citizens alike. Although in the post-Stalin era there were certain improvements 'in terms of accessibility and knowability of the law of housing', there remained significant gaps 'in the availability of housing norms and other important aspects of the law' (Barry 1977: 24). In the following, I present archival cases on informal activities and law-violations of ZhEK employees in the October District and the measures taken by the higher institution of the *raiispolkom*. This allows for zooming deeper into the notorious mismanagement of housing in October District.

In a decree from June 1972, the *raiispolkom* of the October District accused seven ZhEKs of continued delays and arrears concerning the collection of rents and communal taxes of tenants. Among the seven ZhEK offices accused here, I want to emphasise ZhEK-24 whose former director had been fired two months prior to the decree. The arrears came to about 57,300 Rubles (around 47,660 USD in 1972). The arrears of each ZhEK had reached double to three-fold the amount of the annually payable amount. In the decree the directors of each ZhEK were accused of 'unsatisfactory performance' and of 'not taking measures in this issue', although they had been instructed to do so previously. But they were still lucky only to be sanctioned by a rebuke. The *raiispolkom* announced more serious measures if they were not able to forward the money within a two-month period.[67] The documents do not make clear why the arrears had mounted: whether there was an interruption in collecting taxes, dwellers were unwilling to pay, or simply the officials had themselves committed fraud.

In April 1972, the *ispolkom* detected an unauthorised house with two rooms and 30 square metres of living space in the sector of ZhEK-24. Further investigations had shown that the house was built by the brother of the ZhEK's engineer one month previously. This brother, working and registered at the neighbouring industrial city of Sumqayıt, lacked a propiska for Baku. Furthermore, in the same street a member of the militia-regiment had added one room of 14 square metres to his dwelling. These construction activities were 'considered the result of an irresponsible attitude of the ZhEK's director [...] and [of the] engineer [...] towards their official duties'. For the admission of unauthorised construction in his district, the director as well as the engineer who favoured his brother got 'dismissed from office'. Further, the *ispolkom* announced that the source of the purchased construction material was to be investigated and decided to impose 'serious disciplinary action' towards the local inspector responsible for the area.[68]

This case exemplifies well the significance of kin relations in order to serve housing interests. Furthermore, it illustrates the director's responsibility as well as vulnerability because he gets dismissed for his employee's action whether he knew about it or not. That the local inspector

---

[67] *Rasporiazhenie 05/31 po Oktiabr'skomu raiispolkomu* (29 June 1972); ARDABF, f.23, op.1, d.1077a, l.106.
[68] *Rasporiazhenie 05/19 po ispolkomu Oktiabr'skogo raionnogo Soveta deputatov trudiashchikhsia* (18 May 1972); ARDABF, f.23, op.1, d.1077a, ll.124–125.

is sanctioned too, gives an idea of the intricate character of responsibilities and potential sources of illicit action. Thus, there was a constant risk to be included in collective sanctions by higher authorities for the misbehaviour of others. At the same time, it suggests that most of the time, state employees were capable of using their social relations to shield each other from the enquiries of higher administrative bodies.

A final case from 1971 exemplifies how close relatives of ZhEK employees not only enjoyed support in housing matters but were provided with responsible positions in the housing office. On the basis of an official inspection and several letters of complaint, the *raiispolkom* accused the director of ZhEK-32, A. Agayev, of violating his position and authority (ZhEK-32 was also involved in the embezzlement of money by several housing offices in the first example). Among other charges, he was accused of having recruited his brother-in-law, L. Mnatsakanian, together with his wife and her father, for the positions of locksmith, *pasportist*, and gardener of ZhEK-32. The *pasportist* is in charge of residence permits and forwards applications to the district police where the documents are processed (Morton 1980: 238). The passport or registration office (*pasportnyi stol*), according to some of my informants, was where most bribing took place. Another violation of the director's duties was that he had illegally allocated a one-room apartment to his brother-in-law. Finally, several cases of false propiskas had been uncovered. Besides getting dismissed, Agayev and his relatives were to await severe administrational sanctions and Mnatsakanian's housing case was to be transferred to the court for preparing eviction.[69]

These cases exemplify an almost commonplace topic in my conversations with people on their socialist housing experiences. According to them, housing authorities made regular use of their power to favour relatives by granting registrations, putting them on the housing list, or providing them with apartments. This was generally due to 'the continued absence of an effective mechanism of check or independent judgment across a broad range of housing matters' (Barry 1977: 25). Effective control between housing institutions failed on the broader level and left much agency to housing officials. But as I have shown, to a certain degree there is some internal control among and between housing institutions, although on an occasional rather than on a systematic basis. Like many other state employees, they had the power to sanction illegal activities by citizens or colleagues, but they had also the power to turn a blind eye. If they overstepped the normal balance, they ran a real risk of being sanctioned themselves. Oral accounts suggest that local officials in most cases turned a

---

[69] *Rasporiazhenie 05/35 po Oktiabr'skomu raiispolkomu o ser'eznykh narusheniiakh v deiatel'nosti ZhEK-32* (18 June 1971); ARDABF, f.23, op.1, d.1009, l.38.

blind eye (*zakryvat' glaza*) in exchange for informal payments – a situation that has hardly changed in postsocialism. Second, they were often part of the neighbourhood and were entangled in their different roles as state representatives, superiors, subordinates, family members, neighbours, or friends. Like anyone else, they were part of the local web of often conflicting loyalties and social obligations. Thus, officials could be a potential resource and source of social capital, but at the same time they could create obstacles to people's aspirations in housing. Their ambivalent position, their personal use of resources for own ends, or for the ends of others was always a risky endeavour that required social skill to navigate. Finally, media and the press, at least from the 1970s onward, were important actors in pointing to and unravelling irregular practices by state officials who disadvantaged certain people and favoured others in the process of housing allocation.

Conclusion

This chapter has dealt with bureaucracy, issues of allocation, informal practices, and the role of papereality in the relations among state institutions and between citizens and housing authorities. I have discussed these topics through archival materials on the transformation of property and approaches towards the housing question in the 1920s, the formal and informal dynamics of housing allocation in the post-war era, and in the context of Baku's October District in the latter Soviet decades. Starting with Katherine Verdery's notion of 'allocative power' as central to socialist economies, I aimed at demonstrating how housing-related institutions at the national, regional, and local levels sought to enhance and deploy their allocative power. The public discourse on housing shortages and practices related to the hoarding of goods, services, and labour can be interpreted as constituting two sides of the same coin. Public discourse raised awareness of what was 'valuable' and worth hoarding, while hoarding was a means to cope with shortage and enhance allocative power within or beyond formal regulations. Interestingly, the framework for making use of this allocative power seems to become more informal as we move down the hierarchical ladder from the national to the municipal and then to the local level. Also, for citizens, the housing question and the state's ambition to provide apartments to all families in the near future provided an important framework for their own housing aspirations. To achieve these aspirations, families invoked a high level of informality, the use of networks, and other strategies to bypass official rules.

In all these bureaucratic processes and state-citizen interactions the role of representational strategies is of primary importance. I described the façade politics in this chapter by referring to the concept of papereality made up of symbols and written representations that actually become more important than the thing represented. In other words, papers and documents based on defined quantifiable and locatable information (like the sanitary norm and the propiska) had to fulfil the norms; or they had to be interpreted and forwarded in adapted written form so that positive or negative decisions appeared legitimate. As I have argued, for reasons of emphasising such processing, from the initial application to decisions that were cross-checked internally, and then might have been questioned again or leading to official complaint letters, it makes sense to conceive of paperealities.

Finally, by following the housing trajectories described here, it becomes evident that popular conception of any single entity called 'the state' is misleading and simplifying. The empirical picture appears rather blurred. At all levels, state institutions had to deal with challenges, conflicts, and norm violations within and beyond their administrative boundaries. A special position in the socialist housing regime can be attributed to those state officials who served as intermediaries between the district's executive committees and the dwellers. The ZhEK directors filled a broker position in dealing, supervising, and controlling the basic public good of housing, while being under control and supervision of higher institutions. Often, they were part of the neighbourhood and were entangled in their different roles as state representatives, superiors, subordinates, family members, neighbours, or friends. Like anyone else, they were part of the local web of often conflicting loyalties and social obligations. Here, as elsewhere, informal practices required skilfully manoeuvring through the real-world and paperealities.

Chapter 4
Moral Economies of Housing in the New Baku

This chapter moves from a discussion of the ideological and discursive aspects of Soviet housing to a consideration of the wider dynamics and lived experiences connected to urban development since independence. I will present several ethnographic cases to demonstrate some striking tendencies in the housing sector, the role of privatisation, and ways people have responded to new challenges. For most people, houses and apartments after privatisation have served as an important 'base' for making a living (Gudeman 2016). Within urban frameworks, housing provides a space and opportunity for economic activities. Housing also constitutes its owners' major financial asset (Zavisca 2012: 1). When an apartment or house is sold for profit, this, in turn, is frequently reinvested into housing. With a still uncertain labour market, and unsteady and low incomes for most people, housing's role as capital is even more important. Indeed, beyond privatisation, people have found other strategies to generate starting capital for their housing aspirations. In the era of neoliberal market economy, however, the variety in kind and quality of housing (even among Soviet-era privatised apartments) – once translated into economic values – has presented highly unequal opportunities for homeowners.

The presumption of this book is that housing can be seen as a total social fact because it exerts a multiple and efficacious power and impact on various social, economic, and other dimensions in people's everyday life. In the present chapter, I look at people's experiences, efforts, and aspirations regarding the housing question after privatisation with a special focus on the material and economic (but equally moral) dimensions. How can we describe the different economies of housing that emerged under transformation, and the importance of property amidst future uncertainties? I address this question first with a consideration of how people have dealt with the central issue of housing in the era of liberal market economy, and then secondly with a consideration of the social expectations of support among family and kin. Thereby I aim at showing some specific facets of the moral economy of the 'total social fact' of housing in postsocialist Baku. Because, in addition to economic considerations of the 'value' of a house as property, it is largely the house's social nexus, moral issues, dominant images of masculinity, and care for the future well-being and security of children that provide people's primary motivations to engage with housing security and home-making. This is a domain marked by feelings and struggles among people who see themselves as deprived of the means to engage successfully in the new housing market. Houses in Baku are replete with the social, economic, and moral 'tensions' of economy (Gudeman 2008, 2016). Such tensions emerge, especially, in the potential conflicts within kin groups over expectations of social and economic support.

Since the issue of marriage has been raised constantly with regard to housing, the final section describes the political economy of marriages in general and those of weddings in particular. Attending weddings and accepting invitations are not only perceived as a financial issue among households. They also constitute moments where people confirm, maintain, or break social relations. The conspicuous character of today's weddings is compared to how people remembered weddings during socialism. Finally, I describe the ritual aspects and exchange patterns between the involved parties, and the underlying gendered ideology of marriage and home-making. Both men and women hold responsibility for home-making: accommodation is expected to be provided by the husband's family, but the bride's dowry includes all the domestic objects that are required for turning the house into a home.

Housing Economies, Privatisation, and Biographies in Transition

Following his marriage and move out from his parents' home, Azər, whom I briefly introduced in Chapter 2, has moved several times. His family has grown, and there have been changes in the household constellation:

> First, I had a two-room apartment where I lived with my wife and our two daughters. When they grew older, it became more and more uncomfortable to live there as a family of four. I sold the apartment and from that money I bought a three-room apartment, however, five kilometres away, farther away from town where buying a bigger apartment for that price was feasible.

Finally, in 2003, Azər bought his present four-room apartment, again in the centre and closer to his parents. At the time of my fieldwork, Azər lived there with his wife and their 23-year-old daughter Aygün. His elder daughter was living with her husband and had just given birth to Azər's granddaughter. Azər commented on his house-buying, 'We increased the [size of the] apartment all the time, but had to make sacrifices in terms of living close to the centre. But I was very lucky with this apartment'. The price had been almost the same as the sale price of his other one. Azər had made up the difference by selling his car. 'I was without a car, but the apartment issue was solved. Everyone was happy, everything was close. The car was not needed anymore. Still, I got one after three years'. In 2003, when Azər purchased the apartment, it was still possible to obtain housing for a reasonable price, he said. He had paid 20,000 USD for the centrally located four-room apartment:

> Today, you can only dream about such prices. For this amount you cannot even buy a normal car. For young adults purchasing an apartment these days has become a big problem. I can take a loan on my name, make a down payment, and the rest will be paid by the newlyweds themselves for the rest of their lives. Now even if you want to buy furniture, prices have reached European levels. If, of course, the children find work in state jobs, then there may be hope that the state will give them an apartment. And other benefits in due course. Then, parental support is hardly required. A simple man with working class background, however, would need to live with his wife at home with his parents. And families with money can provide for everything that is needed just like this [with a snap of the fingers].

He further emphasised that it was privatisation that enabled him to have capital at all. People today, in contrast to socialism or the early years of independence, he said, are increasingly dependent on credit. Then, life consists of only one problem:

> Paying the monthly mortgage! In return, you have a separate apartment and do not have to live with your parents, which means fewer problems for everyone. No waiting! Time has acquired an essential meaning. Somehow, there were good times back then as there are today. You can't say what is good, what is bad. I don't think credit is a bad thing. It's good for those who have a good education, can get a good job, work steadily, and pay the credit. And the simple workers have basically nothing to rely on. He will have to pay rent for his whole life.

The number of people and families in Baku who live for rent has been steadily increasing over the past years. Although official statistics are far from reliable (since most tenancies are agreed informally), people with less financial means and from various backgrounds pay rent for accommodation. For the many people with precarious and unstable income, it is easier and less binding to pay a monthly rent than a much higher monthly mortgage.

However, living for rent in Baku is widely considered to mark such a low status that my informants mostly described as only a temporary solution.

Azər's case addresses several housing-related issues I will discuss in this section. The first has to do with the importance of property in the form of a dwelling obtained through privatisation. 'When there is money, there is no problem with buying property. But when there is no money but already an apartment, you start to think about what you can do to buy another one'. For many people, although not so clearly in Azər's case, the concern emerges in connection to the prospective marriage of children. His strategy, however, is a common one: 'Sell what you have and buy a cheaper but bigger apartment farther away from the centre; or, if your apartment is big enough, you buy two smaller ones instead. And if there's no money, you have to take a loan'. His property buying and selling was not unrelated to his family's growth, as he too expects to support his children into adulthood:

> In any case, young people receive the support of their family. That's for sure. Family is everything! One person cannot handle everything alone. In the Soviet days it used to be easier in the sense that a stable job, housing health service, kindergartens, education, and everything else was guaranteed. You did not earn too much money, but enough. And you knew that you earn money today, tomorrow, in 10 years … but we had to wait in line for years to receive an apartment. And today, even if I have a good job and earning good money, if I go and get a mortgage … what, if I don't have that job tomorrow anymore? What to do then? Such cases happen very often. There is no guarantee. If you are a specialist, you will quickly find a job. But if you cannot, then you know why family is so important – your parents, brother, sister…

In the case of Azər's married daughter, it was her husband's parents who sold their apartment and bought two smaller ones. Again, Azər emphasises this being a legacy of Soviet times. His daughter's parents-in-law have owned two apartments due to privatisation. They kept one for their son's marriage. When he married Azər's daughter, they sold that apartment and bought another one, which suited them better in terms of location and overall conditions. However, as Azər remarked, 'not all parents got such opportunities – this is the ideal case'. It was ideal because the apartment came from the groom's family and the bride's family provided the furnishings. This was also the case in Azər's marriage in the mid-1980s, with a slight difference. Immediately after marriage, they lived with Azər's parents and registered on the housing list: because the incoming bride exceeded the sanitary norm, Azər's father received a new apartment. He moved into the new apartment with his wife and arranged 'to leave' the old apartment for Azər. 'This is how we started living separate from our parents. But now such options do not exist anymore. And people are looking for all kinds of options to solve the housing issue'.

Housing privatisation turned citizens to *de jure* homeowners. After paying a nominal fee and providing the necessary documents, occupants in state-owned flats obtained their apartments as private property. In some cases, obtaining all required documents could become a long and nerve-racking endeavour, not least because prospective owners had to gain the official consent of relatives who – in reality or merely on paper – were living in the household (see Chapter 6). Azər approached the housing authorities with the required documents and privatised his apartment as soon as the privatisation process started in the early 1990s. As state statistics show, privatisation peaked in 1995 but people showed high initiative for apartment privatisation until the end of the 1990s. In the 2000s, although decreasing in absolute terms, privatisation continued steadily.[70] By 2009, some 69–85 per cent of Azerbaijan's housing stock had been privatised.[71] It is possible that the total figure is even slightly lower, but the more important issues surrounding the levelling-off concern Soviet legacies.[72] People who had not privatised by this time may not have seen any need or advantage to do so, but others had problems with proper documentation, especially in rural areas where local village councils were inattentive with registrations (see Leutloff-Grandits 2006 for similar obstacles in rural Croatia). Certainly in Baku, would-be owners have problems with documentation in areas like Dağlı, where migrants during Soviet times constructed whole neighbourhoods without obtaining any official documents for their dwellings.

By law no one was compelled to privatise. Therefore, in the early years, there were many who – not having an immediate intention to sell their apartment – saw the bureaucratic efforts as a waste of time. At least initially, the only practically perceived outcome was additional financial expenses and

---

[70] See http://www.stat.gov.az/source/healthcare/indexen.php.Last accessed 17 February 2016; http://www.baku.azstat.org/section/labour/. Last accessed 17 February 2016. Between 2010 and 2014 housing privatisation further continued but the rates had sharply dropped around 30 per cent for Azerbaijan as a whole and around 50 per cent in Baku.

[71] The lower range appeared in a newspaper article, '69 Percent Housing Privatized in Azerbaijan'. *Today.AZ*, 20 July 2009. Available online, http://www.today.az/view.php?id =53941. Last accessed 18 February 2016. The higher figure was reported by UNECE (2010: 29).

[72] The general director of a private marketing and business analysis company estimated that only 65 per cent of the country's housing stock had been privatised by 2013. Xalilov, A., 'Zavershit' besplatnuiu privatizatsiiu do 2015 goda'. *Ekho*, 2 March 2013. http://www.echo. az/article.php?aid=36747. Last accessed 18 February 2016.

liabilities. As it is reported for Kazakhstan, the immediate difference was that:

> Now being in legal possession of their apartment, the new owners found themselves liable for a steadily increasing raft of charges for utilities and maintenance that previously, if not completely free, had been so heavily subsidized as to represent a subvention from the state along with housing, education, and pensions (Alexander 2009: 55).

Yet most people Baku had privatised their apartments by the time of my fieldwork. Exceptions that came to my attention were primarily cases in which family conflicts or other problems had hindered people from providing the necessary documentation (see Chapter 6).

My interlocutors privatised with intentions to sell – not immediately – but later. The expected sale was connected to the marriage of children, and they saw selling an apartment as the only opportunity to generate enough capital to buy an apartment for a child. A centrally located apartment, for example, could be sold to buy two cheaper ones – then everyone would be housed properly. Such a practice of 'selling for buying at another location' became an important strategy from the late 1990s. Before that, privatisation had proceeded without a housing market. The early 1990s were politically unsteady and economically disastrous, with the legacies of the Nagorno-Karabakh conflict of the late 1980s and the related war with Armenia in 1992–1994 still looming. For a few years, housing was not 'scarce', and it was difficult to sell property. Altogether, these among other issues led to large-scale demographic changes. Baku's ethnic composition changed due to the large-scale out-migration of Armenians, Russians, and other ethnic minorities in a short period of time (Yunusov 2009: 4). The arrival of hundreds of thousands of internally displaced persons (IDPs) and increasing rural-urban migration led to a significant spatial growth due to people's construction of largely undocumented houses on squatted land at the city's peripheries. Since the mid-1990s, with the countries recovering economy, most urban housing has been of increasing economic value as property, thus facilitating prospective intentions for selling apartments.

Murad, whom I introduced in Chapter 2, was born in 1964. His father was an Azeri from the city of Gənjə, his Russian mother was from Abkhazia. During Soviet times, Murad's father was a biologist at the Azerbaijan State Agrarian University of which, after the country's independence, he was appointed Rector. Murad worked as a viticulturist in socialist times. After independence, he took other jobs, mostly as a security guard in Baku. He was well suited for the role because of his tall and impressive stature. Before independence, he had married and become the father of a son (in 1989), but he divorced sometime in the 1990s and went to Germany to continue his studies in viticulture near Frankfurt/Main, where he spent five years between 1999 and 2004. After his return to Baku, he married a second time and became the father of a daughter. He also found work as a winemaker in a wine factory in the city of Qəbələ. There he supervised the production process and a team of several dozen employees. However, he lost the job when there were changes in the management. He assumes – as is often the case – that his position was to go to someone within the new management's network. Since then, he has been jobless, despite his professional qualifications.

In Murad's financial history, housing played a significant role. In the 1990s, Murad's father had bought a three-room apartment of 80 square metres right in the centre of Baku in a building constructed in 1897 and in a style locally known as *Italianka*. Murad's father died in 2000, and when Murad returned from Germany, he lived there with his mother; he brought his second wife there later. In 2013, the building was demolished to free space for new construction and the inhabitants were compensated with 2,000 AZN per square metre. With the 160,000 AZN of compensation that Murad received, plus a credit of 30,000 AZN, he solved the family's housing question. (Many others who faced the demolition of their houses, as illustrated in Chapter 2, were less fortunate). For his mother, Murad bought a 50 square metre apartment for 100,000 AZN. For his wife, daughter, and himself he bought a three-room apartment in the high-rise near Sovetski. Murad specified that, 'I have looked at around ten apartments together with my wife. It is better to do this jointly. Not that she does not like it in the end'. This apartment cost 90,000 AZN; the credit of 30,000 AZN that he needed in addition to the remaining compensation came partly from a bank loan and partly from money borrowed from relatives. Although he solved the immediate housing issues, Murad has struggled constantly to pay back his debts. At one point he said that, 'If I had the choice, I'd prefer to buy a house instead of an apartment. But I cannot afford it'.

Another widespread strategy for building a house in Baku, in the figurative sense, was labour migration to Russia, Turkey, and European countries. Oqtay serves as example for a successful housing biography in that regard. Without having had an apartment to privatise, as he and his parents came to Baku in the early 1990s as IDPs from Karabakh, he nevertheless acquired property in Baku. Together with his wife and two children he lived close to our own Badamdar neighbourhood in a solid and good quality building from the 1950s which he had recently renovated. He had bought the four-room apartment with 100 square metres in 2002 for 7,000 USD. He generated the funds during his time in Germany, from 1999 to 2002, working 'day and night' in the security service sector in the city of Osnabrück. As he explained:

> I was working all the time with maybe 4 hours of sleep at night. I did not spend any money besides the bare necessities. Part of the money I sent home to my parents every month. The rest I saved for my future marriage as I could not expect any support from home where everyone was struggling for himself. Before I returned home, I bought a Mercedes and took it to Baku, where I sold it for a much higher price than I paid. Soon after, I bought this apartment and got married in 2003. Today I think I was lucky, having bought an apartment for $7,000 USD. Today people would pay far beyond $100,000 USD for it.

Oqtay's story reads like a real success, and he could optimistically look into the future with stable work as the vice security manager in one of Baku's five-star hotels.

The above examples show varied 'success' stories in navigating Baku's postsocialist market for apartments. Even jobless Murad had an apartment, and although he found it difficult to pay-off his debts, he was not particularly worried about losing his house. Given the details of Oqtay's story, Murad could probably still afford to re-buy something relatively large or central, even if he had to sell.

In the following section, I want to describe the housing developments centred around a *həyət evi*. The situation with courtyard houses reflects some similar dynamics to the apartments, but owning a house as a private home allows many ways to approach house economy that are not open to apartment dwellers. I begin with the example of the house where I stayed with my family. It was a new house, built after independence, in Badamdar, on the south-western fringe of Baku. Our landlord Fikrət Qacarov (b. 1964) lived there too, with his wife Sevinc (b. 1970) and their two sons, Fəriz (b. 1990) and Kamal (b. 1992). They lived in a three-storey house which Fikrət had been building continuously over the course of several years.

Fikrət bought his four *sotki* of land in the mid-1990s.[73] During Soviet times, this was a prohibited zone for construction because of nearby oil production, and Fikrət had been among the first to settle in the area when municipal authorities started to sell the land. By the time of my research, Badamdar had become a densely built-up neighbourhood of yard houses and luxurious villas. Along the municipality's main artery, the Badamdar Şossesi, the specialisation of stores and workshops reflected the region's booming house-construction activity. Different kinds of construction

---

[73] One *sotka* is roughly 100 square metres.

material, windows, tiles, raw material for concrete – it was possible to get almost everything needed for house construction here. The same observations held true for the home-making industry. Carpenters specialised in doors, sellers of paint, glaziers who would provide windows of all shapes, as well as furniture stores reflected the importance of local markets for home-making alongside housing construction. Recently built housing complexes hosted western-standard supermarkets on the ground level and provide apartments on the storeys above.

One important observation is that a significant number of apartments are empty and uninhabited – a trend that is not specific to Badamdar but characteristic for many recently built residential complexes across the city. Similar trends, such as the 'social life of empty buildings' and the role of empty buildings in the urban materialities after socialism have been discussed also for neighbouring Georgia (Pelkmans 2003). Observing the windows of apartment blocks is one way to estimate their occupancy. Empty apartments, and sometimes whole residential buildings, are characterised by visible uncleanliness and dirty windows covered with a thick layer of dust. Such windows are a strong contrast to those of inhabited apartments which are cared for and regularly cleaned.

Most important, it is the lack of curtains (pərdələr) which reflect the vacancy of an apartment. This is because curtains are perceived by locals as an indispensable feature of any proper home (see Chapter 5). Furthermore, nightly observations serve as an additional indicator for the use or non-use of apartments. In contrast to the inhabited apartments in Soviet mass residential buildings whose front windows are extensively illuminated, the windows of many post-Soviet apartments in high-rises remain dark – a further sign that they are uninhabited.

Today, the prices for property in Badamdar have skyrocketed and are hardly affordable for people with an average income. The price for one sotka with access to a major road ranges from 40,000 USD to 80,000 USD. Empty plots have become scarce in recent years. Over the last decade, Badamdar has become increasingly attractive for the upper class, ministers, high-ranking state officials, and foreign ambassadors. This trend has extended to foreigners working in the city as well who seek to rent flats in the area – a development that had important impacts on the Qacarovs' opportunities for making a living. Over the course of the years, the family had managed to transform their empty plot into a cosy, homely, and comfortable (rahat) courtyard with fruit trees, a small garden for crops and four separate housing units. They inhabited one 'apartment' and rented out the others to foreigners, including myself and my family.

Within one year of buying the land, they had finished a one-storey, four-room dwelling which in later stages of further construction experienced major modifications in terms of use and spatial planning. But at the beginning, it enabled them to have sufficient living space and Fikrət made effective use of the spacious courtyard for his economic activities. Fikrət had been trained as an *avtoelektrik* (car electrician). He provided the household's main income by repairing cars – he specialised in Soviet Ladas – and through some small-scale car selling. Sometimes he purchased broken cars, repaired them, perhaps drove them for some months, and then sold them for a profit. Additionally, Fikrət started to sell everyday products such as bread, lemonade, sweets, and other things through a hatch in the yard's gate. This addition to the family income lasted for roughly five years until the early 2000s.

Fikrət had aimed early on to shift his activity from car repair towards shopkeeping. As this would require a proper shop, he started to build a second storey to his house. This allowed for important reconfigurations of space. Parts of the ground storey were detached from the living space and transformed into a separate entrance that allowed direct access for customers from the street into the shop. It enabled Fikrət not only to expand his product range significantly, but also to attract more customers. Another part of the ground level was similarly provided with a new door that one could enter from the inner courtyard. This space was then used by his wife Sevinc as a home-based tailor service and beauty parlour through which she was able to contribute to the household budget. In terms of aesthetics, two balconies and a circular staircase into the yard were added. Now, one balcony roofed part of the yard which provided additional shade and also served as an anchor point for a wooden pergola covered with grapevines.

Again, some years later, a third stage in housing began with the construction of a second building. This meant another extension and diversification of the household's economic activities. As soon as the Qacarovs finished the first storey of the second house around autumn 2008, they moved there and rented out their bigger flat to foreigners – an option they realised one day when a shop customer had asked them if they might know of an apartment that could be rented by some friends of friends. With the money they generated by renting out their bigger apartment, the Qacarovs constructed a separate room in the opposite corner of the yard which became the bedroom for Fikrət and Sevinc. Although it was detached from their main apartment, it was the 'only feasible option' at that point for providing their nearly-grown sons with a room of their own. The rental revenues were invested continuously into the construction of a second storey on the second house. When it was completed, they moved back in to the main structure, and turned to let the building that had been their bedroom for occasional use mostly for guests. The steady rental income from the first, two-storey house, allowed for construction of the third storey of the second house which was completed by the end of 2012. And since the separate sleeping room was hardly used, the last step was to transform it into another small apartment. In the end it enabled the Qacarovs to generate income much more efficiently as the demand for rented flats increased after about 2005. The steady rental income allowed for a more constant construction of living space within the yard and by my arrival in Baku they were able to rent out three separate flats.

To sum up, within two decades, Fikrət had managed to significantly improve his family's housing conditions, work, and income opportunities. His investment into the continuous enlargement of housing space enabled a steady and increasing rental income that in turn was reinvested for further construction. By the time of my research, he had constant work and income from his shop, and by renting out three apartments mostly to foreigners, he made an extra monthly income of about 1,500 AZN (roughly 1,900 USD in 2014).[74]

As with the buying and selling of apartments in various sizes and locations, building structures of various size and use enables people to engage productively with the new market economy. In the future, it was conceivable that the extra houses would be turned over to Fikrət's sons; a much-touted advantage of the yard houses is that they allow the different generations to live close together, but under separate roofs. The last section discusses differences and commonalities between apartments and houses with regard to the important aspect of storage, but also in terms of the production of natural goods and how these are socially embedded in practices of sharing and gift-giving.

Whenever we visited the Qarayevs, my former host family, in their socialist apartment, my host mother provided us with gifts of homemade food like pickles and jam, which she stored in the shelves of her balcony. When the Qacarovs visited Sevinc's relatives in Xızı, they too returned home with gifts of seasonal vegetables and fruits. Often, they would additionally buy regional agricultural products being sold along the main roads on their way home. Such produce is supposed to be of much better

---

[74] According to the State Statistical Committee of Azerbaijan (Azstat, abbreviated from *Azərbaycan Respublikasının Dövlət Statistika Komitəsi*), the average monthly income in 2013 was 425 AZN. Although such data hardly represents a realistic income distribution, one can fairly state that the Qacarovs' income from renting out apartments is significantly higher than the official average. See http://www.stat.gov.az/source/labour/indexen.php. Last accessed 23 February 2015.

quality than that sold in urban supermarkets. After returning home, they distributed the fresh produce to us and our neighbours in the common courtyard. The rest was kept at a sheltered location in the yard. In contrast to the Qarayevs, whose storing capacities inside their flat were rather limited to the balcony, the capacities for storage at the Qacarovs' case was never an issue. There was always space, if not in the house, then in the yard. Another important difference between the two families is that the apartment-dwelling Qarayevs must buy most of the products they intend to conserve on the market, whereas the Qacarovs obtain a significant portion of their produce from the parental home in the village and from their own garden.

One important feature in the former socialist context and thereafter has been the capacity of any dwelling to store things. Not dissimilar to the dynamics involved in socialist 'hoarding' and 'allocative power' (Verdery 1991), 'storage', in other contexts, 'implies a capacity to plan, to allocate materials between now and the future, to anticipate needs' (Douglas 1991: 295). Not only in Azerbaijan but all over the former socialist space, urbanites have designated space for storage in their apartments, usually on the balcony. They served to store conserved vegetables, homemade fruit drinks, jams, and other products to be consumed over many months. In the Soviet context, balconies, gardens and dachas served to store numerous goods for daily consumption but also for oddments which 'might turn out to have an unforeseen use' (Alexander 2012: 268). In today's Baku, the market is making necessary goods available nearly continuously, so storage is not so important for existential reasons anymore, but it is still important because people store up gifts for relatives and guests. In this way, storage is important to create, recreate, or enhance social relationships with others.

Yard houses, with their greater possibilities for flexible storage, also provide the capacity to control a greater portion of the cost of goods and products anticipated as future needs. One day in early autumn, our landlord's family returned from one of their regular visits to Şəmkir where one of their sons was stationed for his military service. On their way back, Fikrət bought two young turkeys for which he improvised a cage from available materials stored in various corners of his yard: an old door, old windows, and a broken drying rack.

Plate 9. Improvised turkey cage in the corner of the yard.

Over the next three months, the turkeys grew bigger and fatter, and were finally slaughtered at the New Year. Fikrət's turkeys had cost half the price of one from a butcher in the days before the New Year. As they had eaten kitchen scraps and pecked in the yard, Fikrət bore no 'costs' to fatten them himself. Some of our neighbours, who had similar spatial resources, did the same as Fikrət. Urban dwellers who attempted the same in their apartments would have surely suffered reprisals from their neighbours and, perhaps, the authorities.

During Soviet times, the possibility for urbanites to cultivate products was hardly given. Some people had garden plots and dachas, but these were normally allocated to privileged groups of society. Close family connections to the countryside represented significant advantages for urban dwellers with respect to alternative supplies of food and natural products. Planning capacities, allocation, and potential storage for later consumption or exchange constituted an important strategy to cope with periods of shortage in the state allocation system. Beside social support networks between rural and urban dwellers, another example that points to the varying capacities of houses and urban inhabitants in terms of production was the dacha-economy.

Access to dachas (summer cottages) translated into further economic advantages for the already privileged because it enabled them to engage in the production of vegetables, fruits, and other subsistence goods (see Struyk and Angelici 1996; Lovell 2003; Caldwell 2011). It meant further independence from the state's allocation system, and the state knew it. In the 1980s, the Soviet government even encouraged private cultivation activities on dachas to counteract possible food crises (Lovell 2003: 214). Dacha areas around Baku are mostly located along the northern and north-eastern coastlines of the Abşeron Peninsula, close to settlements like Bilgəh, Buzovna, Dübəndi, Mərdəkan, Maştağa, Nardaran, Novxanı, Pirşağı, and Şüvəlan. Those plots directly located at the seaside have been assigned traditionally to the nomenklatura and most important state representatives. Today, luxurious villas along the shore owned by the president and ministers depict a conspicuous leisure of the elite. Further from the sea have also been more typical dacha areas of former Soviet institutions and companies. Once we visited a friend and scholar who had recently bought a dacha around Nardaran which was located in an area formerly reserved for employees of Azneft. In Soviet times, the company's plots measured twelve *sotki* each. Our friend bought the dacha with money he and his siblings obtained by selling their parents' dacha in Mərdəkan, one of the most privileged dacha areas around Baku. After buying the dacha, our friend and his family, especially his son had invested a large amount of time and effort in the cultivation of vegetables. This was a project that required not only acquisition of basic gardening knowledge but also constant efforts and creativity to achieve satisfactory results with regard to the hot arid climate and the sandy, infertile soil.

To have a dacha, in Soviet or post-Soviet times, required social and material resources but also generated them. Then and now, growing crops was much dependent on performing joint and intensive labour division among family members in their leisure time. Dachas were and are social places where kin-members and friends are frequently invited in summertime, but once they are there, labour becomes mixed with leisure. To visit a dacha means to join in exchange circles including joint consumption, commensality, and sharing with others.

Apart from the cultural ideology and values attached to houses, their pragmatic uses, capacities, and resources differ significantly according to the type of dwelling. Apartments and yard houses provide unequal possibilities to serve as a private social space and a resource for storage and production.

These differences are linked to urbanites'ᐧ various capacities to anticipate future needs, and to engage in socially enhancing activities of consumption, exchange, and personal networks of distribution.

To summarise, let us return to Fikrət's house building in Badamdar. Fikrət has experienced a remarkably upward social and economic mobility, compared to his parents and brothers, since independence. The constantly improving situation of his household economy is linked to the use of financial resources, again and again, for further expanding the spatial capacities of his four *sotki* and increasing rental income. What were the motivations and driving forces behind such behaviours? Are Fikrət and his wife capitalistic, profit-seeking individuals? Yes, when viewed in any short-term perspective. However, they undertake these activities as embedded in the wider sphere of a shared perception of moral commitments that one has towards children's futures.

Fikrət and his wife talk of their building and re-building in terms of securing housing for their sons' future marriages and families. In the words of kinship ideology, it is about the duty to bestow family-continuity over the generations. Fikrət's short and long-term commitments related to investing money for increasing the resource of housing with the aim of securing his sons' future accommodation and, thus, marriage perspectives, fits well with the concept of 'transactional orders' (Bloch and Parry 1989). They are 'a series of procedures by which goods which derive from the short-term cycle are converted into the long-term transactional order' (ibid. 25). Hence, money is converted into the creation, maintenance, and extension of the house as a 'material base' (Gudeman 2016) for the livelihood and reproduction of the family which is equally important in urban settings, even if it is less obvious than in the rural contexts from which the model derives.

Housing, Support, and Moral Conflicts

The cases in the previous section can all be read as being about men who managed to gain profit and to reinvest into more housing space. Such an understanding, however, would neglect other motivations and concerns. In our many conversations, these men also spoke about their actions as securing their children's futures, as acting according to society's moral expectations regarding caring and supporting parents, and as demonstrating shared understandings of masculinity. Let us turn here to the theme of masculinity.

Owning a shop was not just a matter of using housing to generate profit. It was also a source of personal comfort for Fikrət. As it did for many of his male neighbours, who likewise run a shop or service on their house's ground level, the shop provides Fikrət with a permanent work space. Azeri men generally spend their time outside the house. This is an expectation of gendered and spatialised labour that has been common in other patriarchally biased countries, and is religiously and customarily embedded in history. In the Soviet Union, a similar understanding that men should best spend their days outside the house was ideologically fostered, not by emphasising gender divisions, but by underlining the value of work outside the home (and by providing all necessary childcare facilities such that the need for household labour was greatly reduced). On the level of cultural norms, masculinity in Azerbaijan (and not only) extends to the avoidance of domestic chores (Heyat 2002: 118) – as the Soviet government did not tackle this aspect of the 'private' sphere the so-called double burden (of shouldering the bulk of domestic labour alongside work outside the house) continued for women in socialist countries, who sometimes also felt the 'triple burden' of being political (compare Zuo 2016: 67–76). Still, recent patterns should be considered rather as reflecting neo-traditionalised understandings of gendered divisions rather than a straightforward continuity (see Chapter 6). In the 2000s, it is perceived as inappropriate if men spend too much time at home according to both traditional and Soviet ideologies: too much time at home would imply unemployment (i.e. non-work), as well as the inability to provide for one's family with male work. Spending time outside the house therefore serves the representation, enhancement, and display of masculinity. But what should self-employed men, who do not have a workplace to go to during their days, do? A common pattern among my self-employed neighbours was to do exactly as Fikrət did: build a structure adjacent to, but distinct from, one's living quarters and spend one's time there.

Yet as the following description will show, constructing the shop was only one of many housing-related undertakings connected to Fikrət's negotiation of masculinity. Along the way, his family background, inner motivations, and struggles all combined with the negotiation of masculinity.

In buying the plot of land, Fikrət also wanted to escape his overcrowded parental home near the İnşaatçılar metro station some five kilometres north of Badamdar. Since his marriage in 1990 and the subsequent birth of two sons, he had lived with his wife and children in one room of his parent's həyət evi. The house was located in the colloquially named Dağlı (Az. mountainous) neighbourhood that grew out of a squatter settlement as mentioned in previous chapters. Its name not only refers to the neighbourhood's location at the upper part of the city but it is commonly used also because its population is made up by the dağlılar (lit. mountain people) from Xızı Region, who migrated to Baku after the Second World War. Both Fikrət's and Sevinc's families were originally from the capital of this region (also called Xızı), which has a population of around 1,200 inhabitants – 100 kilometres farther north along the coast. In the post-war years, many villagers in the region sought employment and livelihoods in other places. Some, like Sevinc's parents, moved from Xızı to nearby Giləzi, a small town located on the Baku-Quba Highway, which offered better work opportunities due to the presence of a railway station and its important role as a regional centre for trade. Others, like Fikrət's family and many of their relatives, moved to Baku. Some migrants came as part of a state initiative to attract people out of the economically disadvantaged mountainous areas to increase the urban labour force. Those who moved to Baku were given land to construct housing in the *dağlı məhəlləsi* (mountainous neighbourhood). Other migrants came on their own initiative, although often enough with numerous informal arrangements with city authorities and local state representatives. Fikrət never did tell me how his family obtained the land for their house, but certainly they had undertaken all their own construction over many decades.

I visited the house once. It was on the occasion when I had to register for our temporary residence permit. This was necessary for my visa status, but it led to some extended discussions with our landlords who wondered if we might still get out of it (because they would have to pay more fees with additional registered inhabitants), and how we would handle the various other associated bureaucratic steps. It was decided that Fikrət would come with me (in fact he had to), but the notary we chose to verify our documents had an office near his parents' house. He planned to stop by after we completed the registration. On the way, he told me about the bad conditions and crowded living situation, in an almost apologetic way with a slightly embarrassed undertone. Fikrət reminded me that he has three older brothers, and explained that only the eldest, Xalıq (b. 1961), lives with his family in a separate house outside the neighbourhood. The other two brothers and their families are still living with their mother in the parental yard house:

> When I got married, we were twenty people living there and trying to arrange our everyday life as well as possible. But I felt I had to move out because it was too crowded to live there with wife and children. My brother Elçin has two daughters of which the elder one is married, has two kids, and moved to her husband's. The younger one is unemployed and still unmarried. Elçin's son is also without work. They are all sharing one room and there is simply no money to buy a house somewhere else. My brother works in a car-service. His son wants to marry but it is impossible to finance another accommodation for him right now. And for another family there is just not enough space. It is really difficult. My other brother Fərhad, his wife, and their two married sons are also living there.

After the notary's, we paid a brief visit to his mother. When we entered the narrow yard through a small iron door, it was calm and there was no one home except his mother. When Fikrət introduced us, she embraced me, kissed my right and left cheek, and welcomed me warmly while urging us to stay for lunch and tea. However, Fikrət immediately told her that he did not have time and still needed to go for buy things for his shop because he had run out of supplies. When we were leaving, she said with a regretful tone: 'Fikrət also lived here before but he didn't stay. He didn't want to'. At that moment, I did not take particular notice of these words but after some time, I understood that they spoke to a latent tension in Fikrət's relationship with his parental home.

Usually, Fikrət did not talk about his family background and hardly mentioned his father or brothers in everyday conversation. Fikrət's father died of a disease in 1980 at the age of thirty-nine. His grandfather went to fight in the Second World War in 1941 and never returned. Thus, the family had to cope twice with the loss of male breadwinners. According to Fikrət's wife, the early deaths were also responsible for Fikrət's shallow genealogical knowledge. If he spoke of his brothers at all, he complained about their bad economic situation and the fact that they would ask him for money whenever he showed up. 'How long can you support relatives? They think just because I have managed to build a house I am a well-off man. But that's not the case and I am also struggling to support my own family'. Besides Fikrət's frequent visits to his mother, he regularly met his brother at weddings. During my fieldwork, they also came once to celebrate the return of Fikrət's elder son from military service.

In people's daily talk, expectations and obligations of mutual social and economic support among close family members are expressed. These are distinctive and embedded in widely shared notions of moral values and the family. Gossiping about relatives who are too demanding as well as about those who do not lend expected support is common. In Fikrət's case, there were several factors that gave rise to latent social tensions: he had moved out of his parental home, he had established a relatively decent life, and two of his brothers and their families continued to suffer from more limited economic and housing opportunities. Furthermore, of all the brothers, Fikrət was the one most expected to remain in the parental home: he was the youngest son and according to cultural norms of ultimogeniture, he should have stayed in the parents' house and taken care of them as they aged. (In turn, he would inherit the parental house after his parents' death). In practice, this last element of the traditional model is adapted to each family's specific situation, but as an ideal, it can still be invoked to express the discomforts and conflicts among family members.

Fikrət had departed, thus, in many ways from the expected behaviour of the youngest son from a family living in a yard house. In addition, he and his wife maintained a closer and more regular relationship with the wife's family. Sevinc's close female relatives frequently came from the village to assist with food preparation when guests were invited. Sevinc and the couple's sons also paid regular visits to Xızı.

Nevertheless, Fikrət was careful to not live 'too closely' to his wife's family. It was important to him to be the male head of his own family, independent of his own parents as well as of his wife's. Fikrət mostly stayed at home 'to run his shop' when his wife and sons visited Xızı. Surely he could have asked his employee to manage the shop on these visits. When he is invited to weddings, Fikrət asks his younger cousin Həsən (the son of his father's sister) to work longer. In fact, Həsən runs the shop all seven days of the week anyway. Fikrət, opens his shop at around eight or nine o'clock in the morning, spends about two hours there until Həsən arrives, then goes for the daily tour to get needed items and products for his shop. After staying at home during the afternoon hours, he would return to the shop in the evening to replace his cousin, and stay there until he closed at around eleven o'clock at night. This arrangement gives him a certain flexibility and control over his time and social obligations, and it seemed that whenever he felt like attending a social event, he would ask Həsən to stay longer. Conversely, if he did not want to attend a social event, he could cite his work obligations as a legitimate excuse.

Fikrət surely struggled with the moral charges that his brothers levelled at him. He was unwilling – though perhaps also unable – to provide more than occasional financial support to other members of his nəsil (i.e. his brothers). He met some obligations: he gave work to a paternal cousin and he used some of the income generated from renting out his apartments to support others. But there were other things he did not do. For example, he did not offer housing to help his brothers out of the crowded family house that caused so much complaint. He did not offer housing as a solution to the impasse being faced by one of his brother's sons, who would like to marry but lacks the housing to attract a wife. (Of course it should be noted that this was seemingly no option in anyone's mind, but the case below demonstrates that it could have been). Moreover, he gave priority to securing his sons' future in terms of housing and marriage perspectives.

There are other ways to demonstrate masculinity, solidarity with one's brothers, and care for one's own family. A contrasting example that illustrates the solidarity among brothers and their families as part of the nəsil is the case of my friend Tofiq, who moved with his parents into a recently built, luxurious villa in our neighbourhood (see also Roth 2019: 61). His father is a retired economist and the family is far from rich. However, the father's brother is a businessman in the agricultural sector and employs around forty people including Tofiq. Most of the employees, as I learned from Tofiq, are *nəsil* members and their livelihood largely depends on Tofiq's paternal uncle (*əmi*). He was also the one who bought the land and constructed the villa in our neighbourhood. He actively supports his elder brother, Tofiq's father, by taking care of his housing situation. Previously, the flow of support was in the other direction, hence pointing to the generalised reciprocal character of the relationship. Whereas the case of Fikrət rather stands for the care and concerns towards his sons' future, the case of Tofiq's uncle serves as an example for a wide network of kin support in terms of labour and housing. The family's long-term mutual support provides a further example of how extended families may hoard not only housing but also labour.

Tofiq's family is from the rural Göyçay Region where he and his elder brother were born. His father had been working in Baku for some time when the mother and her little children moved permanently to join him. First, they inhabited a two-room apartment on the ground storey of a Khrushchevka in the fourth *mikroraion*. In 1994, Tofiq's father, an economist and later a high official in a state committee dealing with property issues, was allocated an apartment in the city centre close to the later constructed Winter Park. According to Tofiq, these apartments were built for higher state officials whose housing situation was considered unsatisfactory. 'My father received this flat from our former president Heydər Aliyev', he told me. It was in this flat that his father's brother had lived with them for some years. Even after the uncle moved out, Tofiq's parents had had remained there until they moved to the villa in Badamdar in about 2010. It was this very uncle whom they housed previously who had bought a plot in Badamdar years before. Around the time they were living together, the uncle founded a company which today provides employment for about forty people, including Tofiq. He opened another office in Tbilisi, Georgia which is managed by his son. Today, running a successful business, the uncle supports the family of his brother, who, after his state service became an economics professor.

Within five months, Tofiq's uncle had the house built in Badamdar and gave it to his brother's family for their use. During my fieldwork, Tofiq lived there together with his brother and parents. At that time, he told me that his parents 'had finally found a wife for his brother', thereby referring to a longer process that he had also raised in each of our previous meetings. His brother's future wife is also from Göyçay and both families had been known to each other. After the marriage celebrations in Göyçay, his brother and his wife moved into the downtown apartment.

A similar kind of mutual support among the *nəsil* was practiced between Asad and his brothers in the 1990s when they jointly cared for the family business in Russia while supporting their close kin in Baku (see Introduction). These were all examples of solidarity and cooperation among family and kin. So, it is true that housing (also labour in some cases) is hoarded and treated as a 'family resource'. However, what 'family' means depends on specific contexts and circles of kin. In Azerbaijan, there is not even one word consistently used for 'family'. Sometimes it is the nuclear family (*ailə*), sometimes the *nəsil*, that treats housing as a collective resource.

All these stories demonstrate the widespread concerns and tensions faced by men as they struggle to fulfil the social and cultural expectations of them. Conflicts that may arise out of the multiple and entangled expectations concerning support not only for one's own children but for other family members as well. But even as Fikrət complained about his brothers and their demands, he had reached a point of certainty about the future security of his sons as he had successfully provided the basis for their marriage and aspirations in founding a family. As he explained to me on a summer evening when we were both sitting in the yard over a cup of black tea from the samovar:

> When I came here this was desert land. I am turning fifty this year and I have been building ever since then. I am tired but I have managed to do everything possible. Now it is my sons' turn. I have provided them with all I can. It is on them finding proper work and to marry. Of course, I further support them whenever necessary. But most important, when they marry they can live here with their families. There is enough space. I have made sure that in case both of them want to stay here every one of them will have his own house.

Fikrət felt well prepared for his sons' future transition into the life-stage of adulthood which is marked by becoming a married and 'behoused' man and then having children.

A final, much briefer but comparable example comes from a similar discourse with Talıb. Talıb is a former teacher of Azerbaijani literature who became a taxi-driver. He bought a yard house in the same neighbourhood in 2003 (he was actually the one who suggested me to ask Fikrət for an empty apartment). He has one son and one daughter he presented them to me as the main motivation for his housing decisions:

> I have a two-storey house with three apartments. If I finish construction according to my plans, there will be around 150 square metres available on each level. On the first storey there are already

two separate apartments, each with three rooms, kitchen, and bathroom, which I have rented out to tenants. The renovation there is not the best because my financial situation is rather limited at the moment. But when my son will marry, he won't have to worry about an apartment. I will give him the bigger one and the small one I will share with my wife. And the third apartment I will leave to my daughter. In case that her future husband's family doesn't have one, I can provide her with an apartment, too. In fact, the housing question for my children is already solved. You know, the most important thing is a roof! When your sons and daughters have a house, then the heart is at peace (*Samo vazhno – krysha! Esli u synovei i docheri est' dom, togda serdtsa spokoina*).

Beyond the rather material emphasis of the last section, the long-term motivations described in my ethnographic account points to the house's social and moral implications for the perceived future security of one's children. Giving 'peace to the heart', nicely summarises the aspirations and tensions discussed in this section.

Whereas all the above cases are examples of how people were successful in setting an economically secure base for themselves and their children, the final example shows people in much less favourable conditions. For Zahid, poor living conditions, lack of resources, and the diminished marriage perspectives for his sons have resulted in feelings of shame and an inability to provide for his family. In the hillside area close to Nariman Narimanov Avenue there is a lonely standing, triangular-shaped one-storey residential block from the beginning of the twentieth century left amidst independence-era high-rises. Zahid has been living here all his life, for 58 years. Before 2003, the block was inhabited by around thirty people, among them also relatives. Then a construction company bought out the inhabitants to demolish the building for new construction. All but two families left the place, including Zahid's mother and sister, accepting the little compensation of 1,500 AZN per square metre. But Zahid refused any compensation and stayed to seek justice, as he said, though, without success. The demolition started, then the project was halted due to the investor's mismanagement. Zahid ended up without money and without a proper-looking home. Today, only the eastern front is more or less intact while the rest of the building after having been demolished is now overgrown by vegetation. After partial demolition, the breakthrough into the inner yard is guarded by a young security serviceman in a tiny white cabin.

Plate 10. Zahid standing in the entrance of his car workshop ready to check, refill, or repair tires.

When I first met Zahid, he was standing as usual in the entrance of his small improvised car workshop next to piles of old tires. As it says on the hand-written price-list on the building's wall, his car-service includes checking and refilling air pressure and minor repairs of tires. Through a low wooden door, we entered the neat yard, passed by the run-down bathroom, and arrived at a small dilapidated three-room apartment of some 30 square metres, including the kitchen. Here, he lives with his wife and his 32- and 23-year-old sons. While showing me around, he commented that 'if you look at my house, you will be scared of how I live. I live like a tsygan (Gypsy). There is bad smell, mould, and trash everywhere around. I have family, I have grandchildren. It is dangerous for them'. He pointed to a corner of the multi-purpose sleeping and living room where parts of the interior ceiling had crumbled and fallen down recently. A bed stood directly underneath the huge hole. His wife joined us by explaining that 'if there is heavy snow and frost, this part can further break down and only God knows whether someone of us will get up again in the morning. Look here! When it rains, the water pours into the house'. Later, when we had some tea, Zahid continued:

> The furniture was brought here by my wife upon our marriage. Later
> on, we gave some of it to our daughter when she got married
> because we didn't have money to buy her new things. Later, due to

the conditions of the apartment, we had to throw away most of the remaining furniture. Since our roof is leaking, everything became spoiled by the rain and the constant moisture.

Then, his wife Bahar took over the word: 'My sons sleep on mattresses we put on the floor. My husband does the same, lying next to them'. Then, she switched the topic and complained that their elder son, although being already 32 years old, was still unmarried:

We cannot wed him because there is no space. Where should we house our daughter-in-law? Our younger son served in the army and finished his service already some time ago. For him it is also time to get married but we are far from living in human conditions. Look! In here it is not clean, it is not warm. It is not comfortable.

Zahid and Bahar were seemingly suffering from their perceived inhuman living conditions. Their dwelling did not even provide them with physical protection against moist weather which also causes further deterioration. For them, their overall housing condition not only constitutes a threat to health and well-being but also to their very identification as proper human beings and civilised persons. Furthermore, their deficient housing is, contrary to the cases of Fikrət and Talıb, made responsible for their sons' lack of marriage opportunities and everyone's general well-being.

Both Zahid and his wife are deprived of the self-image and role as father/ husband and mother/ wife. Bahar does not blame her husband for their predicament, but it is the house that she feels unable to care for and maintain as a home. At a later point we talked about the differences between the Soviet past and independence. Regarding present insecurities and future uncertainties, the sympathies of both were rather obvious. Bahar said: 'We had a good life back then. My husband worked, went to Moscow regularly. We always had Moscow sweets, groceries, cheese, butter, meat'. Zahid continued by confirming:

Yes! The time of the Communists was good. Young families were given a two-room apartment. But today we have the situation that even both of my sons cannot afford one apartment together. They offered 1,500 AZN and I have 30 square metres. How can I ever afford an apartment for my sons? True, now there is democracy, on the markets you get everything, all the time, Baku has become more beautiful, but people have no money. Back then, we had money, but we could not buy what we wanted.

Others whom I have presented in this chapter and whose present housing situation was rather secure were less nostalgic, though they too emphasised the much-increased uncertainty in people's everyday lives. For instance, once Azər told me that 'housing has always been an issue. Back then people did not need money, but time'. In contrast, 'today, there is no guarantee for anything. In Soviet times, a person was guaranteed a job, housing. But now, to earn decent money and to take a loan, you have to find good and stable work, which has become difficult these days'. A similar statement was made by Mehriban, a friend and NGO-worker who would never want to return living in the socialist past but gave a similar, thoroughly reflected account on how many people perceived the transformation:

> During Soviet times, people had confidence in the future. A woman knew that she would give birth to a child who was looked after in state-sponsored kindergartens, schools, so she was able to work. And you could be sure to have employment later. A worker was highly respected. And he knew that he would get married, that he would be in the housing queue at his workplace and receive an apartment in five to ten years. So, the structures we were living in had already decided everything for us. We had no concerns of what to do tomorrow. There was no uncertainty towards the future.

The nostalgia for the Soviet days described on the previous pages reflects the uncertain housing and employment prospects for many, especially among those like Zahid and his wife, whose present everyday life and future perspective has a strong impact on how they evaluate the present in relation to their past life. Others, like Fikrət or Azər, who manoeuvred their families rather fortunately through the time of transformation were communicating a much more nuanced, differentiated, and less nostalgic picture of the past – if they did so at all (for instance, Fikrət did generally not have to say much in that regard). After having dealt with the economic, social, and moral issues along different housing biographies, one connecting element was parents' (in)ability to pave their children a smooth way to marriage. In the final section I therefore want to discuss the social, economic, and political aspects of weddings.

The Political Economy of Marriage and Weddings

During a spontaneous visit in April 2014 at my former host family, the Qarayevs, Asad started complaining because he had received a wedding invitation for that very evening. As often, it was an invitation from people who were not close, yet also not distant. At either pole, it would have been easy to make an immediate decision about whether to go to the wedding. 'Only in this year I have been to 12 weddings at least. From the money I left there I could have already bought a Lada'. Although he was surely exaggerating, Asad's statement points to the fact that weddings are often perceived as a serious factor in a family's household budget and to their broader economic and micropolitical aspects. The same can be said for weddings everywhere, but in Baku weddings were an almost daily topic of conversation.

Plate 11. Inside an average *şadlıq sarayı.*

Since independence, weddings have transformed increasingly into large and lavishly staged events characterised by strong commercialisation. They are normally celebrated in a *şadlıq sarayı* (wedding palace). These palaces are restaurants with large halls able to host a large number of guests and to provide all kinds of extra services, like the obligatory filming team that accompanies the festive entry of the couple and the whole evening which can be followed from one of several flat screens in the hall. They can also provide the live-band and the moderator who leads the guests through the ritual events of the evening, structured by a continuous flow of all kinds of dishes and non-alcoholic and alcoholic beverages (the latter only reserved for male guests). Guests are expected to give money gifts to the couple – the amount depending on the prestige and reputation of the chosen wedding palace. In the course of the evening, envelopes with money are put into boxes, usually set up next to the entrance to the hall. Envelopes with money were also the standard gift in urban Azerbaijan during socialist times and mark a point of continuity despite other transformations in wedding celebrations. 'People spend much money on their wedding feast. Therefore, money counts as the most appropriate gift because the newlyweds have to pay the wedding palace', Azər remarked. The couple counts on each guest giving the equivalent cost of his/ her seat, and the expenses for most wedding feasts are covered by the money received from guests, not leaving a financial burden on the festive aspect of the marriage. Sometimes, the couple even has some money left. Only occasionally, does a wedding not pay off.

During certain months, families might get invited to several weddings a week. Who attends from the family depends on the social and emotional closeness to the inviters. Both husband and wife will join, including their children, if the relationship is very close. If it is rather a friend or colleague of an individual household member, only one family member is likely to visit the wedding. One must not forget that the greater the number of household members who attend a wedding, the greater the additional financial expense – this must be considered and gauged too, alongside 'closeness'. I also encountered situations in which a son attended as a representative for the whole family, if for some reason the whole family could not join. I, personally, was invited *only* to five weddings in my year of fieldwork – three alone and two with my wife and son. Attending weddings and participating in a kind of invitation economy is based on long-term reciprocal commitments between relatives, families, friends, colleagues, and acquaintances. These social relations are negotiated at weddings and can become confirmed and enhanced, but also challenged and broken. Not only attending but also evaluating each and every wedding is a topic both men and women engage in enthusiastically. On a broader social level, weddings are important rituals of political significance because they should bring together the whole social network of the family.

Akif (b. 1958), a homeowner, self-acclaimed real estate agent in the neighbourhood (among countless others), and hobby historian on Badamdar provided a good example. He became a key person for my integration into the neighbourhood as everyone knew him, and he also made me an active member and protégé of his social network, especially after I supported him once with my English language skills to broker an apartment for a Pakistani family who came to Baku because of a family conflict and in order to find work. In one of my spontaneous visits to his office, located immediately opposite of the bus-stop, he complained of the week's wedding marathon. 'Yesterday I attended a wedding in Kempinski Hotel – not the cheapest place to be invited to a wedding. Today, Məlik [his son] is going to another wedding and tomorrow my wife will'. Referring to the expenses for attending a wedding which includes paying an average amount of roughly between 50 to 100 AZN per guest, but also more, depending on the status and prestige of the venue, Akif referred to his own son's wedding that I had attended only a few weeks previously:

> Some people I invited did not attend my son's wedding, some even
> without excusing themselves. Others were eating and drinking,
> though they did not pay. Since the 1970s, I have been attending
> weddings of others. I don't know how much money I have already
> spent on weddings. For instance, one friend who is pretty well-off
> and for whom I once sold an apartment for 150,000 USD was
> invited. I attended the wedding of their son, but from them, no one
> came to Məlik's wedding.

He pointed to the taxi-driver cleaning his car on the other side of the street
and continued that he also did not join. Entire tables that Akif had reserved
and paid for remained empty because around twenty people had not shown
up. 'But you know what?', he stated, 'on the other hand, I think that's fine. I
have noted down everything. Now I am in the picture; I know on whom I
can rely and on whom not. Also, God sees everything!'

As we have seen, parents feel responsible for the marriage of their
children. They have the role of paving their offspring's way by lending
social, economic, and ritual support for housing, the wedding feast, and the
marriage process in general. This already begins by the active engagement of
parents in finding a marriage partner, especially for their sons. Many friends
and acquaintances, also those having appeared in this chapter, told me about
the role of parents in the process of matchmaking. For instance, Azər, who
was a sailor and therefore hardly at home, was presented with potential
marriage partners by his mother:

> Every time I returned from sea, my mother, without losing any time,
> showed me one or two girls. My parents were arranging my
> marriage. That's how I got to know my wife. My mother
> recommended her to me like she did with five, six, seven, eight
> others before. I did not ask my mother to do so, she just started
> engaging in this. I didn't have time and was also less interested to
> deal with these things as I was always on the ship.

On a more general level, he explained:

> For girls, it worked the same – somehow two parties would approach
> and get to know each other. Through social contacts, a lot of phone
> calls … support of relatives. They are always interested in these
> matters and ask questions. They would recommend suitable guys.
> This was all done by the parents. That's still the case. However, in
> principle, young people can get to know each other on the street, in
> the institute, and at work – but still parents will always go and find
> out who they are, what kind of family it is, what kind of manners
> they have.

Initially, mothers and female relatives usually take the leading role during the matchmaking process. Azər, for instance, stated that he has not meddled in his daughter's affairs, unlike his wife:

> I did not know anything, but my wife was in the picture from the beginning to the end – whom our daughter was dating, with whom she was communicating .... And I was only told after they had been dating for a year and already had certain plans. My wife had every-thing under control [*he laughed*]. Then my wife met my daughter's boyfriend. I did not know him yet. But my wife knew everything about their relationship. Of course, I noticed something.... conversations on the phone.... something was going on. But, according to my wife's reactions, I assumed that everything was just fine. So, I didn't interfere. Then my wife and daughter suddenly told me that the boy's family wanted to visit us.... for the *elçilik* and all these things. First, only women were coming – his mother and aunts. At a later stage, also the men were joining and we introduced each other. When there was the *böyük elçilik* (i.e. the culminating visit), they came with the engagement ring. But do not ask me for any details.... well, women like to observe all kinds of rituals, but I don't, I don't really know much about these things.

Elçilik in its broader sense means 'delegation' or 'mission'. With reference to marriage it denotes the ritual matchmaking when parents and (predominantly female) relatives of the groom visit the potential bride's home to officially ask for the bride's hand. If they agree, the decision is officially disclosed and confirmed by a ritual called *şirin çay* (sweet tea) because the guests are served sweetened tea. Sometimes, the tea is served in a special way of symbolic importance: Black tea is slowly poured into glasses which are half-filled with sugared water. Done like this, it results in two layered liquids. The clear water symbolises the bride's family, the dark layer of black tea on top stands for the groom's family. Both layers are then mixed to symbolise the unification of the couple and their families. Whereas these rituals are also respected and followed by most young people I know, the traditional matchmaking by parents and relatives engaging in the selection of the partner has been changing. But still, parents usually feel a great responsibility for the selection – even if it is expressed merely by making regular references and conversations on the topic or suggesting marriage partners.

Many contemporaries compare the rise of conspicuous consumption and the potlatch-like character of Baku's wedding industry with how people celebrated weddings in late socialist times. The wedding of Azər's daughter in the years before my fieldwork was attended by more than 400 people. 'In our days, though, it was simply impossible to find a place which could have hosted and served so many guests in one place. There weren't such huge restaurants as like today. Maximum for 200 people or so', Azər stated. He continued:

> Huge places for weddings, like today, simply did not exist. People celebrated weddings in the simplest restaurant which had a banquet hall. Normally, around 150 guests could fit in there. They had no capacities for more. We celebrated our wedding in the Inturist Hotel, one of the few places which had several banquet halls. There it was possible to gather 200 people, although it was quite cramped. In the whole of Baku there was only one place with a really huge hall – the Gülüstan Wedding Palace. It opened in 1980 but celebrating there was very expensive. Nowadays, places like Gülüstan exist all over the city.

Therefore, as many people reported, it was much more common in Soviet times to celebrate two separate weddings – one for the groom's side and one for the bride's side. At the groom's wedding, his relatives, guests and only the narrowest circle from the bride's side were invited. And vice versa. Today, however, celebrating only one wedding has become feasible and more popular. Although not comparable with the conspicuous consumption of different kinds and amounts of food and drinks at today's weddings, people often emphasised that, regarding weddings in socialist times, there has hardly been any lack or shortage of anything. Another often-made reference to the better quality of products back then reflects a critical stance towards the recent developments, also because of the financial burden it can create for many households:

> At weddings there was no shortage of anything. In fact, one could get anything. You just had to pay a bit more. But there was *everything*. Black caviar, for instance – although it was expensive in the restaurant. Not the red one as today. But today, we do not have black caviar at all here. A three-litre can of black caviar was sixty Rubles. And three cans were completely enough for serving everyone. Also, there was meat always; and everything else too. Of course, the vodka was much better than today but we – at the same time we had much less variety. However, everything – the restaurants, the food – was cheaper than today. And no one here had ever eaten red caviar – no one! Life was different.

Despite frequent criticism in the rise of conspicuous consumption, basically everyone participates in the enhancement of these trends by aiming at keeping on par with others. Besides the subtle pride and nostalgia for Baku once having been the centre of caviar production in the whole Soviet Union, including the product's affordability for everyone, unlike today, this comment can be read as a kind of justification for a past system that has been misrepresented overtly by post-Soviet political and neoliberal narratives.

Recent scholars of postsocialist transformation have dealt with ritual exchange in the context of wedding feasts – issues that have become dominant features in the Azerbaijani context as well. Anthropological literature on postsocialism provides further examples on recent developments of conspicuous consumption, gift exchange, and the increasingly lavish character of feasts and wedding rituals (see e.g. Creed 1998: 203–4 for Bulgaria; Werner 1997a, 1997b for Kazakhstan; Vasile 2015 for Romania). In this section, I wanted to describe the everyday financial burden of weddings as a structuring element in people's daily life. Besides the long-term investment into future accommodation and home interiors, as described in the previous sections, marriages are a further dimension of future investment. As Akif remarked, people are usually scrupulously noting down how much money was given to whom on which ritual occasion, since not only weddings but also other life-cycle festivities such as a son's circumcision feast (*kiçik toy*), are counted. On one's own celebration, people expect an equivalent return which, if it is not the case, may result in people re-ordering the quality of relations in their social networks.

Finally, I want to provide some brief background information on the ritual links between house, home, and marriage for better understanding in the following chapters. A marriage is characterised by ritualised forms of exchange between the two uniting families in terms of male and female aspects of home-making. Such gifts are said to provide for a successful transition of the newlyweds into the status of a new *ailǝ* on which their future as an independent family are based. Besides the rather pragmatic considerations of providing young people with material and economic support, the ritual complex of marriage in Azerbaijan is a symbolic representation of how concepts like house, home, home-making, and marriage are understood locally. Moreover, although the term *ev* does not distinguish between notions of house and home, both conceptual parts are nevertheless presented as gendered concepts. In analogy to a new family (*ailǝ*), a new house only emerges as a proper whole through the unification of husband and wife, their families, and resources. As probably has become clear with regard to the 'political economy of Azeri weddings', it is generally the case that the bridegroom's parents 'are expected to provide [...] separate housing for the married couple sometime after the wedding, either through buying a house or a flat or building one' (Yalçın-Heckmann 2001: 28). But today, as it was during Soviet times, the young couple is likely to move to the husband's parents' house until there are sufficient resources to move into a separate apartment. Anyway, it is the groom or men more broadly who are again associated with the physical structure of the house. The bride's family, however, is expected to provide for all the interior necessities of the house or apartment as part of the bride's dowry (*cehiz*), including furniture, carpets, curtains, household items, china, chandeliers, and more. Such marriage transactions include pragmatic reflections and are often considered long before the wedding becomes an issue.

Among some of my informants, mothers have started to accumulate and store future dowry items for their daughter years in advance. In turn, parents of sons are often considering the dowry of their future daughter-in-law (*gəlin,* lit. 'incomer') with regard to their home interior. Instead of buying new furniture themselves to replace the older one which the mother once obtained as *cehiz* herself, they may wait for the *gəlin's* dowry. Shortly before a son's marriage, households often carry out major renovations in their apartment and make space for new furniture (see Chapter 5). These marital transactions between two future affinal families, and their material and spatial associations with the bride and the bridegroom respectively, are a ritualised way of expressing the social values and meanings of house, home, and family *qua* marriage. All these notions, by local understandings, are integrated in the term *ev*. At the same time, *ev* constitutes (1) the house which is associated with its 'male qualities' and represented as male duty and responsibility as well as (2) the *home* which expresses its female counterpart. The immovable and movable objects of the house have become, historically, signifiers and symbols for the ideal conceptions, roles, and duties of masculine and feminine personhood. Both male and female aspects are required to make a proper *ev*. It is only the *cehiz* that makes the house a home. Vice versa, there cannot be a home without the house as its complementary counterpart. It is by uniting both these aspects through marriage that the family comes into being.

However, these are ideal representations within a ritualised context that eclipse the challenges that many of my low-income informants encounter in the framework of an increasingly unequal, precarious, and excluding housing regime which is perceived as an immediate limitation for successful marriage negotiations. As I have shown, there are a variety of conflicts, tensions, and obstacles that people are coping with in their aspirations to perform according to changing socio-cultural expectations that have gained an implicitly competitive character. For rural Azerbaijan, the political economy of Azeri weddings, including aspects of conspicuous consumption, large expenses, and status negotiations, has been described by Lale Yalçın-Heckmann (2001; 2010: 138ff.).

The adventurous and sometimes troublesome *cehiz*-negotiations are illustrated by the experiences of Saleh (b. 1983). In contrast to most other people I have met, he rigorously rejected the 'patriarchal character' of his society and the parents' influence on marriage decisions. His father is Azeri, his mother Ukrainian, and they share the liberal attitude of their son. Six months before we first met, he married Alina, his second wife, whose parents have the same mixed-marriage background. Both come from families who exclusively speak Russian at home. Still, he held enough common assumptions about the respective roles of the groom's side and the bride's side that a conflict he had with his first wife's father-in-law led to divorce after only eight months. The conflict occurred because Saleh's father-in-law, according to Saleh, broke the rules of respectful behaviour towards Saleh and his father but attempted to forge a publicly superior status and position. Our conversation over some beer with the obligatory chickpeas started around the topic of marriage and housing:

> The day before my father went to meet my future father-in-law, he asked me whether and how I could finance an apartment. He wanted to know my plan in order to negotiate. By that time, I had a well-paid job at British Petroleum and I told him that I could provide for an apartment within two months. So, our fathers met and the other side promised to bring the *cehiz* as soon as I got the apartment. We married. As promised, I bought an apartment after two months. I paid 45 per cent of the price immediately. For the rest, I took a bank loan for a period of ten years. Then I went to my father-in-law, put my apartment keys onto his table, and told him that it is time to bring the *cehiz*. We went to have a look at the apartment but instead of just getting the *cehiz* he said he wanted me first to do some interior renovations. Since it was still empty, he expected some painting and wallpapering to be done. Well, so I hired five guys who finished everything that he wanted within twenty-five days. After that I approached him again and he assured me that the *cehiz* will arrive within the next few days. However, nothing happened for months. After half a year he called me on a Friday and told me to come with my wife to his dacha on the next day. We went there and met a lot of my wife's relatives who had been invited, too. I thought it would be the usual kind of barbecue. Then, after we had finished eating, my father-in-law suddenly stood up from his chair, held a brief speech on his daughter, me, and our marriage. He publicly handed me the keys for a car and solemnly announced that this was the *cehiz* for his daughter. The car was a five-year-old *Peugeot 206* – it was really a joke! By that time, I already owned two cars – a Mercedes and a

Peugeot. Apart from the fact that we were not in need of a car, this whole act was so ridiculous and I was literally speechless. I asked him whether I could sell the car to buy instead all the furniture and other stuff for the apartment that we desperately needed and actually expected to receive. This he denied because the car was registered on his name. I found that outrageous and got really angry in front of all guests. 'We agreed on a *cehiz* in order to furnish our apartment and to finally being able to move in there', I shouted at him.

Apart from that, what felt most embarrassing for me was the fact that he acted not the way he agreed with my father. He did not even invite him, maybe because he knew very well that my father would get even more angry than I did. All in all, *his* behaviour was simply disrespectful not only towards me but especially towards my father. I got so angry that I immediately left that place. I asked my wife whether she was coming with me. When she replied that she would stay one more night at the dacha and return to me only tomorrow, then I told her that 'when you stay now, my door will remain closed for you – not only tomorrow but forever!' That was the last day we've been together.

In the end he contrasted all these difficulties with his later experiences in the marriage process with his present wife and her parents. Alina's father, he said, was completely different as he was not teasing him with wrong expectations and volatile demands. Saleh and Alina had been engaged for three years before they finally decided to marry. Saleh stated that:

This time my father told her father to negotiate with *me* because I was already an adult person making my own living and financially independent from my father. My future father-in-law asked me a simple question: 'Where do you want me to bring the *cehiz*?' That was it. And that's the way it is supposed to work.

Saleh's story illustrates, according to my experience, a rather exceptional case in which a young man is endowed by his father with the right and agency to engage personally in negotiations concerning his marriage and related housing arrangements – an issue that is mostly dealt with by parents as the ones handling most of the financial issues.

Conclusion

Based on ethnographic examples from people with different housing, social, and economic backgrounds, this chapter has addressed the role of property, apartments, and houses after privatisation. In some of my cases, privatised housing constituted the major asset for people to engage in the housing market and to improve their living conditions. In other cases, it was the possibility to acquire land and to build a house which served also as an economic base and income generator. Either way, the house enhances economic prospects which in turn enhance the house's growth. Different forms of housing are further discussed with regard to storage and production of natural goods which enhance the family's capacities to engage in practices of sharing and gift-giving. Furthermore, the housing question in all cases was crucially related to social and moral issues of providing one's children with promising prospects for a secure future.

In some situations, housing creates tensions and conflicts regarding people's different priorities of providing support among kin. In the most extreme cases, a lack of proper housing results in a feeling of deprivation from society. Not being able to provide adequate housing, let alone financial perspective, significantly reduces the chances of getting married. Feelings of shame among parents unable to support their children are another consequence.

The overall connection of housing to the issue of marriage has led me in the final section to describe the political economy behind these important rituals more closely. The issue of frequent wedding invitations has been raised frequently as an increasing economic challenge for many of my informants. Weddings also contain a socio-political dimension that is enacted and negotiated along understandings of long-term reciprocal support that defines the quality of social relations. More generally, the conspicuous consumption and market industry around Azeri weddings are compared against the context of wedding celebrations during late socialism. This implicitly serves as a way of criticising recent developments against the background of past experiences. However, such criticism remains rather a lip service as people's embeddedness in their social context hardly allows for flexibility in how to celebrate a wedding. It would also mean to illegitimately escape the long-term cycle of reciprocal hosting and ritual gifting. The final example shifted attention to conflicts in the dowry negotiations and challenge of the other party's status and respect. Social interaction along unwritten rules was a significant factor. To a great extent this will also play a role in the next chapter.

Chapter 5
Private Spheres and Public Display: Façade Politics between Exposure and Concealment

This chapter describes spatial and social processes of how residents imagine, act, and negotiate private and public domains in their everyday life. Although people I met generally imagine the private and public as clearly separate conceptual spheres, in everyday practice both are related to and constitute each other in concrete social settings. The complex and ambiguous character of the widely popular public/ private constitutes 'one of the "grand dichotomies" of Western thought' (Weintraub 1997: 1). Hence, any attempt to clearly distinguish and demarcate the public from the private points to the widespread tendency of 'ideological simplifications' (Alexander et al. 2018: 128), and 'obscures the extent to which some public is embedded in every private, and some private is embedded in every public' (Hirt 2012: 15). These ambiguities will be unpacked in light of several ethnographic cases concerning how people with different housing backgrounds imagine and enact privacy by material, social, and symbolic forms. Walls, doors, and curtains as the primary thresholds between inside and outside serve as examples. I describe people's relational and socio-spatial understanding of private spaces, which can refer to the house/ home, the courtyard, or neighbourhood. With regard to their social surrounding but equally directed towards the state, dwellers exercise control by regulating the movements and intrusions of persons and objects from the outside (see Douglas 1966). At the same time, I will describe strategies and controlled ways of setting up occasional permeability of porous private spaces for the sake of public display in order to confirm, reinforce, and negotiate social relations. I will also discuss the local social practice of 'maintaining the curtain' (*pərdə saxlamaq*) that describes the proper enactment and performance of daily social interaction among people of different genders, age, and status within and beyond the family home. It is the context of home (*ev*) and its shifting meanings through time that allows a nuanced approach to public/ private conceptions which are constantly made at the crossroads of dominant ideological, socio-cultural, and political frameworks. The practice of home-making, the role of home interiors, and the widespread practice of *remont* (home renovations) will then be described in relation to marriage, the ascribed meaning of hospitality, comfort, and (conspicuous) consumption.

Scholarly studies on the concepts of public and private have long constituted a major body of literature within the anthropology of the Mediterranean and the Middle East. Classical works on differences between public and private domains were strongly linked to issues of gender, space, patriarchy, intra-family or citizen–state power relations (see e.g. Papanek 1973; Nelson 1974; Bourdieu 1976; Gilmore 1982). Similarly, in Azerbaijan, my male company conceived of the home as a gendered space attached to women rather than men. Male responsibilities towards home and family involved providing for and representing the home, such as going to work or engaging in other kinds of *biznes* to earn money – all things which largely depend on an extended social network and demand additional time for fostering and maintaining it (see also Roth 2020). Later anthropologists have adopted a more dynamic approach gendered spaces and considered such categories according to the fluidities and ambiguities in people's everyday practices (Joseph 1993a, 1993b, 1997; Singerman 1995; Vom Bruck 1997; Mazumdar and Mazumdar 2001; Meneley 2007 [1996]; Ghannam 2013). With regard to postsocialism, only a few anthropologists working on the different impacts of economic transformations on men and women have given attention 'to the culturally specific ways in which public/ state and private/ kin/ domestic domains are mutually constituted and differently valued' (Liu 2011: 117). These have challenged the ideological dichotomy of public and private, describing how for both spheres 'the principles associated with public and private coexist in complex combinations in the ordinary routines of everyday life' (Gal 2002: 78). The boundaries are thus not stable, but fluid and dynamic. They need to be set in their specific contextual frameworks. Furthermore, it is by the use of the public/ private dichotomy that people 'can subdivide, recalibrate, and thus make recursions in their categorizations of cultural objects and personae' (ibid.: 79).

According to some literature on Soviet and post-Soviet societies, constructing privacy vis-à-vis the public, is largely shaped by the performance of physical and visual protection, concealment, secrecy, and intimacy (e.g. Shlapentokh 1989; Kharkhordin 1997; Habeck and Belolyubskaya 2016; on Azerbaijan see Tohidi 1996; Heyat 2002). This is largely due to the fact that the public and private were political and politicised categories. Their shape at a particular moment tells a lot about prevailing state-citizen relations. People protected and concealed the 'private' (usually including the home and much of everyday life) because it was subject to the Party-State's ideological and political intrusions.

In the present chapter, I shall introduce Azerbaijani meanings of privacy and ways of constructing physical and social space with a special focus on the house and home while equally considering the political and ideological impact of socialist experiences. The Soviet state's approach towards the home and people's private life after the Stalinist era was unsteady. Especially in late socialism, these shifts largely followed the different approaches of the leader and enabled a variety of 'new forms of life, publics, persons, lifestyles, temporalities, spatialities, imaginary worlds and visions of the future' (Yurchak 2006: 295), a process that was said to be 'largely external to the party' (Humphrey 2008: 9).

I start the chapter with a description of how private space is architecturally and symbolically constructed and protected by means of boundaries and thresholds such as walls, doors, windows, and curtains. I then describe their importance as mediators and signifiers of moral values, status, and wealth. I illustrate the effort, time, and money people invest into making and beautifying such thresholds, as well as the visual and symbolic transformation actors undergo when crossing them. The next section discusses the emic concept and distinctive feature of the curtain (pərdə) which is perceived not only as an essential element of a proper home but constitutes a central metaphor for describing appropriate and respectful ways of interaction between houses, between household members, and other primary social relationships. I argue that the local concept of pərdə and the practices of maintaining it allow us to grasp the complex negotiation of privacy in different contexts. Finally, I explore contemporary processes of home-making among Baku urban residents. Elsewhere I have compared the widespread practice of caring for one's car as the publicly performed male counterpart of women's care for the home (Roth 2020). Here, I focus instead on the practice of remont and transforming homes according to personal taste and newly emerging standards of interior design.

I argue that remont, which is widespread across the Soviet successor states, can be understood by considering people's past experience of shortage. During socialism, housing and people's efforts in making, furnishing, and aestheticising the home were shaped by policies towards the private sphere of home as well as by citizens' strategies to bypass structural limitations and the scarcity of domestic goods. With the privatisation of housing after 1991, newly gained freedom in designing home-interiors resulted in dwellers' inflationary practice of remont. Besides being a pragmatic form of investing money into the home in order to increase its market value, I further argue that such practice constitutes not only a strategy to personalise standardised dwellings. It is also of crucial importance in the context of marriage and the seemingly competitive field of hospitality. Thus, apart from the popular trend of interpreting home-making as an individual expression of social distinction, I show that the cultural values attached to marriage, dowries, and hospitality are additional motivations for dwellers to transform their domestic space. So far, these aspects have not only remained marginal in existing literature on how privacy is constructed in wider socio-cultural contexts. They also demonstrate that the home, as private space par excellence, can occasionally turn into a stage of semi-public display in a controlled and ritualised manner. In all this, sociality is constructed by a skilful staging of the private home, which is an essential part of the more general yet subtle social politics of representation.

The Wall and the Door: On Boundaries and Thresholds

'For Azerbaijanis the home is like a fortress', Reşat, a 55-year-old friend and academic told me. 'We highly appreciate our privacy and do not want others to observe us in our daily life. That's why the first thing we do is build a wall around our property even before we start building the house'. During my fieldwork in Baku, I soon noticed the walls: they were widespread, and not only in private residential neighbourhoods. In public space, the state (as landlord of the national home) built walls to hide poor and unfavourable areas alongside major roads. These undesired urban spaces are concealed from the eyes of visitors and local inhabitants likewise, and even from the eyes of the country's president. For me, this form of 'cultural intimacy' (Herzfeld 2005) shows many parallels with how people in Azerbaijan represent, talk about, and act around homes including their physical and symbolic barriers such as walls, doors, and especially windows. It follows the argument that 'state ideologies and the rhetorics of everyday social life are revealingly similar' (Herzfeld 2005: 2). The building of fences and walls in Yakutsk has been described as a 'micro-practice of dividing space' based on the 'materiality of those objects that actually restrict and regulate access' (Habeck and Belolyubskaya 2016: 119). My ethnographic material in this section similarly explores the material and symbolic meaning of walls.

Reşat's statement on Azerbaijanis' concerns about privacy was supported by the impressions that my wife and I gained during the first months after moving to Baku. Within 25 years, the previously unbuilt space on the urban periphery where we rented our small apartment in a *həyət evi* had become a densely built low-rise housing neighbourhood. The streets and small alleys were flanked by high limestone walls and closed metal gates, shielding the property from curious gazes. For an anthropologist interested in the changing housing strategies and home-making efforts, this was not the most encouraging observation. Indeed, even at the end of my fieldwork there were still many neighbours whose houses, courtyards, and family life remained a well-kept secret from me. Reşat's remark was further confirmed by the observation that even vacant and unbuilt lots were protected by walls or improvised alternatives. In one case, there was a twenty-metre-long and three-metre-high patchwork of rusty metal sheets in different sizes, colours, and stages of corrosion. Another plot was enclosed with scrap parts of train wagons in yellow, greyish, and rusty colours – a surprising contrast to the rather monotone impression of unplastered limestone walls in the area.

Plate 12. Wall constructions of various materials in Badamdar ranging from solid limestone (front left) to 'recycled' scrap metal and discarded train wagons.

Even as walls and the visible exterior of buildings blocks out some view of the social lives within, they draw attention to other socio-economic information. Hence, our Baku neighbourhood represented an extensive mixture of dwellers' social standings and economic situations. Our landlords' home was of average quality within the neighbourhood (though much better than the homes in other parts of the city). However, up the road there were also luxurious villas of the nouveaux riches (Humphrey 1997). Often, these homes appeared like fortresses because of high walls around the houses, huge gates for huge cars, and window grills even on the houses' top storeys. There was a distinct sense that all these details were meant to 'show off' the possibility that what lay beyond the gates and doors was particularly desirable, and needed to be protected from theft. Wealth was not be disguised by architectural modesty.

Reşat's statement, however, was meant to stress the value of secrecy and the functional protection of family privacy and intimacy. Similar conceptualisations of protecting privacy are found regionally and across the Soviet Union. They are reported for Armenia (Fehlings 2014: 126–27). They also were integral to life within the Soviet communal apartment, 'Secrecy is one of the most important ways of keeping the illusion of privacy' (Boym 1994: 146). On a broader level, such understandings of privacy protection relates to still vivid memories among families, related to the times of Stalinist terror and the constant threat of denunciation by neighbours (see Fitzpatrick 1999; Hooper 2006). The Baku *məhəlləs* from pre-Soviet and Soviet days that were dominated by courtyard houses (*həyət evləri*) constituted an extreme contrast to the state's mass housing and micro-districts. The Soviet housing provided collective space for outdoor leisure and activities only in the middle of the architectural ensemble; it was semi-private not for one household, but for dozens.

However, Reşat's statement can be interpreted as also referring to the roles played by fences in providing material and symbolic protection against violations of property rights. Such violations are frequent and perpetrated even by the state and state-backed investors. Hence, walls also constitute an important safeguard for the owners of empty plots who may well be labour migrants spending most of the year in Russia, Turkey, or elsewhere. Still, the protective powers of the physical walls rest on the power of paper documents.

At the Baku Branch of the State Archive of the Azerbaijan Republic (ARDABF), which files all copies of land-ownership documents in the Baku region, I learned that one pragmatic aspect of such filing is to vouch for the authenticity of ownership documents. On public reception days, many people approach the archive to check the ownership status of land they intend to buy. According to the archive's lawyer, a young man in his late twenties, cases of falsified documents issued by professionalised criminal circles have increased significantly over the last years. These fake documents are often of such good quality that most people cannot distinguish them from genuine ones, and so they visit the archives to cross-check the documents they have been shown.

False land sales are undertaken in many cases by real-estate agents, or other individuals with significant knowledge of housing bureaucracy, who offer property that belongs to a third party, who by reason of physical absence would not even take notice of the transaction. The lawyer at the archives told me about a case involving his best friend's father-in-law. The father-in-law lives in Germany but owns land in Binəqədi – a suburb and administrative district of Baku at the city's north-western fringe (first built up in the 1920s), and now inhabited by around 240,000 people who settled there mostly after independence. His plot was not at all protected by a fencing device. One day, on a return visit to Baku, he saw that a house had been built on his plot. He enquired within and learned that the owner of the house thought he owned the land, but his documents were false. Settling such a dispute is a long enduring and complicated process. Walls are no guarantee against property fraud, but they do provide a material and symbolic barrier which prevents easy access by strangers and demarcates otherwise empty space as property.

Walls hide and protect, but they also expose and display. Anthropologist Francesca Bray has elaborated on the overall importance of walls and gates around traditional houses in late imperial China. On the one hand, they 'provided protection as well as privacy for its inmates'. On the other hand, they revealed much to outsiders:

> The Chinese house presented a blank face to the outer world. It was surrounded by a high wall, usually unbroken except for a high and elaborate gateway. 'You can tell the opulence of the rich and the misery of the poor by the walls of their houses', wrote Li Yu. 'As they say: one house builds a wall but two houses enjoy looking at it; it is the only object in a house that is in fact public' (Bray 1997: 92).

Unlike Simmel's assertion that the door speaks to the outside world, but the wall is mute (Simmel 1994 [1909]: 7), historical evidence and my own ethnographic observation suggests the contrary. Walls and gateways are relevant not only for the construction of private space but in many cases, they equally serve the public display of status and wealth. Walls immediately objectify and communicate the house's materiality and the dwellers' social aspirations to the outside public. So, what Simmel suggested for the door, similarly holds true for the wall, namely that it 'represents [...] how separating and connecting are only two sides of precisely the same act' (ibid.). Still, the wall pretends to be mute, while attention is drawn to how the doors and gates constitute a threshold and borderline to the intimate family space of the yard. It seems that the permeability of private space to things and information is strictly controlled by the inhabitants. At times, the gate's role is explicit; it communicates 'between family and outside world, first as a physical threshold, and second as a kind of notice board' (Bray 1997: 92). In Azerbaijan, a red ribbon tied on yard gates and doors, even on apartment doors in residential blocks, signifies a recent wedding and the bride's arrival into the household. Similarly, a black ribbon signifies a recent death in the household. The inhabitants, however, do not control fully the permeability of their private space. Walls do not keep out many sounds, conversations, and arguments.

Plate 13. The gate and its message: the decoration signals the recent arrival of the *gǝlin.*

When talking to people about the quality of different Soviet apartments blocks, sound and noise were among important markers for the evaluation of quality. For instance, the poorly soundproofed *Khrushchevkas* with their thin walls do not perform as well as the *Stalinkas* with walls of up to 80 centimetres thick.[75] In addition to size, ground plan, and general convenience, stark differences in insulation inform the hierarchy of housing

---

[75] One legacy of Soviet mass housing is that a variety of building types exist and are colloquially known, and assigned value, as Stalinka, Khrushchevka, Leningradski, Minski, and Kievski, among others. As I summarised elsewhere, 'the solid stone walls, high ceilings, convenient layout and usually central location in contemporary Baku similarly contribute to the high standing of the Stalinkas, as does the fact that such apartments were typically allocated to the political and intellectual elite of Soviet society. Khrushchevkas, in contrast, occupy the negative extreme in the housing hierarchy – an association that was quite different during the Khrushchev era itself, when such new housing projects provided many families with a separate apartment for the first time in their family history. Today, they are associated with low ceilings, small kitchens, small bathrooms, an inconvenient passage room and thin walls, all of which could be rapidly assembled from industrially produced panels of concrete' (Roth 2019: 62).

in Baku. Soundscapes also played an important role in our neighbourhood of detached houses. Nearly every morning I woke up from our neighbours' lively rooster. Without having seen these neighbours throughout the time of fieldwork, they nevertheless took more and more shape just by the sounds that freely transgressed the walls. Impressions ranged from one neighbour's regular family gatherings, loud conversations, and extensive barbecuing, to another neighbour's ceaseless shouting at his chickens while in turn being shouted at himself by an authoritative wife. Seen from another angle, the soundscapes point not to the separation and protection of private space, but to the social connectivity, interaction, and communal aspects of neighbourhoods.[76] Still, people observe the intent of the wall while making use of its permeability to sound. Non-kin do not enter a courtyard uninvited. Instead, they stand outside the gate, shout out the name of an inhabitant, and wait for an invitation before they enter the property.

Although such descriptions provide a good sense of the general materiality and social interaction within *hayat evi* neighbourhoods, it is important to note some differences in the public life of these neighbourhoods. In Baku's Sovetski neighbourhood, for example, the narrow roads are confined by walls as in Badamdar. However, the intensity of social life in the streets appeared quite different as well as the size of the inner courtyards and the quality of the dwellings.

The detached housing neighbourhoods in Badamdar, as well as the vast housing settlements in the city's peripheries, are characterised by a relative abundance of space in terms of plot size and the height and space of dwellings compared to Soviet and pre-Soviet standards. In Sovetski, as for similar parts of the 'other Baku' (see Chapter 2), space has been scarce since the early Soviet years. There, houses and courtyards are much smaller but at the same time inhabited by many more family members. That is one of the main reasons why much social life takes place out in the streets. The much older history of these neighbourhoods that were home to four or five generations, paired with traditional residence patterns, contributed to the contrasts with the relatively new neighbourhoods like Badamdar. There, I hardly encountered extended families cohabitating.

---

[76] The importance of soundscapes in neighbourhood life has also been described with reference to the Kyrgyz city of Osh where sounds convey the 'thickness of neighbourhood social life' and allow for an 'auditory co-presence of neighbors' (Liu 2012: 132).

Plate 14. Sovetski courtyard consisting of several small apartments and inhabited by members of one extended family. Parts of the first storey were extended continuously, detached and transformed, usually due to the marriage of sons.

To summarise, the concealing and separating character of walls, gates, and doors is a common quality of courtyard houses across time and urban space. However, these structures communicate status and economic situation to the outside. Even for Bakuvians who spend little time 'enjoying' the walls of either neighbourhood, Badamdar tells the story of a recently emerging lower middle and upper middle-class neighbourhood whereas Sovetski embodies quite the opposite, with inhabitants of lower socio-economic status. In the rest of this section, I devote attention to doors and their meanings as thresholds.

Four weeks after we had arrived in Baku, I went to buy bread from our landlord's shop after a night of heavy rainfalls. I had to go out of the yard to enter the shop from its outer entrance. As soon as I stepped through the yard door out onto the street I saw Fikrət and his son Kamal kneeling next to a pile of sand and a sack of cement. They were cutting tiles to renovate the floor outside the shop's roofed entry area. What caught my attention was that they were not the only ones engaged in such an activity. Several neighbours along the road had piles of sand in front of their yard gates too, and they were all carrying shovel after shovel into their yards. First, I thought the sand had been provided for a communal improvement of the street's appearance. When I sought Kamal's affirmation, he laughed at me. No. He explained that the rain had washed the sand down from a huge pile somewhere in the upper area of the neighbourhood. Because there were no drains, water (and anything it picks up – sand in this case), flows through the streets and accumulates in the numerous street depressions, and potholes. This was a seemingly welcome form of natural redistribution as people claimed the deposited sand for themselves by either moving it into the protected spheres of their courtyards or, as was the case with Fikrət, by putting it right away to repairs and building improvements. Fikrət's spontaneous initiative to beautify his shop's entrance area by plastering it with red tiles and to extend the small steps further into the street reflects two important dimensions. As with walls and yard gates, doors and the adjacent outer area are perceived as 'high value' points of a property, not only because they constitute a threshold between inside and outside, between spaces of different private and public character, but also because they stand *pars pro toto* for the house. The attention given to these points reflect the overall home-making aspirations of dwellers and their socio-economic status. Doors protect the home from outsiders' views while simultaneously evoking expectations on the apartment's quality among those outsiders. Second, the neighbours' move to use sand can be interpreted as a kind of material and symbolic appropriation of (semi-)public space into the private sphere of the home.

Anthropologists should not be surprised by the attention given to doors, gates, and walls by Bakuvians. Already in his 1909 published classic *Les Rites de Passage*, Arnold Van Gennep described the crucial significance of social and physical thresholds and doors as 'the boundary between the foreign and the domestic world [...]. Therefore, to cross the threshold is to unite oneself with a new world' (2004 [1909]: 20). Other authors working on post-Soviet cities have also described the prominent role that people attach to doors and thresholds between public and private spaces in general (Abrahamian 2007; Liu 2012; Fehlings 2014, 2015).

Nor should it be a great surprise that one of the important qualities of the home in Azerbaijan is its capacity to protect inhabitants from contaminating objects that have a polluting and tainting effect. The house is conceptualised as a space of purity, and dwellers care about its capacity to allow them to control the flow of people and things from the outside to the inside, and vice versa, and to prevent unwanted intrusions. As has already been emphasised by Mary Douglas, people are engaged in 'separating, placing boundaries, making visible statements about the home that [they] are intending to create out of the material house' (1966: 68). Such a view rests on an oppositional distinction between the house and the outside world which has been described by anthropologists in terms of a spatialised gender cosmology (Bourdieu 1976). One main characteristic between the house and the street is that 'people have created social, physical, and symbolic barriers to prevent their different qualities from mixing uncontrollably' (Robben 1989: 575).

In Baku, pollution, dirt, and dust are not only imagined. They are the physical companions of everyday life. Azerbaijan's arid climate and strong winds make dust a common companion. If we opened a window, the floor of our apartment would be covered shortly with a visible layer of fine dust. We had almost a bad conscience when our landlady visited us because it seemed impossible to us to keep pace with her effectiveness in keeping the home clean. When she noticed our son entering the apartment without taking off his shoes, or leaving our apartment door open, she would kindly remind him of the proper procedures. When it was raining, most streets immediately turned into muddy and slippery terrain. Across Baku, not only in our neighbourhood, the water is not drawn off by canalisation but instead transports dust and dirt to depressions. There it remained until the water evaporated, leaving behind sediments that started a new mobility cycle. While my shoes became dirty within fifty metres of walking down the street, the shoes of locals were amazingly clean. In bad weather, people used wet tissues or small accessories with shoe polish to touch-up. They applied it even on public transportation. A whole assortment of shoe polishes was kept near the door of nearly every household.

That is to say that 'dirt' had clear material forms, and there were a number of common everyday practices to keep it at bay. These were important as symbolic barriers between the house and the outside world. It also shows that people and objects become mobile representatives of an immobile house, hence underlying its very principles in public accordingly. Most important, these examples show well the emphasis that locals attach to the impression they create in public and the efforts they take to manage the appearance of their bodies, their property, and representative objects.

Another striking example is an observation with the doorstep as threshold – similar to the case described above. As with many other socialist housing blocks in post-Soviet cities, apartment buildings in Baku tend to have a run-down appearance marked by a decrepit condition of staircases, corridors, elevators, electrics, and other technical infrastructure. Dark entries, occasionally broken light bulbs, broken staircase windows, or crumbling wall plaster point to a serious lack of maintenance of building infrastructure, especially since the end of socialism. Although apartments were privatised, the buildings were not – neither the corridors nor the spacious courtyards – hence their maintenance largely remained the responsibility of municipal or central state institutions. These, however, lend insufficient care and resources to routine upkeep and maintenance. A further issue is the low taxation of housing space – a problem that had been debated already by Soviet housing officials and economists (for details see Andrusz 1984). Generally, the lack of maintenance is said to be a result of 'an underdeveloped taxation system in which property taxes are extremely low, while State properties, including common areas, are not taxed at all' (UNECE 2010: 2).

Plate 15. The apartment door and its immediate surrounding in a socialist residential building. Dwellers often apply extensions to the threshold in front of their apartment doors.

An outstanding visual contrast to the building, however, are the apartments themselves, starting with the door. These cover a wide range of different styles, qualities, and material value. Within the building's dull monotony, it is the apartment doors which represent a personal touch and alleged socio-economic distinctions among the apartment dwellers. From simple steel doors with peepholes to the more elaborate ones, layered with imitations of expensive wood, often embellished with iron doorknockers, each door has its unique appearance. Another observation in the dim staircases is the immediate corridor space in front of many apartment doors. As Fikrət did with his shop, many apartment owners have beautified the thresholds and tiled six to eight square feet of the corridor as if they were aiming to appropriate or privatise the collective space of the corridors. Together with the door, the whole threshold area can also be interpreted as an anticipated display of the private realm behind. As it is mentioned by others, 'The door, being an important part of the home, its safeguard and presently its calling card, often represents the home as a whole, especially under the conditions of modern house planning on a mass scale' (Abrahamian 2007: 272–273).

Levon Abrahamian's discussion focused on the importance of the house and its parts in ethnic and national terms. In order to underline the door's ideological meaning, he told the story of an Armenian soldier in the Soviet Army shortly after the capitulation of the Germans. While 'other marauders had robbed different types of valuable things, this soldier carried a heavy, beautifully designed door on his back'. As we learn, 'he removed the door from an abandoned house and wanted to take it back with him to his native village [...] to build a new house for his family' (Abrahamian 2007: 273). However, I am not convinced that the soldier's decision should be overemphasised as an example of 'the *Armenian* attitude toward the door-and-house' (Abrahamian 2007: 273; my emphasis). My objection is not because Azerbaijanis share much of this attitude – although they do, and therefore this might become problematic as so many other elements of shared and contested culture between the two peoples and states.

Much more important, it seems to me, are the soldier's materialistic motivations. Certainly there was a constant shortage of construction material within the Soviet republics, including doors and windows, especially after years of war and times of crisis more generally. Long practices of hoarding these materials was made visible in Sovetski during August 2014, just after the city administration had given the green light to start demolishing houses (see Chapter 2). In the area's upper parts, adjacent to Nariman Narimanov Avenue, excavators first torn down a significant number of houses. Over the following weeks, they moved further into the neighbourhood and continued demolition street by street. Dwellers were busy clearing out their houses and put all kinds of furniture out onto the street. I noticed different kinds of doors, doorframes, windows, wooden planks, and other building materials leaning against the house walls.

Plate 16. Public scene in Sovetski neighbourhood. Doors and frames from soon to be demolished apartments awaiting potential buyers.

On one walk, I encountered a group of fifteen men, ranging in age between their twenties and fifties. They were sitting out on the street around a table and playing domino, some were sitting on a couch waiting for the samovar tea to be ready. Another neighbour cleaned his silver Hyundai car with a hosepipe, occasionally informing himself about the game table's progress. Everyone was dressed as if at home, and the public street seemed to have spontaneously transformed into a private living room or courtyard. After having introduced each other, I was invited to join for tea.

I took a seat and learned that they intended to sell all possible parts of their houses to make some money. The doors and windows, they said, would bring the greatest sums. Here seemed to be the limit of the so oft-applied narrative that the home represented a man's 'universe, where he plays the role of the creator' (Abrahamian 2007: 271). Although I was documenting how Azerbaijanis attach deep meanings to homes, doors, and thresholds (not unlike their geographical and cultural neighbours, of Armenians, Georgians, Turks, and many others), such an essentialising view also obscures the complexities of contemporary societal, economic, political, and historical processes involved in the construction of national identity and home-making. Here, the male 'creators' were about to sell the stars of their universe piece-by-piece. In this case, they meant to rescue some material value from the approaching demolition.

A final observation that I want to discuss in this section are the visual and behavioural transformations connected to the dwelling's threshold that expresses a passage from private moral contexts and normative frameworks to public ones. Urban Baku dwellers arriving at home from their public business put on clothing to be worn only in the private sphere of the home. As described below, these clothes convey comfort or cosiness (Az. *rahatlıq*), concepts that are strongly connected to the corresponding Russian term of *uyutnost'*. Hence, any person crossing the threshold of a dwelling actively undergoes a visual transformation. Some examples and little details I observed were similar to elsewhere in the world, such as not greeting a guest across the doorstep of an apartment until after he or she had entered the home, or to put out shoes when entering the private space of the home (a habit that in Baku even applies to the craftsman or electrician entering a client's home). Bodily transformation expressed by changing clothes, however, had a distinct political and moral notion strongly promoted by the Soviet state. In the present, I perceived the power of such considerations unabated – but strongly embedded in rather traditional or conservative notions of cultural appropriateness. I frequently observed how men (like women) engaging in public activities outside their neighbourhood are very well dressed. When working for the state they wear a uniform, and even construction workers, taxi, or truck drivers at work often are well-dressed in serious looking blazers, pleat-front trousers, and black leather loafer-shoes. I was frequently reminded of images and depictions of Lenin's typical bureaucrat-style dress which also dominated the dress code for Party members and the nomenklatura. Only at home people do enjoy a kind of freedom concerning their style, look, and bodily impressions. Working men, after arriving at home, put on jogging trousers and a T-shirt (or a sleeveless undershirt in summer). A man wearing a sleeveless shirt – let alone an undershirt – in public is considered taboo; shorts too are out of bounds. Such clothes are only acceptable at home. As a common explanation, I was told that there is a cultural expectation that men should not expose their shoulders and knees in public. For men, to keep these body parts covered is similarly considered the normal state as is women's veiling in neighbouring Iran.

The contemporary importance of differently appropriate clothing resembles the 'functional principle' propagated by Soviet fashion magazines since the 1960s, 'which distinguished clothes to wear at home, at work, and for different types of leisure' (Zakharova 2010: 102). Women who grew up in Soviet times would put on the typical multi-coloured or flowery housedress (*khalat*) that became common all across the former USSR. Notions of space including its different qualities thus become inscribed onto people's bodies. According to social scientist Olga Vainshtein (1996), the *khalat* enjoyed universal usage among women in the Soviet Union who basically always wore it at home when engaged in housework. Also, despite all economic difficulties and shortages 'Soviet manufacturing went on producing *khalaty* in [...] the most diverse (sometimes insane) color combinations, in order to encourage women's enthusiasm for domestic work' (Vainshtein 1996: 84, emphasis in original). The *khalat* became 'the standard image of the ideal housewife' and 'the symbol of coziness' (ibid.: 85).

I vividly remember my second day in my host family's home in a late-Soviet Baku suburb residential building in August 2008. The Qarayevs immediately felt responsible for reminding me, the western anthropologist with long hair, beard, and earrings about his inappropriate appearance: 'Here at home you can look like that', my host-mother kindly remarked, 'but when you go outside, tie up your hair and put off your earrings'. My host father added that I should shave myself properly in order not to look like a 'Wahhabi'. As he told me later, these instructions were meant to prevent any gossips by neighbours as well as to protect me against potentially intolerant folks. A more detailed and illustrative case occurred in summer 2014, when we occasionally met with my former host-brother Aslan and his family to go to the beach. He had married three years earlier, and his wife Ayşe had moved into his parents' apartment where they shared one room with their two-year-old son Raoul. We were waiting for them with Aslan's twelve-year-old sister Səbinə in our car in front of the apartment block. As usual, Ayşe was wearing a long dress over her beach leisure clothes – shorts and T-shirt – which she would take off as soon as we drove out of the courtyard. Accordingly, on our return in the evenings, she would put on the dress again before entering the courtyard, covering her beach clothes with something more appropriate for public view. One night, however, shortly before we were about to enter the courtyard she realised that she had forgotten. The dress was out of reach in one of the bags in the car trunk, and she began to panic. Səbinə tried to calm her, referring to the darkness outside, but Ayşe insisted that I stop the car before we entered the courtyard so she could pick out her dress from the trunk. She explained to my wife that she did not want the neighbours to see her in shirt and pants because they would be highly disapproving and start gossiping. 'You know, people here are just like in the village', she said, and Səbinə, while turning to us, briefly added 'this is only because she is our *gəlin*'. On this issue, another female friend told me that 'people here constantly talk and gossip about their relatives and neighbours. It is not only old women's business but something that literally everyone does'. This case well reflects the overall importance of maintaining the curtain as an important concept in social interaction. This is the topic of the next section.

'Curtain Politics' and Negotiations of Privacy: The Material and Social Representation of *Pərdə*

Referring to Mary Douglas (1966), the anthropologist Irene Cieraad states that the window can be understood as a 'gendered borderline' between a 'private female-oriented' and a 'male public-oriented space' (2006b: 32). In presenting a 'history of female involvement in Dutch window arrangements' (ibid. 33), the author provides a historical account on the evolvement of opening up windows in Dutch urban spaces. For a non-Dutch person, 'It seems a strange habit of exposing not only one's interior, but also one's intimate family life, to the eyes of passersby' (ibid. 31). This Dutch peculiarity where windows are 'passionately decorated' and 'left uncovered day and night' (Vera 1989: 215) stands in contrast to many other societies including Azerbaijan in which similar practices of constructing transparency would be considered as socially inappropriate.

Windows and curtains are not only indicators for whether an apartment is inhabited or not. Like walls and doors, they communicate added information on the socio-economic standing of households. In the context of home renovations being discussed in the next section, for instance, windows attain functional and representative functions. The wooden window frames of Soviet housing blocks are among the prioritised devices to be replaced with plastic frame windows which are not only perceived as being modern but also as providing better insulation. Most attractive to many of my acquaintances are German brands because of their supposedly superior quality. Displaying the high quality of one's windows led to the widespread practice of keeping the security foil on the window frames for years instead of removing them (as per installation instructions) within three months. By this, homeowners show off a qualitative part of the home to passers-by as well as to guests granted access into the apartment. One also has to keep in mind that good quality windows belong to the costly parts of apartments to be renovated. Windows, like walls and doors, are functioning not only as protective devices but as symbolic markers of status and wealth. This is further illustrated by the many recently constructed villas in our neighbourhood. Many have large windows that stretch across two storeys but provide visual protection either by a reflective coating or luxurious curtains, and sometimes both.

In Azerbaijan, the window is immediately associated with its most important feature – the curtain (*pərdə*). It is a standard practice, especially among middle-class people, to attach two or three layers of curtains of different materials and transparency. Besides the domestic object, the term also describes a social and moral borderline. In its active and processual usage of *pərdə saxlamaq*, 'maintaining', 'keeping', or 'protecting' the curtain refers to one's own individual and family privacy, as well as the show of similar respect for another person's privacy, intimacy, and secrets. Hence, analogous to properly setting up the window curtains, which is about the skilful physical and visual protection of private space and affairs from public view, *pərdə saxlamaq* simultaneously stands for similar skills and requirements in social interaction.

The metaphor is linked to concepts and practices in Islam, and less importantly among those of cultural and geographic neighbours. In historical depictions, for example, the Prophet Mohammed is sometimes shown with a veil on his face that equally serves the purpose of 'saving the face'. The analogy is visible, too, in the widespread practice of Muslim women wearing a veil. In many Muslim and Hindu societies, the term *purdah*, which is of Persian origin, means veil and curtain (Papanek 1973; White 1977). The Azerbaijani term *pərdə* has the same root; but whereas in other contexts the term describes the physical seclusion of women from non-kin-members and, thus, maintaining the family honour, in Azerbaijan this meaning has been transformed significantly. Also, in Christian Georgia the term for curtain is *parda*, however, its meaning is restricted to the window curtain and lacks further social or religious connotations.

Curtains can be understood as a symbol for the protection of privacy and the intimate sphere of the home towards the outside world. But in what sense? As I will demonstrate in this section, privacy has many nuances and ambiguous notions. In many of my conversations on privacy, I received similar answers like the one by Vüsalə, one of my students in a seminar: 'In Azerbaijan there is no privacy!' – a perception that I could confirm from my own experiences living in different kinds of dwellings embedded in the social spaces of host families, landlords, and neighbourhoods. It was rare to be alone, rare to have individual privacy. However, this did not seem to be the reference of Vüsalə's, or others', complaint. On the contrary, when I probed my interlocutors about the value of individual 'private' space, I received many comments similar to the one made by my friend Nazim, who lived in a shared flat with many other men, a contemporary widespread form of the past communal apartment living in Soviet times. 'Your whole lifetime, you share sleeping rooms with others: as a child at home, in the dormitory when you study ... that's normal. Being alone is just considered weird and boring. Man is a social animal'. Moreover, there were countless occasions, when men and women seemed to enjoy an enormous level of privacy, though in rather collective and spatially separated ways. I came to understand that the kind of privacy that Vüsalə referred to was the collective privacy enjoyed within the home. It was the kind mentioned by Reşat at the beginning of this chapter when he explained the meaning of walls as protection from the curiosity of other people. But how could Vüsalə claim that there is no privacy in Azerbaijan when people's own emphasis, as well as the architecture and materiality of homes and neighbourhoods (e.g. walls and thick multi-layered curtains), point in the opposite direction?

Vüsalə herself explained. 'People in Azerbaijan constantly talk about their relatives and neighbours. Here, everyone is into gossiping – not only elder women'. Indeed, among my friends and acquaintances it was common practice to gossip about and compare one's self with others, which seemed to constitute an everyday topic in conversations. Especially weddings offered plenty of fodder for conversations, comparison, and criticism with regard to the number of guests, the location, its prestige, quality of food, live music, etc. Since talking about and comparing with others plays a prominent role in today's society, people in turn place high value on protecting close family members from becoming subject to gossiping or criticism in public. But the more something is considered to be endangered, the more likely people attach special meaning to it. Thus, the home ideally enables families to enjoy privacy, protection, secrecy, and control from the outside world. Furthermore, it is a space that ensures a kind of mutual loyalty, trust, and integrity among its dwellers. This is well captured in a telling proverb a local linguist shared with me: *evin sözünü çöldə deməzlər!* (the word of the house must not be told in the desert).[77] At the same time, because privacy is so important to maintain, in daily conversations, people also engage in strategically telling secrets about family members, friends, and others as a way to convey and deepen trust in other social relations. In this way maintaining privacy involves an ambivalent performance of social politics.

Akif who also appeared in Chapter 4 serves as a good example. As we spent countless hours sitting inside or outside the office together, mostly with his partner Pərviz, he told me personal details about neighbours, friends, and clients who passed by or paid a visit to his office. After people had left our company, Akif would lower his voice in a typical manner and start telling about private affairs. Once, his brother who was engaging in occasional driving jobs was sitting together with us and chatting. After he had left, Akif started to rail against his brother as someone not being able to stand on his own feet, always coming and asking for money, and above all, drinking too much. The latter observation was partly true but with no

---

[77] The proverb is taken to stem from earlier times when many Azeris were nomads (i.e. home would have been a tent and the outside world would have been the desert).

difference at all to Akif and Pərviz themselves who were far from being role models for abstinence. On another occasion, the three of us lunched in a neighbouring restaurant. We sat outdoors, in a 'compartment' – a table surrounded by wooden walls on all sides with an entrance to provide a private atmosphere to the mostly male visitors. As usual, a bottle of vodka accompanied the lunch for purposes of toasting and enhancing sociability. Among many people who were raised in Soviet days, such a lunch was perceived as a normal thing. After lunch, we returned to the office and Pərviz left soon after for home because he desperately needed a rest. After he left, Akif started to complain heavily about his colleague's vodka consumption. He talked about his bad health, family problems, and other topics that made me embarrassed to hear from Akif. This was his decade-long friend and so much was being told to me as someone who had only met him very recently.

These observations point to an important anthropological moment in dealing with secrets, as the 'revelation of a secret is performative. Comprising or informing a personal narrative, conveying a secret does not simply reveal what [is] hidden; it reveals the politics behind it' (Manderson et al. 2015: S186). Akif's play with revealing secrets and intimate information not only served to supposedly signalling a deepened level of trust in his relation towards me. Also, and referring to similar situations in general, this serves to position individuals morally in their relation to those people whose secret is being told or, in other words, whose curtain is raised. The Iranian Azeri anthropologist Farideh Heyat describes 'the secretive, complex nature of the Azeri society' as being the result of the Soviet system (2002: 39) because the ideological nature of that system led to a double code of official/ unofficial conduct and speech (ibid.). Moreover, though this 'promoted a culture of concealment and dissimulation', it was enhanced by a culturally existing dualism between the self's inside (içəridə) and outside (zahirdə), similar to Iranian and Islamic religious-philosophical notions of batin and zahir (ibid.). In my view, notions of pərdə are far more important and common in people's everyday life than the religious-philosophical concepts illustrated by Heyat. Thus, I argue that the notion of pərdə shows how such principles are translated and find expression in the lived reality of socialist and postsocialist everyday life.

At another level, I contend that 'maintaining the curtain' can be understood as the negotiation of individual privacy among family members in a society in which notions of an independent self are said to be of marginal importance. Instead, Azerbaijani society is characterised by 'a notion of personhood that prioritizes kin relations rather than one that is based on Western ideals of a bounded and independent self' (Goluboff 2008:

82). It would be, however, wrong to assume the non-existence of individual privacy just because there is no equivalent term in Azerbaijani.

How can the concept of *pərdə* empirically be conceived? I first got acquainted with this concept when I spent one evening with our landlord's son, Kamal, in a nearby *çayxana* (teahouse). When our conversation was about joking relationships, he told me that 'serious jokes' are possible only with one's closest friends. He further explained that this kind of joking requires an outstanding degree of closeness to the other person – a relationship that is distinguished from others by the fact that there is no *pərdə* between them. Kamal told me about his perception of *pərdə* and the challenge to actively maintain the curtain within but also outside the family home.

Overall, maintaining a curtain implicitly entails the selective and controlled display of the self in front of others, including close family members. This practice of presenting the self in everyday life is hardly exclusive for Azerbaijan but a widespread phenomenon that the sociologist Erving Goffman (1959) described on the level of the individual with his concept of 'impression management'. In the present context, however, similar mechanisms of representing the self are applied within private family frameworks, strongly governed by social norms. This simultaneously includes the maintenance of private matters according to prevalent socio-cultural expectations but also by respecting a person's secrets. It is about mediating and accepting an image of the self or the other that acknowledges less the 'factual reality' than the verbal and performative idealisation of the person's role and the expectations of that person as ascribed by his/ her socio-moral environment. The moral concept that underlies such social interaction is *hörmət* (honour, reputation, respect).

Three crucial principles that are at work in 'curtain management' are gender, age relations, and seniority. For young people, this means the avoidance of habits such as smoking and drinking in front of parents and other elder relatives, as well as openly criticising or challenging their authority. When a son chats, talks, or dates with a girl via Facebook or smart phone, he would never admit this to his parents, but instead pretend to have talked to a cousin or a friend. Most parents would still know about what is going on because they have gone through a similar life course and because they are informed by gossip.

The same relationship and avoidance of certain practices and topics in social interaction applies between the sexes, including spouses. A popular topic that I often encountered among older men who grew up during Soviet times is that of the mistress (Ru. *liubovnitsa*). When my family left to spent some weeks in Croatia, Rahib immediately enquired about whether I planned to have an extramarital affair or take a *liubovnitsa*. He considered this an appropriate action for a man of my age and in my situation being alone, temporarily without family and familial responsibilities. Still, men were finding it difficult to conduct their affairs in private, and they talked rather openly about these problems. In part, there was no place at home a man could call his own: all rooms serve a multi-functional purpose. This is one reason why cars have such important meanings for young adults. As elsewhere, cars generally provide alternative space for individuals, couples, and peers to enjoy a certain privacy (Roth 2020). In Azerbaijan, the privacy, as well as the mobility, of cars especially allows young people to engage with the other sex in a discrete atmosphere. Already for men in the late Soviet Union, 'the interiors of cars ... served as refuges from the crowded conditions of apartment dwelling' (Siegelbaum 2008: 7) and provided alternative spaces for enjoying privacy.

A close friend, married and in his mid-fifties, met occasionally with his *liubovnitsa* in a close-by apartment. Another neighbour around the same age, also husband and father, was constantly complaining about how difficult it had become to meet women with whom one could have sexual affairs. He talked nostalgically about the Soviet days when Baku was a cosmopolitan city, and that today, in contrast, the city had become rather prude after the large-scale emigration of Slavic residents in the 1990s. Azeri women, he and also others had insisted, are not 'that kind' because they have a superior morality that makes dating a difficult issue. Once we met after a longer period of absence, and he told me about his recent visit to Kazakhstan where he had found a wonderful Kazakh *liubovnitsa* with whom he had spent nearly one month. To hear such stories openly told by male friends, acquaintances, and even strangers such as local taxi-drivers constituted an atmosphere of normalcy that I could hardly imagine in my own society. These examples should not create a false picture of a generalisable male attitude towards extra-marital affairs. Many of my male friends and acquaintances in Azerbaijan distanced themselves from such narratives. They pointed out that such talk related to a certain generation, social background, and an implicitly performed nostalgia towards a less traditional and more international Soviet past. They agreed that it mattered that the city had become much more homogenous in ethnic terms. Furthermore, they stressed, Soviet military service meant that many older men had spent a certain amount of time in places all over the USSR, and had been exposed to different gender relations and opportunities for early sexual encounters in a discretional setting outside the home.

When talking to women about these issues, they often joked about male attitudes and seemed well aware of men's affairs – sometimes even those of their husband. Occasionally, some joked that they felt sorry for men's very nature; a perception rooted in popularised notions of biologically determined behaviour. As one popular Azerbaijani scholar wrote in his book on mentality, *The Archetypical Azeri*: 'He [the man] leaves the house in order to return with gifts, trophies, earnings [...]. At home, he does not have any tasks but can only relax without a possibility or expectation to confirm and increase his authority' (Kuliyev 2002: 42). I was surprised to find how popular this author was among local scholars and how his primordialist ideas corresponded to public and media discourse on the Azerbaijani culture and nation. While some colleagues at the Academy of Sciences criticised its rather popular scientific approach, others advised me, in my profession as anthropologist, to read the book in order to understand culture and family life. Such patriarchal biases do not go unchallenged by women. In female spaces that are protected from public male scrutiny (e.g. beauty salons or bathhouses), women do criticise males and may well blame their husbands for incidents of infidelity. Still, public criticism is muted. Referring to the joking comment by my former host-mother, the previous quotation can be read alternatively as follows: 'As long as my husband returns home with gifts and earnings, let him have the female trophies he needs in order to feel like a proper man'. Superficially, women deride men for their potential amorous escapades, but excuse them as long as the men care and provide for the family. A husband – but also his wife – is expected to maintain the secrecy of his affairs, or at least of the stress they cause and reveal in the marriage (i.e. *pərdə saxlamaq*). When marital conflicts become public, and in cases of divorce, people may criticise the husband, but more frequently, they criticise the wife for not having maintained the curtain. Indeed, female lawyers and human rights activists point out that it is often the wife who is blamed by society and relatives in the first place for her husband's infidelity.

These patterns of public criticism point to the more severe aspects of *pərdə* in terms of power relations and economic dependencies between family members. Many women in Azerbaijan are simply dependent on their husband in financial, supportive, and moral matters. Not to confront husbands with issues that might lead to severe family conflicts, or even divorce, constitutes a coping strategy that serves the maintenance of family integrity and personal security. A woman's agency in such matters depends much on the strength of her relationship to her parents and the latter's will and capability to emotionally and financially support their daughter in case of divorce. But a divorce can still lead to social marginalisation because customary law and increasing patriarchal biases handicap significantly women's position in society.

On a broader level, the concept of *pərdə saxlamaq* refers to protecting a person's and family's honour (such as 'to save face' in many other Eurasian contexts). It is constitutive for the everyday processes of negotiating social closeness, intimacy, and quality of relationships among social groups. While other authors reasonably describe Azerbaijani society as holding concepts of personhood primarily embedded in kin relations (Goluboff 2008: 82), the notions of *pərdə* show that such a family-centred conceptualisation of the self does not exclude the much less visible individual aspects of personhood, but allow us to better make sense of how differently represented values are enacted in everyday practices. Furthermore, the social politics of the curtain again emphasise that the boundaries between private and public are fluid and constantly negotiated in social and spatial relations. In the next section, I will discuss examples which illustrate the opinions by the people above that the private space of the home in Azerbaijan is rather to be considered 'the public space of the household' (Prost 1991: 62).

DO-IT-YOURSELF the (Post-)Soviet Way: Home-Making, *Remont*, and their Social Nexus

After having approached the house from the outside, through the wall and the door, I now enter the home and discuss processes that unfold with regard to home-making (see also Roth 2020). What I describe is not limited to the sphere of cultural ideas of how people conceptualise a proper home and try to transform it through *remont*. What I describe is equally shaped by historical contexts and changing attitudes related to the Soviet state, class, economic constraints, and media representation of the domestic sphere.

Above, I have elaborated the gendered aspects associated with the social, material, and symbolic dimensions of home-making with an emphasis on the ritual process of marriage (*evlənmək*) and founding a family. Elsewhere, I have described how *evlənmək* is a gendered term which literally means 'to become enhoused'. It is mostly associated with the male perspective as a more common term for the marriage of women is *ərə getmək*, which literally translates as 'going to the husband'. I have maintained that the term home-making serves actually an appropriate and most direct translation of *evlənmək*, if seen in a gender-neutral way (Roth 2020: 57). The dowry and other gifts that are associated with the female domain of making a house into a home are part of a longer-term engagement with home-making to create the state of a comfortable and cosy (*rahat*) home. According to local understanding, *rahat* means comfortable, cosy, and tranquil, but it entails a far deeper meaning that underlines feelings of 'home' or 'homely' in many Western contexts. Long-term planning and considerations for obtaining, maintaining, and improving the home constantly require the joint efforts by family members. Again, such activities are strongly connected to marriage, especially towards housing the future *gəlin* – major home renovation activities, therefore, are usually implemented in the context of an upcoming wedding, the birth of a child, and other rites of passage that change the household's composition over time. At the same time, when looking at aspiring middle-class families, home renovations serve another important purpose: deliberately enhancing the home's capacity to display the family's status to third parties – often future in-laws and extended family members. The frequent and widespread renovation of dwellings is also characterised by an underlying competitive spirit in which successful home-making represents a successful family. Such competition is enhanced but also naturalised by being embedded in an encompassing discourse on the moral value and national feature of hospitality. It is only by *practising* hospitality that the protected sphere of the private home opens up its curtains to others – it temporarily transforms the private home into a semi-public space, though in a strictly controlled and orchestrated manner.

I have previously pointed to the stark contrast between badly maintained common spaces of Soviet residential houses and the embellished make-up of the apartment threshold. Such striking contrasts between dilapidated socialist buildings and well-maintained apartments has been similarly described across post-Soviet space, including Armenia (Fehlings 2014: 126), Georgia (Bouzarovski et al. 2011: 2693), and Tajikistan (Sgibnev 2015: 57). A key-concept that allows us to approach the pervasiveness and high degree of renovations, as well as dwellers' continuous commitments, efforts, and investments regarding the realm of their private homes, is the concept of *remont*. It is interesting to note that the term was originally applied in the French military context for compensating losses in the cavalry with new horses before it entered the Russian language as a term that refers generally to any required repair or upkeep (Sgibnev 2015: 55). As in the Tajik case described by Wladimir Sgibnev, however, in Azerbaijan the term is applied to the repair and upgrade of an apartment; it also refers to the overall status and condition of a dwelling.

Remont is often taken to refer specifically to renovations taken after privatisation. Indeed, much of the renovation undertaken in the last thirty years reflects well people's new socio-economic and political circumstances. *Remont*, however, was already a widespread practice under socialism. Russian researchers have described Soviet society as a 'repair society' (*obshchestvo remonta*) because of chronic shortages and the constant need of dwellers to counteract the unsatisfactory maintenance and service by the state (Gerasimova and Tchouikina 2004; see also Chernyshova 2013: 175). Beyond its connections to temporally specific material conditions, *remont* can also point to continual processes of refurbishment, and the interlinking aesthetics and performance of refurbishment. I therefore agree with Catherine Alexander who points out that *remont* has importance beyond the Soviet and post-Soviet contexts since 'repair and adjustment, as labor on the self, the world and the body politic, are symptomatic of the human condition' (2012: 265).

Today, *remont* has enhanced the dimension of representation through obtaining and displaying exclusive domestic materialities in subtle competitive manners. (This was also the case, though to a lesser degree, in the later consumerist era under Brezhnev). Among the factors which enhance the prestige and ascribed value of such practices is the foreign origin and style of utilised materials reflected in the contemporary emphasis of *evroremont* (see Alexander 2012: 257; Fehlings 2014: 223; Sgibnev 2015: 60) – renovations of supposed 'modern', European standard and quality. In Azerbaijan, I have encountered even more nuanced and differentiated terminology for advertising renovations and apartment conditions on Baku's housing market (see Roth 2019). Housing advertisements frequently apply expressions like *srednii remont* (average renovation), *khoroshii remont* (good renovation), *otlichnyi remont* (excellent renovation), *superremont* (super renovation), or *super evroremont* (super Euroremont). Further specifications such as 'Spanish/ Italian/ German sanitary installations' signal added aspects of modernity, aesthetics, and quality. Here, when we look at the sphere of the housing market, economic and monetary considerations also play an important role. As, for example, with regard to apartment extensions, others have pointed out that it is an important strategy for people to invest surplus capital into their apartment in order to increase its market value, especially when banking sectors are underdeveloped (Bouzarovski et al. 2011: 2702; Sgibnev 2015: 58). This points at one important economic motivation for why many people invest in elaborate *remont* for reasons of selling or renting out apartments.

However, not unlike the state's high profile construction projects, *remont* is often not of the high quality that is promoted. A widespread feature in Baku, as in other post-Soviet spaces, is the visual upgrading of buildings' outer and inner appearance without a corresponding functional upgrading. Such optical renovations of usually inferior quality are commonly known as *kosmeticheskii remont* (cosmetic or aesthetic renovation). Such regularly conducted 'cosmetic renovation' is opposed to *kapital'nyi remont* that describes the 'general overhaul' necessary for full and large-scale renovation. Interestingly, the latter term appears commonly in official documents since the 1920s, but I have never seen the former in any archival document. The necessity of *kapital'nyi remont* in Soviet official documents was invoked with reference to the many privately-owned houses in desperate need of renovation. With reference to the rapid urban transformations in cities like Baku or Almaty, locals are reported to be well aware of the artificial character of urban *remont*: everything appears new at the surface, but underneath things remained pretty much as they used to be (see Alexander 2012: 269; Grant 2014: 509). In such public contexts of maintenance and material impression management, it is essential to ask for 'the specificity of *remont*' and 'how it is performed, aestheticized and moralized, and has come to domesticate broader economic and political changes' (Alexander 2012: 265).

Similar questions arise when looking at the often underemphasised relation between renovation activities and life-cycle rituals, specifically marriage (see also Sgibnev 2015). When I first arrived at the Qarayevs' home in 2008, they had just finished an extensive home renovation of their four-room apartment partly financed by a bank credit under much better conditions than usual due to their son's state military employment. The large investments which, according to Asad exceeded 25,000 AZN (roughly 30,000 USD), were explained by the engagement and soon expected marriage of their son Aslan. The floor in the entire apartment was replaced with solid wooden flooring and new tiles in the bathroom. The latter was further equipped with new ceramic devices, water tank, and heater. A filigree-patterned and noble-looking wallpaper had been put up in the living room, and it fit well with the stucco-imitate on the ceiling and the two-layered white curtains with golden stitchery. The parents' bedroom was decorated similarly, just with penetrating pink-coloured wallpaper and curtains – features that continued even more strikingly in the other bedroom that I was supposed to inhabit during my stay. Another significant step in the renovation process was buying a new front door and exchanging the older, wooden windows with expensive, German-branded, plastic-framed windows. The family kept their old furniture, however, because they expected new furniture to arrive with the bride's dowry.

Oqtay, a 40-year-old friend, bought his three-room apartment in a two-storey, high-quality post-war building in 2002 right before his marriage. The first thing he did was *remont*. He had worked in Germany for four years and had saved a comparatively large sum for his marriage and to support his parents. He said that he had worked non-stop because he anticipated these costs. From his parents, both teachers and with only a small salary, he could not count on any significant money. Before returning to Baku, he bought a car in Germany in order to re-sell it in Baku for quite some profit. Ten years later, he conducted another *remont* in 2012 for about 8,000 USD. Rahib, whom I have introduced earlier, has engaged frequently in renovation of his three-room Khrushchevka-apartment – windows, floors, wallpaper – roughly every five years. The last time was when his son got married and moved his new wife into the apartment. Then they divided the apartment and made two separate entrances.

In these examples all the *remont* activities were not carried out in a random manner but in most cases corresponded with life-cycle events which were accompanied by long-term considerations. It is notable that, among those who can afford it, the increasing commercialisation and conspicuous consumption around wedding rituals have extended to processes of home-making. Some of my informants (especially the less well-off) lamented on the increasingly lavish character of not only weddings, but also expectations towards renovation standards and expensive *cehiz*. This becomes increasingly problematic for the less affluent households and reduces chances for young couples of different socio-economic backgrounds – often by the resistance of their parents. In most cases, however, efforts are turned to providing the young family with a smooth start into their new life-stage even if some normative social expectations are not met in full. This flexibility was demonstrated in Talıb's case which I illustrated in Chapter 4.

It is the principle of virilocal residence after marriage that is much less flexible. For most, it is no question. It is a tradition and ritual part of wedding celebrations that the bride will leave her parental home and move to her husband's family. Moving to one's in-laws is always perceived as subordinating one's own status to the new family. An Azerbaijani proverb exemplifies that issue by pointing out the sensitive contestation of masculinity in such a case: *arvad evinə girənin, qapısı alçaq olar.* That is, if a groom enters the wife's house, the door will be too low. It means that the man must bend his head to enter, and so subordinate to the head of the household, loses his honour. It can be possible for the bride's father to provide the young couple with land so the husband can build his own house. Still, even this is not a popular solution because it can provoke the groom's sense of masculinity and reverses the usually superior status of the bride-takers. Moreover, ownership of the land may be retained by the bride's father, which deprives the groom of full legal rights to his home.

Lale Yalçın-Heckmann has shown that the political economy of Azeri weddings, including dowry negotiations, is increasingly prone to conspicuous consumption, showing off, and the negotiation of status between the two families (Yalçın-Heckmann 2001, 2010: 122–123). This can happen easily when the occupational and financial background of the two parties differs, but I found most striving to choose or agree to a match only from within their own socio-economic strata. This desire was most pronounced among the wealthy. Yet, especially among wealthier families, the large expenses for *remont* and dowries can be interpreted as embedded in subtle notions of conspicuous consumption, display of status, and impression management. The following case provides an example.

Elbəy, born in 1986 in rural Sabirabad, never had to worry about money. His father was a well-off businessman, and Elbəy and his brother had joined the family business activities –importing German cars, construction of large-scale cowsheds in the countryside, investing in real estate and tourism. At the age of nineteen, he married Gülnar, whom he had known since primary school and whose parents were well acquainted with Elbəy's. Immediately after they married, they moved into Elbəy's paternal home in *mikroraion* 7 of northern Baku. It is a spacious five-room apartment on the fourth storey of a nine-storey Leningradski constructed in the mid-1980s. After Elbəy's wedding, his parents moved to their villa in the sea-side settlement of Mərdəkan.

At the time of the wedding, however, the parental apartment underwent major renovations, as if it were going to accommodate two families instead of one. The long front balcony was modified into an enclosed apartment extension as was the smaller balcony on the backside, thereby increasing the living space. A large living room was created by transforming two rooms into one. The whole apartment was paved with highly ornate, oakwood parquet-floor. Entering the living room from the hallway, the left side was arranged with two black armchairs with golden ornaments and dark blue velvet cushions and a small table. Next to these stood a huge two-metre-high longcase clock, covered in gold and supplemented with a golden young child in the middle part that was holding the golden bowl with the clock over its head. All these pieces were part of a furniture-set that continued throughout the salon. On the right hand there was a long sofa with a table and other pieces of furniture including china decoration – everything in black and gold. On the other side of the salon there was a large table including chairs for eight persons. On the wall behind, there was a cupboard with fine-looking dishes behind the glass as well as a sideboard with a generous mirror. The golden chandelier with numerous glass crystals and the rich three layers of white, golden, and blue curtains corresponded to the overall interior. The chandelier still had a tiny red ribbon from the wedding, almost ten years before. All the furniture was part of the bride's dowry. It was paid for by her father, a successful car businessman, but he had allowed Gülnar and Elbəy to choose it. It had been made in Italy and had cost 38,000 USD, plus transport from Europe to Azerbaijan.

Plate 17. Parts of Elbəy's renovated apartment interior and *cehiz*. This is only a small part of the large living room and some furniture that was given as dowry to his wife.

Such an example about home-making through *remont* and *cehiz* not only points at issues like taste, ideas of consumption, and aspiring representations of the inhabitants' selves. It equally becomes relevant with regard to the outstandingly ascribed moral value of hospitality towards third parties during which homes are transformed temporarily into semi-public spaces as a selected circle of guests is granted the right to step over the threshold. To me as a foreigner and supposed professional on 'culture', Azerbaijanis' outstanding hospitality was among the numerous lessons I was given from my informants. Usually, a first-time conversation ended with an invitation from my interlocutor. However, it soon appeared that people attached more importance to the performative aspect of speaking out invitations than whether this would really happen in the future. A typical response used several times a day not only to less concrete invitations but to offers, hopes, and wilful intentions in general is *inşallah* (if God wills), that subtly communicates the offer's acceptance, without factually confirming or agreeing on it. With the exception of close family members and friends, men more rarely receive invitations into a home than women, thus, pointing to the gendered and spatial dynamics of hospitality. In a similar way as described by anthropologists on the Middle East (e.g. Vom Bruck 1997; Meneley 2007 [1996]), it is rather women who mutually visit each other at home. Among men, meeting at restaurants is much more common. Such 'private banquets' in the discrete and physically detached atmosphere of a public restaurant were among the frequent situations during my fieldwork. Eating out (and drinking) with friends and colleagues constitutes a regular part of everyday life for many of my acquaintances. This is not, however, just an expression of commensurability between equals. Invitations are made in a reciprocal pattern of inviting all the others, making the eating-out a form of hospitality that is marked by distinctions, not only of gender, but also by differences in the class and occupational backgrounds of those who eat together. At home and out, the performance of hospitality can gain competitive character across different strata in a society where the newly rich are perceived as a role model for lower occupants in the socio-economic hierarchy in terms of consumption patterns, status display, and prestigious consumer goods.

Among the first scholars to write about the appropriation of upper-class fashions by lower strata of society was the German philosopher and sociologist Georg Simmel (1904). Even a few years earlier, Thorstein Veblen, who coined the influential concept of 'conspicuous consumption' in his book *The Theory of the Leisure Class* (2009 [1899]), had stated that 'the usages, actions, and views of the well-to-do leisure class acquire the character of a prescriptive canon of conduct for the rest of society' (Veblen 2009 [1899]: 132). Despite the fact that roughly a century has passed since these ideas – critical of the capitalism of their own time – were formulated, they are still telling today. In my own observations, I felt often reminded of the *Tournaments of Value* and consumption of wealth described by anthropologist Anne Meneley (2007 [1996]). In her Yemeni example, it is the elite who are considered to 'have the leisure and resources to […] offer gracious hospitality'. 'None of these practices are exclusively elite, but the elite are able […] to conduct these practices in the most admired style, and thus embody most fully the values held by all' (Meneley 2007 [1996]: 6).

I observed such trends in contemporary Baku, too. People tried to follow the elite's practices of staging lavish wedding feasts in a prestigious *şadlıq sarayı*. Certainly wedding guests engaged in a distinct effort to rank the prestige of the venue, the quality of the food, service, entertainment, and so on. Countless street sellers and shops offered cheap copies of clothes, watches, and perfumes from prestigious labels. In the post-Soviet context, many scholars still explain present patterns of consumption with regard to Soviet-era shortages. The historian Larissa Zakharova, for example, has argued convincingly that, at least with regards to textiles, 'vertical dissemination' was key: ordinary Soviet citizens followed the fashion trends of the elite, partly because of the highly charged symbolic significance of 'luxury' in a society of shortage (2010: 113–115). Linking these ideas to the larger topic of this chapter, it appears that '[D]omestic display – as the management of appearances, the other half of which is concealment – plays a part in the construction of privacy and the presentation of individual or household identity for the limited "public" allowed over the threshold' (Reid 2015: 209).

As I learned over time, the extension of a formal invitation to someone's home included unwritten expectations among hosts and guests. Bringing gifts for the hosts, such as chocolate or sweets and toys for the children, is an important gesture which is usually accompanied by the hosts' initial and emphatic refusal of the gift. The hosts divide their responsibilities towards their guests and each of them is equally concerned to provide appropriate entertainment. Food, eating, drinking, and consumption in general are characteristic features and it happens regularly that guests are shown around the apartment or house. Activities are usually gendered. Female guests often join the hostess who is preparing food in the kitchen to exchange news and gossip. Males sit together in the living room and follow their own topics of interest, talking about *biznes*, work, financial challenges, *remont*, or wedding expenses. Eating together, sometimes while men raise several glasses of vodka for friendship, family, their caring wives, approaching weddings or births, is the centre of the event and can take several hours. While the male head of the household often shows off his skills as a good host by being entertaining, creative in toasting, and providing his guests with a joyful time, women show off and get regular compliments for their food-preparation skills.

Offering hospitality, however, also requires the skills to display the home and its interior in the most comfortable and cosy manner for guests. The ability to provide a *rahat* experience in a material and social sense is accompanied by a temporary and controlled dissolution of normative distinctions between inside/ outside and private/ public spaces. Nonetheless, it is of equal importance to emphasise that perceptions, meanings, and the construction of *rahatlıq* itself underlies historical shifts and reformulations which, in the Soviet context, were shaped by different state approaches, media, and consumer trends. That is why in the following, I will draw attention to changing political measures by the Soviet state towards issues of home, home-making, and the domestic sphere within the wider context of consumer culture in late Soviet society.

The home had long played a primary role in the state's aspirations for creating 'the Communist utopia' and constituted a political category, 'an instrument of ideological exertion and a cultural construction site' (Chernyshova 2013: 162). During the USSR's history, however, the state's handling of this most private space was an ambivalent and volatile process, ranging from utopian to pragmatic measures, from active intrusion to withdrawal. In short, mirroring trends in housing construction, the Soviets increasingly had to grant compromises to home interiors, which became an 'important instrument of social differentiation'. Especially in Stalinist times and later again under Brezhnev, 'the Soviet authorities saved some ideological face and showed that the socialist project could be unexpectedly flexible' (ibid. 183). In her monograph, *Soviet Consumer Culture in the Brezhnev Era,* historian Natalya Chernyshova gave a detailed account of the shifting political and aesthetic grounds surrounding ideals of appropriate furniture and domestic interiors for the Soviet home (2013: 162 ff.).

The literary scholar Vera Dunham (1976) has argued that, already in the 1930s, Soviet literature promoted ideals of socialist domesticity which were imbued with bourgeois middle-class values, and in which the model home was characterised by comparably spacious, richly furnished apartments with decorative elements. She called this an element of the 'Big Deal' which was neatly summarised by later scholars as 'an accommodation between the Stalinist regime and the Soviet social stratum of educated professionals and state administrators, which saw the regime accept and promote the middle-class values of private happiness, materialism and careerism in exchange for political loyalty' (Chernyshova 2013: 58). The Stalinist model stood in sharp contrast to the Bolsheviks' initial aim to enforce a communist utopia with an 'ideology of everyday asceticism' (Gurova 2006). This 'Great Retreat' (Timasheff 1946) from the Bolsheviks' communist ideals during the 1930s resulted in bourgeois-like, conservative ideals and established a new middle-class elite which 'wanted to lead a "cultured way of life"' (Gerasimova 2002: 209–210). It was in this period with its idea of 'culturedness' (*kulturnost'*) that material goods, the role of consumption, taste, daily necessities, and even luxuries were rehabilitated, legitimated, and promoted as part of and right for socialist society – these, then, were needs that the Party was obliged to satisfy (see Kettering 1997; Gurova 2006; Crowley and Reid 2010; Gronow and Zhuravlev 2010; Chernyshova 2013). This understanding of *kulturnost'* promoted the value of cosiness and a cosy home, which was rehabilitated as 'an echo of pre-revolutionary bourgeois life' (Gurova 2006: 94). It can be forgotten easily, though, that the 'Great Retreat' was a luxury for rather privileged groups of society. 'A genuine private life was [only] attained by a select few. A separate apartment, a home, privacy, personal transport [...] were luxury goods' (Trudolyubov 2018: 43).

With Khrushchev, this political approach of a quasi-bourgeois Soviet home experienced a major twist following the radical shifts in construction and architecture. The new mass housing campaigns, characterised by industrial and standardised construction techniques, emphasised an ascetic, minimalistic, and functional style of the home and its interior. The promotion of such newly politicised home aesthetics, domesticity, and socialist mass consumption made the home a 'soft power' and 'weapon' between the Soviet Union and the USA at the start of the Cold War in the late 1950s (Castillo 2010). Furthermore, new ideals of home were mediated and advertised to citizens by newspapers, journals, encyclopaedias, and book publications (Buchli 1997: 164). For instance, an illustrated book from the early 1960s, entitled *The Apartment and its Decoration* (Baiar and Blashkevich 1962) provided templates of appropriate furniture arrangements and aesthetics for each room in the newly available standardised separate apartments. The depicted interiors all followed the style of Khrushchev's propagated functionalism in the Soviet home. As with the apartments themselves, available home furniture for ordinary Soviet citizens was similarly standardised, hence, book illustrations of room arrangements contained accurate measurements of room-space, interior objects, and sequences of dwellers' everyday motions which conveyed to readers a most economical use of apartment space with the available materiality.

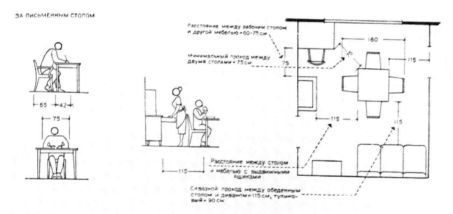

Plate 18. Example for interior arrangement in standardised apartments from 1962 that illustrates how to place the writing desk, including measurements of required space in centimetres.

With Leonid Brezhnev becoming the new General Secretary of the Communist Party of the Soviet Union in 1964, the Khrushchev-era ideal of the modern home gave way to a revitalisation of a Stalinist-type home. This was not a political turn, but withdrawal: after Khrushchev's politicised stance against 'bourgeois' cosiness, 'the Soviet regime gave up on its ambition to shape citizens' habitat; the consequence was the eventual de-politicization of the home' (Chernyshova 2013: 164). Values of comfort and cosiness returned. The imposition of taste norms was now considered the wrong approach, and dwellers were encouraged to 'reshap[e] standard interiors according to their own ideas. This individual approach was hailed as medicine against the monotony of mass-produced single-family flats' (ibid. 166–67). On a much larger scale, the relatively prosperous Brezhnev era, for the first time in Soviet history, came to be associated with a culture of mass consumption and the availability of consumer goods for a broader Soviet public. And home interior and domestic space became one of the prime symbols for the new consumer society.

Whereas in Western capitalist contexts the home has been considered crucial in the production of individuals' social selves, similar questions have been posed for the standardised mass housing under socialist modernity. Answers point to the ambiguous character and inconsistencies in the official discourse. While petit-bourgeois mentalities and material fetishism continued to be disapproved of in ideological terms, consumption for the home and concerns with beautifying and personalising private space in other aspects of official discourse was seen as legitimate. This development led to what can be called 'the hypertrophy of domestic exhibitionism' and eventually to a kind of 'private publicity':

> Transforming their domestic interiors into sites of conspicuous consumption and everyday aesthetics through material practices of decoration, display, and concealment, occupants made these standard spaces their own. At the same time, they made themselves at home, creating meaningful selves and coherent narratives of their lives that they could present to others on their own terms (Reid 2015: 228).

By looking beyond the confines of Soviet Russia, these carefully observed aspects of late Soviet home-making practices get accompanied by several other dynamics that are of crucial importance in the Azerbaijani context, such as life-cycle rituals, gender relations, and the value of privacy.

Compared to socialist times, people today have gained much more autonomy in terms of furnishing, modifying, and beautifying their homes. In practice, the freedom supposedly provided by the market economy strongly depends on a family's ability to mobilise the financial means to participate in the home-making and consumption industries. Therefore, we can assume at least three distinct continuities between late socialism and the independent era: first, there is a continuity of scarcity although of different character. Compared to socialism, people have now a free choice to make their house and home according to their own ideas. But scarcity of money came to replace the former scarcity of goods. Second, there is a continuity of what was once called a 'bourgeois' lifestyle (i.e. the value people ascribed to the role of consumption, domestic display, and cosiness of interior design). In Baku this trend has been significantly enhanced and reinforced in the 2000s after the economic hardships of the 1990s. Third, a high symbolic value, alongside the economic one, still adheres to imported western goods because they are perceived as being endowed with an aura of exclusivity. The preference for exclusive foreign furniture, as in the case of Elbəy, is not new. It was present too during the Soviet period because it enabled people to feel distinct and to symbolically construct their home as superior to the limited choice and supply of Soviet goods that were perceived as being of inferior quality (Chernyshova 2013: 176–81). Goods from East Germany, Poland, Romania, Yugoslavia, or the Baltic states were always in high demand during the Soviet years. In the context of the domestic sphere, especially my female interlocutors often expressed the Odyssey-like character of getting access to rugs, china, trays, or salvers of good quality. As the mother of one of my close friends, a lady in her fifties, told me:

> Such items were almost exclusively available on the black market. In Baku we usually went to Kubinka for this. Under the counter with good luck and some extra Rubles you could get most of the items that were usually under short supply. If you wanted to get anything of foreign origin and good quality then you went to Kubinka. Today this has changed. You can buy anything you want, but there is no money.

By making use of informal markets and networks, many people strived towards obtaining exclusive goods and commodities in order to personalise their standardised dwellings or to collect items for a future dowry or wedding gift. In Baku it was Kubinka – an old neighbourhood in inner-city Baku. There, people from all social backgrounds, commoners as well as high-ranking Party-officials, obtained foreign goods.

To sum up, there are various aspects to the phenomenon of home-making and consumption that reach from individual concerns of personalising the aesthetics of standardised apartments, managing one's presentation to others, or to collective and socially relevant interactions such as hospitality, conspicuous consumption, and the controlled display of the home. As I have argued, these processes were predominantly embedded in the social context of marriage which at the same time marked the most important among several life-cycle events to engage in home-making activities, especially since, according to local notions, home-making is equivalent to the meaning of marriage. Without the latter, home-making loses many of its crucial aspects.

Conclusion

In the first part of this chapter, I have described the material and social construction of home boundaries and thresholds such as walls, doors, windows, and curtains and how they shape local perceptions and enactments of private and intimate spaces. Here, I described how supposedly fixed spatial categories are blurred and become permeable as dwellers control and regulate the traversability of thresholds. The protection of privacy as well as the representative and displaying functions of thresholds were interpreted as confirming, reinforcing, and negotiating social relationships. A prominent metaphor for expressing the material, social, and symbolic qualities of privacy is the 'curtain' which is not only constitutive for a proper home but is also a crucial concept in the everyday management of privacy within as well as between houses. The widespread socio-political practice of maintaining the curtain (pərdə saxlamaq) describes the ideal of properly enacting social relations within and outside the family home along principles of gender, age and, more generally, notions of respect. In these enactments of sociality, the boundaries of private and public become regularly blurred and renegotiated. This became also evident in the final part of the chapter where I have finally traced contemporary notions of home-making by giving special attention to practices of home renovation, hospitality, and consumption, their embeddedness in people's experiences of scarcity in Soviet times, as well as in cultural notions of life-cycle rituals. The most intimate sphere of the home can be transformed temporarily into a semi-public space for domestic display, conspicuous consumption, and impression management – a practice that has become increasingly important among better-off families since independence. At the same time, I have pointed to the commonalities with the political and social dimensions of mass consumption in the late Soviet Union.

Chapter 6
The Contested House: Property, Patriarchy, and the State

With regard to housing security, the end of socialism, the transformation of the previous housing regime according to market principles, and the privatisation process led to important changes in intergenerational family relationships and modes of support (e.g. Pine 2002; Semenova and Thompson 2004; Read and Thelen 2007; Attwood 2010; Heady 2010). Until then, young families, whose post-marital residence was with the husband's parents, could apply for a separate apartment, usually through their work place. If they fulfilled the necessary criteria, their names found ways onto the waiting list. In many cases, it was normal for young couples to live with the husband's parents during the first years after marriage until finally receiving the *order* for a separate apartment. As one of my interlocutors aptly put it when we were talking about the contemporary pressure for purchasing housing for the son's marriage:

> Under Soviet rule, no one talked or asked about whether you got an apartment or not. Your son was working, applying for, and receiving an apartment from his workplace – that's it. There was the certainty that in five to seven years you would definitely receive an apartment.

In these accounts, the socialist past and its urban housing regime serves as the framework against which people interpret and evaluate the present and the transformations after the USSR's collapse. With privatisation, however, housing property in Azerbaijan was transferred to those age-groups who now constitute the parental and grandparental generation. The end of an era of 'free housing', welfare and state institutions meant a turning point for parents since they felt now responsible for their children's post-marital housing prospects. This feeling of responsibility has been exacerbated further by rising living costs, low salaries, and a generally precarious and unstable job market – all of which stand in sharp contrast to the paternalistic Soviet cradle-to-grave welfare system.

With regard to housing, a further difficulty is the increasing pattern among many young families to live for rent. The rental sector today, as in the Soviet past, is socially and economically stigmatising. During Soviet times, renting a room (usually in unreputable neighbourhoods dominated by privately owned homes) was a widespread and often informal arrangement for the lower segments of socialist society. In addition, today, young couples' choices for housing are seldom autonomous but dependent on the financial and moral support of parents. In other words, children who marry usually rely on their elders' financial and property resources to obtain joint or separate dwelling. With the end of socialism and the privatisation of property, it was housing that became 'the chief source of household wealth in the new economy' (Zavisca 2012: 1). In a similar stance, other studies on the South Caucasian republics argued that after privatisation it was the older generations who maintained control over housing. As a result, parents were able to exert power continuously on their children's 'family formation sequence' of getting married and becoming parents themselves (Roberts et al. 2009). Whereas this argument points to an important dimension of property and power relations, it generalises such dynamics in the South Caucasus too quickly and overlooks two important issues: first, the power and control that parents have in deciding about their children's future, especially marriage choices and questions of housing, is also dependent on a family's socio-economic background. Wealthier families have more interests in securing their achieved wealth in the long-term and in controlling the distribution of their property. Second, I hardly encountered young adults who perceived their relationships to parents as a dependency characterised by control and the exertion of power. In turn, I perceived parents rather than their children as being predominantly concerned about and exposed to the new challenges of providing the latter with housing after independence.

Such conflicts and related dynamics provide the basis for the present chapter. The wider framework is to ask how families, their close kin, and in-laws cope with conflicting interests regarding the housing question and aspirations to acquire property. Such conflicts may erupt along social or cultural differences, families' long-term strategies and aspirations, and diverging economic interests – but also recent developments within state and society. In light of anthropological debates on property and patriarchy around the empirical field of housing, I ask how different generations in the household cope with such tensions and negotiate their dependencies and freedoms amidst normative power differences such as gender and age.

The end of the Soviet Union marked some profound changes in the urban housing regime, as with the conceptualisation of property and ownership more generally. In social terms scholars have discussed the impact of the new housing situation after privatisation on different groups of urban inhabitants, households, and families. In urban Russia, for instance, young people who want to obtain separate housing have become mostly dependent on their parents and close kin. The sociologist Jane Zavisca (2012) has shown that after privatisation, households' financial constraints limited the choices and opportunities for home-ownership, especially for young families who are forced to continue co-residing with their parents. The author illustrates families' collective efforts to secure housing and the supportive role of parents towards the younger generation. However, such mechanisms of support are prone to conflicts and can lead to de facto dependencies of young couples because they, like other household members who lack ownership rights, 'may have few prospects for obtaining housing elsewhere and, correspondingly, may experience housing insecurity and dependency' (Zavisca 2012: 12). Such lack of ownership rights and the resulting dependencies of some family members are usually biased towards specific groups within society not only in terms of generation and age, but also with regard to gender. Whereas in Zavisca's Russian examples these are mostly men, in Azerbaijan, it is mostly women who are most vulnerable. An important anthropological study on postsocialist urban housing (Höjdestrand 2009) deals with the production of homelessness in Saint Petersburg and describes cases of people who have no accommodation or propiska because they lack family support or have been deprived of access to housing by their relatives. In most cases, people:

> were deceived by close relatives or by spouses using authorisations, forged papers, or bribed officials to secure the official right to the living space of their victims. [...] Most of them are divorcees (usually wives) who left home without caring about any formalities, or elders who escaped the violence of younger members of their household (Höjdestrand 2003).

How do such processes unfold in the Caucasian context that is said to differ from Russian society by its strong association with patriarchal bias, male domination, and supposedly traditional gender roles? What are the similarities and differences in their postsocialist trajectories despite a shared Soviet past, and can we detect further social dynamics that have not yet been considered sufficiently?

Such questions entail important dynamics, as previously described, of the moral notions entailed in urban property. Earlier I have pointed to the important difference of whether we approach housing as the property of individuals or of families. As was argued for housing in Soviet times, 'In the medium term most families sought to enlarge and improve their housing resources. For most practical purposes dwellings belonged to families rather than to individuals or the state' (Roberts et al. 2000). In other words, Soviet housing was turned into a 'household asset' (Zavisca 2012: 40). But such assertions generate further questions on the meaning of family in specific contexts. Which family members are included when we talk about housing as being owned by families? Does it make sense to assume a clear distinction between individual and collective or communal property rights (Hann 1993: 300)? Thus, from an anthropological viewpoint there are two crucial issues that need to be considered for a deeper understanding of housing- and family-dynamics in Azerbaijan after independence: First, we need to consider people's normative comprehension of housing as property and its relation to social practice. Both, I argue, cannot be fully understood without reference to the Soviet housing-regime because notions of property do not immediately follow the introduction of new property regulations and legal bodies. Second, the parental control over housing the young invites further scrutiny on the various faces of patriarchy in the Azerbaijani family, society, politics, and law. Such 'focus on the relationship between power and property' is a crucial endeavour which, unfortunately, was mostly limited to 'the state as the sole legitimate font of property rights' (von Benda-Beckmann et al. 2006: 5).

Another widespread development discussed among scholars on Central Asia and the Caucasus is the active effort of governments to replace former Soviet narratives and state-citizen relations (of a socialist and equal society) with recourse to supposedly national values. While it was previously the government that guaranteed the right to housing, education, and health care, these responsibilities have shifted mostly to the sphere of the family. This triggered a general development across the former Soviet republics of Central Asia and the Caucasus. Issues like gender, authority, religion, and tradition have been discussed anew under notions of neo-traditionalism, retraditionalisation or 'traditionalisation' and its alignment with nationalism (Beyer and Finke 2019).

On a broader level, and implicitly linked to debates on neo-traditionalisation, this chapter is concerned with questions on the impact of 70 years of Soviet social politics on present society. Today, Azerbaijani society is strongly characterised by a patriarchal bias in various domains of everyday life. This observation stands in stark contrast to socialist ideology and the Bolsheviks' attempts to overcome the patriarchal structure in its Muslim republics. Indeed, in Soviet times, 'patriarchy served as a loose concept into which any practice considered questionable within Soviet ideology would be placed and labelled as "backward" or "survival"' (Roche 2017: 14). The emancipation of women – guarantee of equal rights, access to educational institutions, and incorporation into the workforce – are perceived as a fundamental achievement of socialist systems. Thus, how can we make sense of the apparent 'paradox' (Kandiyoti 2007) in the recent history of Central Asian and Caucasian republics that patriarchal developments in politics and society have (re)constituted a crucial element in local lives (see e.g. Akiner 1997; Constantine 2007; Ilkhamov 2007; Ismailbekova 2014)?

Vulnerable Property, Social Conflicts, and Legal Discrimination

In Chapter 3, I have argued that Soviet citizens largely perceived and used housing as a collective family resource that was hoarded and that conveyed moral expectations towards solidarity and cooperation among close kin. After the death of an apartment's main tenant, the ownership rights could be inherited, usually, by one of the co-registered persons. If no registered co-residents were at hand, the dwelling fell back to the state housing fund. Thus, in order to secure long-term use-rights and legal entitlements to an apartment, it was common practice to register at a relative's place without eventually residing there. In fact, housing became an important resource allocated by the state to its citizens and was, therefore, hoarded by kin groups. As I have illustrated, the practice of hoarding resources, including dwellings, translates into social and moral expectations of solidarity and cooperation. However, as the title of this chapter indicates, housing can become a contested resource that is prone to conflicts within families – thus challenging the moral notion of collective ownership. This is because even though houses are to be seen as being de facto collectively owned, it does not mean that the degree of influence and control in decision-making processes are distributed equally. Furthermore, instead of running the risk of seeing housing as only a material property that enables elder, materially superior generations to exert power on the younger ones, scholars should give more focus to the 'embeddedness of property' (Hann 1998) in its regional and social contexts. This means that, rather than sticking to a conventional association between subjects and objects, 'property relations are consequently better seen as social relations between people' (Hann 1998: 4). It is especially the sphere of housing in the present context that fits to Chris Hann's definition of property as 'the distribution of social entitlements' (ibid.: 7). Such processes unfold around ideals, changing moral discourses, and historical shifts which have to be included in the overall picture (ibid.: 34). Hence, questions and conflicts over property discussed in the present chapter turn out to give little emphasis to the legal relationship of a person to an object. Seemingly higher importance is ascribed to property as representing the quality of social relations within and among families in the context of privatisation as it constituted a redistribution of social entitlements. Apart from the legal changes of privatised property, it is mostly moral concerns, historical experiences, and an increasingly patriarchal promotion of the post-Soviet government that have a fundamental impact on how people negotiate access to property.

One issue that had an important impact on how people initially evaluated privatisation was the experiential difference between ownership rights and use-rights. When the privatisation programme began, people privatised apartments usually in the name of one person. Although many people had been registered to an apartment, only one person became the legal owner of the dwelling, and this was usually the senior male. This was not required by law. According to Article 5 of the Privatisation Law, ownership entitlements of housing could be transferred to either one person in the household, to several of them, or jointly to all those who had reached majority age; the choice was to be made with the consent of all registered full-aged members in the household. Furthermore, the law was handled differently elsewhere: In Russia, it was common to privatise apartments by distributing equal shares to all the registered household members (Zavisca 2012).

Although the post-Soviet property law enables other models, many people in Baku continued to apply the Soviet practice, according to which there was only one main tenant. Every registered co-tenant (predominantly family members) had to agree formally on privatisation since they had equal use-rights to the apartment. The legal document required for privatising, selling, or otherwise changing the property rights of a dwelling is the so-called *forma dva* (Form 2) which can be obtained from the local *ZhEK*-office. It lists all registered household members in the apartment and proves the residential address of a person. The same document is needed in other administrative contexts, such as applying for a new passport. *Forma dva* is of crucial importance because only with the legal consent of all co-registered tenants can the owner dispose legitimately of his or her property. It also means that, in practice, property transactions get encumbered because owners who want to sell their property fail to provide the notary with the necessary agreements of registered cohabitants who might not even live in the apartment.

Azerbaijan's Supreme Court has issued a number of resolutions dealing with these problems. For example, it was decided that those cases in which people were registered before the year 2000 are regulated by the Housing Code while those having registered later are to be dealt with by the Civil Code. While the former procedure has just been described, the latter involves granting a right to monetary compensation for those who de-register from the dwelling. Thus, conflicts between the owner's and the users' interests are expected to decrease because of the stipulated compensation; non-owners are expected to relinquish use-rights for money, speeding the ability of the owner to dispose of property. In that regard, the distribution of housing entitlements is still connected to official registrations, which under such circumstances, can lead to property conflicts between co-registered family members. Later in this chapter I detail some extreme conflicts, but first address the continuity of practices, knowledge, and assumptions around property, use, and registration from the Soviet period.

In Chapter 3, I have already discussed the power of the Soviet propiska system and how citizens bypassed this means of state control to meet their housing and family interests. Basically, this power of registrations continues to the present (see Höjdestrand 2009), however the legal and societal context has changed tremendously. Thus, we can observe other dynamics of conflict related to the propiska today. For instance, in neighbourhoods such as Sovetski or Dağlı there are many dwellings in which ten to twenty people are registered, though most of them moved out long ago. Even Fikrət Qacarov and his family are still registered in his parental home although they moved to Badamdar twenty years ago. Instrumentalising the propiska was such a widespread practice for access housing, work, and welfare services that people have been slow to de-register from old dwellings until – as in the past – they feel a clear need to do so. In some ways, there is even less need to do so now. Today there is no rule which obliges people to de-register from a dwelling they do not inhabit, but during Soviet times, any tenant's absence in excess of a certain period of time was a common reason for eviction:

> According to Article 60 of the Housing Code, municipal tenants who are proven not to have resided at their place of residence for more than six months may by a court decision be evicted and deprived of the propiska, and their flats or rooms are then given to people who presumably are in more need of them (Höjdestrand 2009: 26).

In practice, however, authorities were hardly able (or interested) to check and control violations against this law unless there were complaints from co-dwellers. And although such regulations could be strategically used against close kin and family members in cases of property conflicts, the law mostly affected dwellers in communal apartments. Besides this, certain groups of Soviet citizens were directly and precariously affected by such rules. Throughout the late Soviet period, and until 1995 in the case of Russia, the Housing Code did not differentiate between voluntary or involuntary absence, such as cases of long-term hospitalisation (e.g. for mental health issues) or criminal conviction: 'People sentenced to more than six months incarceration were automatically deprived of the propiska, and if they had a

place of their own before the conviction, they were deprived of it'
(Höjdestrand 2009: 26).[78]

Another point on which customary practice continues Soviet-era
norms, despite adjustments in the law that appear to be more 'Western' is
property inheritance. As specified above, during Soviet times, only a co-
registered tenant could inherit the main tenancy and use-right following the
death of the previous 'owner'. In Azerbaijan, co-registered tenants were, and
remain, almost always relatives. And still today, rather than dividing
property into equal shares among the children – as the law encourages as a
default pattern – it is common practice to transmit it only to the youngest
son. Azerbaijanis perceive this as a 'traditional' (not Soviet) practice and
consider it part of their 'culture' that the youngest son should stay with his
parents in one joint household after marriage. In exchange for the care that
the youngest son (and his wife) gives to the parents as they age, he inherits
the dwelling. This is not perceived, however, as an unequal inheritance, but
rather explained along the lines of what Jack Goody (1970: 45) termed the
'devolution [of property] *inter vivos*': ideally the older sons move into a
separate place, which mostly is provided by the parents, at or shortly after
marriage. These properties can be perceived as a kind of pre-mortem
inheritance. Jack Goody used the term with reference to the dowry a
daughter is given at the moment of her marriage, but it would apply to sons
in this case too. At any rate, Azerbaijanis do not consider that one son is
more favoured than the others by the parents in material terms – though it is
recognised that some will enjoy more autonomy from the parents than
others.

Knowledge and use of the law, as well as the invocation of 'tradition',
is uneven. According to Article 1159 on Equal Heirs in the Civil Code of the
Republic of Azerbaijan, approved on 28 December 1999, the property of a
deceased person in the first instance is to be shared equally among his or her
children, spouse, and parents. The law does not discriminate against either
sex. Yet, most citizens have not followed the law in distributing property. As
a female lawyer put it in one of our conversations:

---

[78] In the case of convicts, the state directly de-registered them from their former dwelling.
After they had served their terms, the local administration was supposed to help ex-convicts
find jobs and housing, but the system was inefficient and employers were usually unwilling to
take on ex-convicts. The result was that even though they were 'rehabilitated', former
prisoners often turned to informal arrangements for housing and work, such as renting a room
within a private house. Under such conditions, they often continued to lack a propiska and
were thus vulnerable to charges of violating passport laws, vagrancy, and other such problems
linked to their exclusive reliance on informal arrangements. The large number of private
houses in neighbourhoods like Sovetski may well have attracted ex-convicts (and thus given
some reality to their reputations of being 'full of criminals').

After marriage the daughter leaves the parental home while the son thinks 'how could I dare to leave my parents?' In fact, our laws are sufficiently democratic in that sense, but in practice many families still cannot depart from their mindset. And it is also the case that many just do not know that they can hand on their property not only to their son but as well to their daughters. They think it is only possible to pass it on to the son who should stay with them. Thus, many old houses were passed down from father to son for generations.

As the lawyer underscores, people normally do not differentiate between use-right and legal ownership: the daughter 'moves out', so it is assumed she cannot inherit or be the owner, while the son 'should stay' because he is assumed to be the one who will inherit. Yet, the distinctions can be made, and are made when there are different expectations and interests among family members.

On a rather pragmatic level, my conversations with lawyers and others showed that property is registered in the name of a man's parent (usually his father) with the knowledge, and strategic intent, that this will protect the husband against claims of legal entitlement to the property that his wife and her family may make in case of divorce. Many people know and apply all kinds of legal tools to prevent their spouse from acquiring legal rights to property. People are very creative in that matter. For instance, if a young man with real estate property marries, his family can decide to re register the property in the name of one of his close family members – not only that of his father, but also of his mother, brother, or sister. In case of divorce, his wife could not claim any of the property because, officially, her husband does not own it. Thus the pooling of property within families extends beyond the concern for ensuring adequate living space for family members. Against this background, mutual cooperation within the family, but also cases of conflict over property, invite further analysis on how intra-familial loyalties are actually negotiated according to cultural dispositions.

The positive examples for solidarity, support, and cooperation among brothers on issues of housing and social security that I illustrated in earlier chapters, contrasts with the strong gender inequalities faced by women, especially daughters-in-law, as they marry in to structurally disadvantageous positions. For a bride who moves to her husband's place, it is likely that she will never have any legal entitlement to ownership of the property. She will have legal claims to ownership only on any property that is acquired by her husband (or, of course, herself) after the marriage. In fact, she has no entitlement to any immovable property her husband acquired *before* marriage, because it is not considered joint property. The same applies to property which was acquired as inheritance or as donation. In such cases, it is not subject to legal division in case of divorce (see Family Code of the Azerbaijan Republic, Article 34.1). This might make the substitute registration of properties under the names of other family members appear unnecessary; however, this still provides extra protections to the owning family. Spouses, like the parents and children, of the owner may enjoy use-rights to a property after divorce (see Civil Code of the Azerbaijan Republic, Article 228.5). Here, we see that the Civil Code approaches housing as something more like the collective property of a family than as individual property because it leaves the legal owner to bear the moral responsibility of providing access for all those who are, or have been, family members.

If a marriage breaks down, and especially if the relation was not approved of fully by her in-laws, a wife runs the risk of losing housing and registration. Her civil rights are unlikely to be protected, pursued, or upheld. After divorce, women commonly go back to their parents' house, but this is perceived as socially stigmatising.

During fieldwork I spent time regularly with Nazim, a divorced man in his mid-forties who had rented a room in a house near İnşaatçılar. Besides working as an animal doctor who was regularly sent on business trips to the regions, his passion was singing *muğam* – the traditional folk music popular in Azerbaijan. I accompanied him several times to his concerts, also because he needed a driver, and as a friend, it was clear that support role fell to me. On these occasions, I also met İlahə, a woman in her early forties, who was a singer too. As I learned after some time, she had been married to a bank director but divorced because her husband disapproved of her budding career as a singer. He did not like that she appeared in public in revealing dresses. According to him, a wife exposing herself to the public was shameful (*namussuz*) and a sure reason to get divorced. Interestingly, when explaining the issue to me, Nazim agreed with İlahə's husband. In his role as a colleague and friend, he had no problem with İlahə's role as a female singer and successfully maintained the curtain. He did not disrespect her (which made much sense to me as he was also benefitting from the extra singer jobs she landed). But as a husband he would have been unhappy, he said. This double standard is no contradiction. As her husband, Nazim would be considered responsible for how his wife was looking, behaving, and being perceived in public. Since she is not much representing expected female virtues, this would be felt by Nazim as a serious challenge of his masculinity and role as head of the household. But as a colleague engaging in joint public singing, he seemed not to worry about these things. İlahə had chosen to follow the possibility of a singing career; her two sons and daughter stayed with her husband. In the end, her career did not fulfil the promised outcome, and she still lived with her father in an apartment in Yeni Yasamal, a large area of postsocialist high-rises in Yasamal District.

Nazim told me more. İlahə, he said, sometimes engaged in prostitution to earn desperately-needed extra money. This was how he had met her. He had been her client, and only later did they become friends who shared some opportunities for live performances in restaurants or at weddings. When I asked Nazim how she could receive her clients when living with her father, he replied that her father was alcoholic and that she would send him to get some wine or vodka. During roughly an hour of her father's absence, she would perform the business. Truly, their relation was complex. Nazim was concerned that İlahə was often not paid by her clients. But on other occasions, he spoke disapprovingly of her. She was a woman without *namus*[79], he said, and you could not trust her, among other reasons, because she sold herself to men.

This account gives only a glimpse on the power relations, the role of patriarchy, and the vulnerability of women in social, economic, and legal terms in contemporary Azerbaijan. These, along with ethnicity, are illuminated in the following case. I have reconstructed the example from a lawsuit I encountered during my archival research. It demonstrates women's precarious position regarding housing and social security because of a lack of legal security paired with patriarchal biases in the home and in administrative institutions. This case crosscuts issues which all have a specific link to housing and property conflicts, and shows how norms of gender, patriarchy, and authority can underwrite extreme forms of domestic violence and ethnic discrimination. Most important, it provides insights into how state and legal institutions are embedded in contemporary discourses about morality and national values that accompany retraditionalisation campaigns. Because this archival material is of relatively recent origin, the names of the victim, the perpetrator, and other people involved are anonymised. Furthermore, I decided to desist from a reference to the source material out of ethical concerns and to protect the anonymity of persons because the case represents a serious crime.

From the case documentation, we learn details about the ethnic Russian woman, Anna, based on accounts written by herself and her sister in their correspondence to Yasamal District Court officials and to the Russian embassy in Baku. We get acquainted with the increasing emotional burden and of the physical, psychological, and emotional violence that Anna experienced from her Azeri husband and in-laws. Eventually, the conflict

---

[79] Unlike the more commonly used term for honour, *hörmət*, *namus* is often perceived as something related to women and their public actions, and it is a kind of honour a man can lose because of his wife's or daughter's inappropriate behaviour in public.

escalated into Anna's murder by her husband on 6 December 1999. The murder turns out to have involved a property conflict, but it is quite some time before this was revealed by the legal proceedings. In short, Anna's husband and his family attempted to appropriate property that belonged to her as their own. Due to her ethnic background and lack of effective social networks, Anna became a clear victim of society's patriarchal bias as it has been translated into serious shortcomings within public institutions. This legal case is of special value because it allows access to intimate family conflicts that usually lay beyond the view of anthropologists. It enables a glance into the darkest side of the home which most people would eagerly try to keep confidential and well preserved behind closed curtains.

On 27 December 1999, Larisa, the sister of the murdered woman, wrote a statement (*zaiavlenie*) addressed to the Chairman of the Commission for Custody and Guardianship which is responsible for youth welfare, of Yasamal District:

> In February 1991, my sister, *Anna R.* [*1972] married *Elnur R.* [*1960]. Two children were born, *Nihal R.* [*03/06/1991] and *Nargiz R.* [*05/01/1995]. The relationship between the spouses became worse and was accompanied by violent behaviour of the husband who frequently beat my sister. On this issue you can find statements at the Baku City Prosecutor's Office, at the Russian Embassy, and the district's police office [...].
>
> In November 1999 they were legally divorced by the Yasamal Court. After that, my sister approached a [female] friend for temporarily providing her with shelter. There she was living with her children until she got murdered. Despite the divorce, her former husband did not leave her in peace and paid frequent visits. While pretending to be interested in the children's wellbeing, he instead raised a scandal with *Anna* and beat her up in front of the children. In the night of December 6th *Elnur R.*, after barbarically beating *Anna*, cut her throat with a broken glass right in front of the children and took them with him. Today, my nieces are with *Elnur R.*'s mother, a woman in her sixties who had never shown interest for her grandchildren nor any participation in their upbringing. She rejected her daughter-in-law and her children because my sister was of foreign nationality [Russian]. *Elnur R.*'s mother and sister have tried to split up the relationship in every way possible [...].
>
> One cannot entrust the fate of my underage nieces to the mother of a sadistic son. By virtue of these facts [...] I ask the Commission [...] to provide me, *Larisa S.* with the right to custody of my nieces.

Finally, the applicant was granted the children's legal guardianship. The whole process, however, required the support of the Russian Embassy. Ten days before Larisa wrote the above application, that is on 17 December, she wrote a letter to the Russian Embassy for advocacy and support in seeking custody as her first request to the Yasamal officials, made within days of the murder, had remained unanswered by the Azerbaijani authorities. Then, the Embassy wrote an official letter to the Yasamal Commission for Custody with the request 'to assign for checking the indicated facts and, in case of confirmation, to take appropriate steps and to inform the Embassy about the outcome'. Larisa approached the embassy because she perceived that her efforts to gain custody were being thwarted by severe ethnic and gender discrimination from a state executive representative. That this was just the tip of an iceberg becomes clear in the divorce documents from her murdered sister.

In the divorce certificate it says that Anna endorsed the decision to split on grounds of her husband's inhumane and violent treatment. He 'threw her and the children out of the apartment and only after a court order could they return there'. The same document describes how Anna's husband and mother-in-law took advantage of her legal property by using it as a resource for their own ends. Another severe conflict arose out of Anna's lack of a propiska for her marital home and its further socio-economic implications. These issues – domestic violence, property fraud, and denial of registration – were described by Anna in two almost identical letters. The first one she wrote to the Yasamal District Court but because of the indifference and lack of support, she applied to the Russian Embassy two weeks later, again describing her case and asking for supportive advocacy.

She first states that, after marriage and moving to her husband, he and her in-laws did not register her in the apartment which officially belonged to her mother-in-law. By that time Anna herself was registered at her parents' apartment, and that was why she had not insisted to be registered at her husband's apartment. Her parents, both ethnic Russians, had resided in Baku for most of their lives until moving to Russia in 1996 (five years after Anna's marriage). When they moved, they left their four-room apartment in the Baku outskirts to Anna and her sister. Anna's husband insisted that the women should sell the apartment and share the money. They did so, and Anna's share of 3,600 USD was appropriated by her husband who told her that he and his mother desperately needed the money. They promised her very soon to buy a separate apartment. Anna's mother-in-law, however, used the money to appropriate the apartment of her mentally ill sister. Because she was at a psychiatric hospital, the woman was not entitled to make a legal deed of donation. However, her sister, Anna's mother-in-law, used Anna's money to bribe the notary to prepare the documents anyway and became the legal owner of her sister's apartment, who died shortly afterwards in 1997. The mother-in-law not only refused to return Anna's money, but even denied Anna and her children registration in the apartment where they lived. They desperately required this registration because they had sold their former place of registration, and Anna's in-laws gained tremendous power and influence over Anna's daily life by withholding the propiska that entitled her to a whole bundle of social entitlements. She wrote, 'three years have passed since then and I and my children are still without registration and therefore without any rights. As a result, I could neither find any work nor participate in elections'.

But what were the motivations for denying the propiska? According to Anna's sister, it was because the mother-in-law had never accepted Anna because of her non-Azeri ethnic background. But even if the mother-in-law had no objections to the marriage (especially when it took place), she may have had motivations to continue to exclude Anna's legal registration. As I have shown, strategic inclusions and exclusions of individuals with regard to registration are common. I think what could be relevant in this case is that the mother-in-law did not necessarily want to deny Anna the civic entitlements (to work, voting, healthcare, children's education) that concerned Anna so much, but that she wanted to consolidate control over property. As previously said, a legal owner who wants to sell his or her apartment, or take up a bank loan, has a completed Form 2, which documents the agreement of every registered adult with the planned action. If we can imagine the possibility that Anna and her mother-in-law often disagreed in matters of property, finance, and family strategies, it would not be hard to see how denying Anna the registration could be interpreted as a strategy to secure and maintain decisional power. It is, however, a strategy that equally excludes her from full social and legal incorporation within the house, and denies her the social entitlements that are accorded to those who are considered 'unconditional' members of the family.

The workings of patriarchy cannot be limited to a simple dichotomy of superior men to subordinate women. In this case, the mother-in-law seems to have been the all-controlling decision-maker in the household, while her son did not challenge his mother's authority and superiority. The case is also not without evidence of sometimes complicated relations between the predominate constellations of hierarchy and power. We have learned already about the husband beating his wife and children. In more detail, Anna described another incident in which her husband severely beat her, then ran into the kitchen to get a knife. She escaped in that moment from the apartment into the staircase, hid at a neighbours' apartment, and called the police. When the police arrived and detained her husband, the mother-in-law begged Anna to not let her son go to prison, and promised to buy a separate apartment within the next ten days so that Anna could move out with her children. This description of a mother so desperate to protect her son from legal consequences that she is prepared to grant Anna concessions stands in stark contrast to her usually dominant role described above.

However, seven months after the incident, Anna had neither received the promised apartment nor a propiska, hence, she applied to the court to finally get a registration at her husband's place. As soon as her mother-in-law received the summons, she threw Anna and her children out of the apartment notwithstanding the presence of a police officer. Regarding the denial for registration, the husband once again was on his mother's side. Finally, the court confirmed Anna the right to be registered at her husband's and mother-in-law's place. Shortly after, she finally decided to file for divorce. In front of the court, her husband promised to sell his mother's apartment to buy a separate one for his ex-wife and their children and additionally to pay her back the 3,600 USD. Later, after having obtained his wife's consent (which was needed now that she was registered) on selling the apartment, they sold it for 16,000 USD. The mother-in-law took 10,600 USD for herself and her son and moved to her daughter's place. Anna and her children were given only 5,300 USD, as her in-laws decided to make the share between three parties instead of two. They also insisted that all debts were cleared. In short, she neither received an apartment nor the adequate share of money as was promised to her at the court. That is why Anna announced once again that she would approach the court. As a compromise, on the next day her husband offered to support her in finding an apartment for the money share of 5,300 USD that she received. If necessary, he would even pay the additional money for a decent apartment. As a result of this promise, Anna felt compelled to search for a dwelling together with her husband. After he had found an apartment for 7,300 USD in the region of Bailov, he agreed to pay the additionally required money – but only if the contract were issued in his name – a step that Anna decisively rejected. He then said that if she did not agree to purchase the apartment in his name, he would not pay the additional sum, and if she complained to officials, he threatened to 'deal with things in a way that would make her even lose the 5,300 USD'.

Within days, the husband presented himself to the authorities as a victim and took active measures against Anna by accusing her of theft. He complained to the city's Main Police Department that he was being robbed by his ex-wife. Some days later, when she was at home, Anna wrote that she was seized by two police officers who neither introduced nor identified themselves but instead forced her into the police car. Anna had no idea what was going on. She feared that the two men were criminals because her husband previously threatened her to hire outlaws in order to kill her, or at least to make her life in Baku impossible. Anna was kept at the Police Department until midnight, full of concerns about her kids whom she was unable to pick up from school. In her first application, which she addressed to the district court, she expressed concerns about not being supported by the police: 'I have no idea what will happen next and I do not think that the police will take appropriate measures to support me according to law. Although I constantly asked the police for help, they did nothing. Every charge on my husband was closed inexplicably'. Anna felt that she and her children were left completely unprotected and unsupported from her husband's illicit behaviour. She wrote: 'He constantly threatened to bring me into jail or to kill me. He assured that he was able to do so because of the influential contacts he had due to his father's regional origin from Nakhchivan'.[80] However, as Anna felt she was supported neither by the Yasamal District Court nor the Police Department, she finally wrote to the Russian Embassy: 'I ask for your help and support by considering my case in an unbiased way'.

This whole case describes a mother of two children, significantly maltreated by her husband and in-laws, who by various means aimed to extend their own property and financial resources very much at her expense. Furthermore, the descriptions point to serious discrimination by state institutions against a female citizen of non-Azeri ethnic background. Against official law, the involved administrative and executive powerholders denied their support. In light of the widespread corruption and bribes that are perceived as a necessary requirement to enforce one's rights against state institutions, Anna seemed to be in a disadvantageous position compared to her husband and in-laws. At the very least, she lacked access to any significant sources of money to pay the bribes so often necessary to secure assistance from authorities, and especially from the police. Moreover, she perceived, probably correctly, that her Russian identity was hindering her bid for support and assistance. In public discourse, Russian women are

---

[80] There are two regional groups predominantly associated with the concentration of political and economic power: The *Nakhchivantsy* (people from the Nakhchivan Autonomous Republic) and the *Yeraz* (Azerbaijani from Yerevan, Armenia). The majority of the president's apparatus was born in those regions and it was *Heydər Aliyev's* strategy to mobilise regional networks in order to incorporate loyal compatriots as the ruling elite (see Sidikov 2007). I want to add that people's increased consciousness and mobilisation of their regional identities gains importance when they migrate from their regions into the city. Therefore, I would argue that even though regional identification has played an important role during Soviet times, it became even more crucial after independence.

depicted as being morally inferior to Azeri women, largely because of their presumed sexual 'looseness'. Therefore, Anna finally approached the Russian embassy for support. It is not clear whether this strategy would have helped or not: in the official letter sent by the Russian Embassy to the Prosecutor of Baku City, we find the diplomatically expressed 'gratitude' for the prosecutor to enforce 'appropriate' measures to resolving the case:

> *Anna R.* fears that the law enforcement organs are not going to react to any subsequent appeals about bringing her husband to justice. Therefore, she requested us to enquire about any progress in that matter. In that regard we were grateful for rechecking the assignment and the mentioned arguments and, if substantiated, to enforce appropriate measures. Please inform the Embassy about the outcome.

In the end it is hard to speculate on whether such advocacy by the Russian embassy would have helped solving the issue. Probably, it would have all depended on the individual attitudes or shared opinions among the responsible decision-makers. Besides the above explained moral stereotypes concerning Russian women, the wider political relations between Azerbaijan and Russia have suffered in the previous years, not only because Azerbaijan's increasing relations with the West. Much more because of Russia lent military support to Armenia as an ally in the Nagorno-Karabakh conflict. Manifold interests and dynamics could have played a role on all levels mentioned.

As a final step, I want to engage in some interpretations, partly based on the documented information, but also on my experience and observations during fieldwork, concerning Anna's probable relations with her husband and in-laws. By my estimations, she entered the marriage from a vulnerable position, beyond the usual dynamics of male superiority/ female subordination. That is, Anna was only nineteen years old, and her husband was eleven years older than her. The marriage may, indeed, have been undesired by one or several parties, as she was pregnant at the time of marriage, and gave birth roughly four months later. Moreover, her children – both the first and the second – were daughters, not sons, giving her little chance to gain merit in the traditional patterns recognised for new brides.

Instead, we see that Anna's 'value' in the family shifted to a question of property. It was after Anna's parents moved to Russia and left their apartment to their two daughters in 1996, that the records note the beginning of increased physical violence and constant conflicts over property among the cohabiting in-laws. Treated merely as a means to an end, Anna was exploited financially, and then she and her children were denied the indispensable registration, and were even thrown out of the apartment. As far as this was reported to the authorities, we learned about her mother-in-law's aspirations for accumulating and securing entitlements to real estate at the expense of her lateral and affine kin – her mentally ill sister as well as her daughter-in-law.

However, it is also instructive that Anna's treatment deteriorated *after* her parents moved away. The withdrawal of the bride's parents exposed their property to the interests of their affines, but we can see in this case a number of the tensions that exist (albeit less extremely) in most marriages and that both sets of parents are concerned to control for at the point of matchmaking. As mentioned previously, parents' consent on their children's marriage choice is considered indispensable. Several factors are taken into consideration in evaluating a potential match, including ethnicity, region of origin, age, whether and how a man will provide for his family, and whether a woman conforms with ethnic ideals of being modest, shy, a virgin, and so on (see Heyat 2002: 144–50). Interethnic marriages are rarely favoured, and in many cases I know, the parents' favourite matchmaking option would be a spouse from the same region of origin. Second, when the newly-weds move in with the groom's parents, the *gəlin* is expected to be subordinate to her mother-in-law, to fulfil domestic tasks, and to give support generally within the household. She is also expected to give birth within one or two years after the wedding, preferably to a son. When a bride does not meet these expectations, they can become factors of conflict, but this is most likely when there were tensions even before the marriage. In Anna's case, the marriage never received the mother-in-law's consent (*riza*), but seems to have been rejected and actively disturbed on account of Anna's non-Azeri background.

Another factor adding to tensions between parents and children is the marriage age. According to Azerbaijani standards, Anna's husband married late – a man of thirty years is considered old already. Usually, parents push their sons to marry in their mid-twenties – that is, as soon as they have completed their education, military service, and found employment. However, since well-paid and stable employment has become more difficult since the end of socialism, men have been marrying at a later age than women, who still often marry after they have finished their education. According to official statistics, the average age for marriage in the last twenty-five years has increased for both sexes while the age difference between the spouses has increased as well. In 1990, men were on average 26.2 years old at marriage, while women were 23.2, which makes an age difference of exactly three years. In 2014, men were already 27.6 years old, while women were 23.7 years, an increase to about 4 years in age between spouses.[81] A similar trend of rising marriage age due to a prolonged period for young men to accumulate the financial resources and housing has been discussed in Middle Eastern media and scholarship (e.g. Singerman and Ibrahim 2001; Ghannam 2002: 18, 145; Drieskens 2008).

In Anna's marriage of 1991, not only was the husband about four years past the average groom, but the age difference between the spouses was nearly four times that of more typical matches. We can surmise that significant tensions already existed between Anna's husband and his parents because he had remained unmarried for so long time. He was also the only son in his family, which presumably raised both stakes and tensions over any potential mate. His bride would necessarily be the one to take care of his parents.

Finally, he married a *Russian* girl, and this most certainly added to his mother's discomfort. In local public discourse, Russian women are often presented as prostitutes, or at least as ignorant of the dominant socio-moral expectations that a girl should protect her virginity until marriage. It seems likely to assume that Anna's mother-in-law considered her son's relationship with a Russian woman (if she knew about it) as merely a sexual affair, and did not intervene earlier because she did not expect it to lead to marriage. The bride's pregnancy was presumably a complicating factor, precipitating a marriage that the groom's mother might have prevented otherwise.

Marriage to a Russian woman might be prevented because of her presumed lack of shame. In Azerbaijan and many other Caucasian and Central Asian Republics, Russian women are commonly depicted as the morally inferior counter-image of one's own women. This postsocialist expression of nationalism and ethnic pride reverses the Soviet Union's long-standing approach towards civilising and developing its Muslim populations. It is an inversion of past ethnic hierarchies governed by a superior and privileged class of Russian and Slavic people in the new light of still young but independent and sovereign nation-states. Such a pattern, which I also encountered among males, was well expressed by one of Heyat's female informants:

> A woman is not like a man. She does not have an animalistic attitude to sex. She needs to feel affection and love, and it takes time to develop love, to appreciate it. We are not like the Russian women. [...] For them sex is like any other physical activity. If they fancy a man they don't hesitate to sleep with him (Heyat 2002: 160).

It might equally be prevented because Russian women are not expected to accept the supportive and subordinate role of the *gəlin*. In everyday

---

[81] See http://www.stat.gov.az/source/demoqraphy/indexen.php. Last accessed 11 September 2015.

conversations, ethnic differences were certainly held responsible for mismatched expectations and behaviours between mothers- and daughters-in-law when they occurred. Thus, in public discourse, interethnic marriage is discouraged with reference to deeply-rooted differences in ethnic mentalities and lifestyles.

For all these reasons, we can presume that Anna's mother-in-law tolerated the marriage as long as her son's in-laws were still living in Baku. However, after they left, she 'tried to split up the relationship in every way possible', did not protect her daughter-in-law from the increasing violence of her son, and even added further harassment. Worse, for Anna, is that her mother-in-law succeeded in enforcing a real subordination beyond the culturally 'idealised' structural one. By not granting Anna a propiska, the mother-in-law made her a non-being, an invisible citizen, deprived of most civil rights and social benefits. Without a propiska, Anna had no access to proper employment, no legitimate mobility outside the domestic sphere, was economically dependent on her husband, and became subject to increased control. The powerful position of the mother in the household, her authority over the son, and her emotional rejection of her daughter-in-law shows, as well, her active effort to keep her son's loyalty directed towards herself. As Kandiyoti remarked of patriarchy, 'sons are a woman's most critical resource, ensuring their life-long loyalty is an enduring preoccupation' (1988: 279). Patriarchy ensures that even the most powerful women – women with sons – are vulnerable without men's protection. In the presented case, the one detail that goes almost unmentioned in the documentation is that Anna has no father-in-law. Even with property in her own name, without a husband, Anna's mother-in-law surely needed her son's loyalty even more dearly than most mothers-in-law.

I have reconstructed and told this case at length in order to illustrate intra-family conflicts about the distribution (or retention) of social entitlements and to show its relationship with a variety of power dynamics. It also pointed to the subtle negotiations of social relationship embedded in patriarchal bias and its wider ramifications in contemporary society which I will focus on in the next part of this chapter.

'Differing Patriarchies' and Bargaining for Power

'Patriarchy' as a concept and tool for analysing society, gender, and power relations has passed its heyday in feminist scholarship (see Beechey 1979). In the late 1980s it was said that 'patriarchy is probably the most overused and, in some respects, the most undertheorized' concept within feminist theory (Kandiyoti 1988: 274). Although it has become less popular, since the 1990s, anthropologists have also refined the concept and our understanding of how patriarchy operates, especially with reference to Middle Eastern and Arab contexts (e.g. Joseph 1993a, 1993b, 1996).

My own approach to patriarchy follows Kandiyoti, who remarked that 'the term *patriarchy* often evokes an overly monolithic conception of male dominance, which is treated at a level of abstraction that obfuscates rather than reveals the intimate inner workings of culturally and historically distinct arrangements between the genders' (Kandiyoti 1988: 274–75; emphasis in original). Instead, a thorough contextualisation of patriarchy and its relationality in social interaction is strongly connected to other experiences of social difference as well. Above all, age is important, as 'a person may be both a junior and a senior entailing shifts in positionality and power' (Joseph 1993a: 460). Patriarchy, then, is better defined as 'the dominance of males over females and elders over juniors (males and females) and the mobilization of kinship structures, morality, and idioms to institutionalize and legitimate these forms of power' (ibid. 459). Following this definition, the patriarchal ideology, including its hierarchies, inequalities, and power structures, is perceived as something normal and natural by most members of society (see also Yanagisako and Delaney 1995: 1). This naturalisation of patriarchy is related to the 'symbolic violence' described by Pierre Bourdieu (2001) as 'a gentle violence, imperceptible and invisible even to its victims' or, 'the domination exerted in the name of a symbolic principle known and recognized both by the dominant and by the dominated' (1–2).

Defined as such, patriarchy is not confined to the institution of the family but entails many 'differing patriarchies' (Joseph 1996: 14). As Anna's case above illustrates, patriarchy characterises Azerbaijan's public institutions, as well as other realms of everyday life. Therefore in the final section of this chapter, I follow the lead of other anthropological studies that have demonstrated how patriarchal notions of kinship, gender, and the nation shape the relation between citizens and the state (e.g. Delaney 1995; Bryant 2002).

Regarding aspects of property and housing related to power dynamics, it is helpful to distinguish between 'differing patriarchies' like social, economic, or political patriarchy (Joseph 1996). A clear distinction is often difficult and all of these forms play a role in different sections of this chapter. In the present context, the concept of 'economic patriarchy' is most suitable with regard to property because it also underlines the active role of men and elders in supporting the young. Hence, I refer to:

> 'economic patriarchy' to discuss the privileging of males and elders in ownership and control over wealth and resources, including human resources. Patriarchal kinship is the primary source of eco-

nomic security, and males and elders are considered to be financially responsible for women and junior relatives (Joseph 1996: 15).

In the Azerbaijani case, as elsewhere, such power translates into socially and morally defined responsibilities for parents that, especially for the less privileged, have become far more challenging to meet since the advent of neoliberalism and the end of the socialist welfare state. It is important to note that patriarchy can be experienced as a system of equitable relations, as well as one with the potential to reverse patterns of domination, because those who are supported as juniors or subordinates find themselves in a role with similar capacities to exert symbolic violence on their parents and relatives whose social status and recognition will much depend on their reciprocal support later in the life-cycle. In the everyday contexts discussed here, recognising and acknowledging patriarchy, power, and control, thus, is always related to responsibilities and duties to the dominated. Otherwise hierarchies might lose their legitimacy. Hence, patriarchy as a concept is not something to be observed as such but can better be characterised as a constant negotiation.

In the following, I will give some examples of intergenerational support and power with regard to housing and finances. Within the prevalent patriarchal structures, I hope to show that young adults are not only dependent and controlled but have some agency to negotiate parental domination. Kandiyoti introduced the term 'patriarchal bargain' to describe the set of concrete constraints within which women strategise in patriarchal societies (1988: 275). The following examples illustrate the dynamics of such bargains. However, I do not share Kandiyoti's argument that women alone need to bargain with patriarchy; men equally have to strategise within the constraints of patriarchal ideology.

Günay (b.1983), who is married and has a five-year-old son, is among the few people I know who live in a rented apartment. Both the families of Günay and her husband are from Sabirabad Region but moved to Baku in the late 1990s. After marrying, they began living with the husband's parents but later negotiated with them to move into a separate apartment. When I asked Günay for the reasons of moving out, she explained that living together was too difficult and stressful for her. She evasively described the situation by the phrase *Heçür öz oğluna olan məhəbətini gəlninə bölməyi istəmir*. The meaning is ambiguous as it can mean both that the mother-in-law does not wish to share her son's love with her daughter-in-law; or, that she does not extend her love for her son to her daughter-in-law. Additionally, 'love' does not only imply sentimental liking or attachment, but also recognition, acceptance, and respect.

Surely there was more to the story, as there is nothing about the financial or material situation that speaks to moving-out as a desirable option. Günay works at a university and earns 140 AZN per month. Her husband works as an accountant in a restaurant. Their joint income is barely enough to meet the monthly expenses. Previously, they were living in the four-room *həyət evi* of his parents, together with his sister in Xırdalan, still within the municipality of Baku at its north-western fringe. Since her husband is the only son in the family, Günay explained that according to custom they definitely should have stayed with his parents. Initially, his parents vehemently disapproved of their plans and criticised such an act as 'being disrespectful' (*hörmətsizdir*) while referring to the gossip of the neighbours and their prospective son-in-law: *Qonşular, damad bizə nə deyər?* ('What will the neighbours and son-in-law say about us?'). By 'son-in-law', they refer to the future husband of their daughter and his family, who might judge the whole family as shameful on account of the one son's behaviour. It was largely due to Günay's husband's skilful negotiations with his mother that she finally gave her consent. As Günay hardly mentioned her father-in-law's position, I enquired, but she only commented that it was all about convincing her mother-in-law because she was the master at home. Her father-in-law would usually agree with his wife's decisions.

So, they finally rented one room for 130 AZN per month in a two-storey house in Yasamal District close to the metro station İnşaatçılar. All in all, the house is inhabited by fourteen tenants, among them three male students who share one room, a family from Moldova, and some others whom Günay hardly knows. The tenants pay for their room but on each level they share the kitchen, bathroom, and toilet. Such housing arrangements have become increasingly common in recent years especially among students, low-skilled workers, migrants, and others who have to balance their housing needs and limited financial resources. A prominent example of this development is the area around İnşaatçılar in the city's western part including the Dağlı neighbourhoods. Usually, such housing is densely populated and people often live there without being registered because the owners try to bypass the payment of taxes and local fees that are set based on the number of registered inhabitants. For many homeowners it also has become a profitable business to partly rent out their property. Some, like Nazim's landlord, are even constructing houses, often below security standards and equipped with only improvised and unfinished installations, explicitly to rent out. Such low-status housing is regarded by tenants as a temporary solution. Günay told me:

You know, we could live in a better place but we prefer to save as
much money as possible for buying our own house as soon as
possible. Renting an apartment is not comprehensible for my
parents. They would like us again to live with my parents-in-law.
For them it is hard to see their only daughter not being housed
properly after marriage. In Azerbaijan, owning the place where you
live is considered a must. Well, after some really hard time they
finally accepted our decision.

Actually, Günay's parents themselves were struggling to ensure proper
housing for their sons. Her parents, together with their two sons and the
older son's wife, live near İnşaatçılar, too, ten-minutes walking distance
from Günay. It is usually her mother who takes care of Günay's five-year-
old son during the day, thus enabling both spouses to work. I asked Günay
why her married brother does not have a separate apartment and whether he
and his wife plan to move out before the younger brother marries. She
answered that her family did not have the financial means to buy a house at
the time of the older brother's marriage. Now, as they have the resources,
they want to buy an apartment for their younger son. They plan to sell their
present house in Baku and buy two houses near the city of Sumqayıt instead.
One is intended for their younger son and his future family, the other one for
themselves and their older son's family.

Then Günay started to laugh. 'Actually this isn't right and not
according to our tradition'. She explained that her younger brother was very
smart and 'had spent some time' already in Russia. But her older brother was
the contrary, and despite being married was interested in other women and
would follow often the wrong track. That is why her parents want him to
stay living in their house. 'This is the only reason for such an arrangement',
she said, 'my mother would actually prefer to stay with my younger brother,
but she'll do differently only to have some control over the other one'.
Günay's story illustrates well not only the patriarchal bargain of the young
couple with their parents, but the latters' capacity to bargain and negotiate
within the constraints of traditional ideas. In these linked families, the
daughters-in-law are also valued enough that their interests are also
considered and protected. In terms of living arrangements, it demonstrates
the flexibility which is applied against the background of everyday
challenges. Similar dynamics of patriarchal bargain can be observed in the
following example but from a male perspective.

Anar (b. 1978) enjoys the privilege of coming from a well-off family
background. His father has a high position at the State Oil Company of the
Azerbaijan Republic (SOCAR), the successor of Azneft, where he
'organised' a well-paid accountant job for his son. Anar studied economics

and spent three years working in Texas. Due to this experience in a foreign country, he said, he became more critical and reflective towards the cultural peculiarities of his home country. He asserted a largely autonomous life from parental control, which, however, came from a long troublesome process to make his parents accept his 'individual lifestyle'. Even before marriage, and rather unusually for local standards, he lived in a separate apartment which was owned by his father. Interestingly, he always spoke of it as his own apartment, indicating that he could dispose of it as he wished, despite the fact that his father was the legal owner. Regarding the strategy of hoarding and housing as a collective resource of families mentioned earlier, this is a further example how, in everyday perception and practice, distinctions between use-rights and legal ownership are of secondary importance. The distinction appears primarily with conflicts in the social relations between the people involved. For Anar, living independently was a crucial value that he emphasised on several occasions, like in the following case:

> I want to be independent and enjoy my *own* life before I get married. One friend of mine got married when he was 21. He never had a life on his own as is the case with most young Azerbaijanis. Between the ages of 20 and 25 your life is determined by the topic of marriage. I first want to live my own life and earn some money before I think seriously about marriage.

However, in other contexts, he was less successful at resisting parental control. While living in Texas, he thought about staying there for good. However, it was his mother who persistently tried to dissuade him from the idea. Finally, he received a call from his father saying that his mother was seriously ill and that he should return home urgently. From other relatives, he learned that his mother was not ill, but he decided to return anyway out of respect for his mother's desperate feelings. This incident can be extended by another example which demonstrates not only Anar's ambiguous approach to 'individual freedom' but also the subtle symbolic violence (Bourdieu 2001) of patriarchal ideas:

> When I marry there will be the usual *elçilik*. Although it has a rather formal character, I feel obliged to follow our tradition first and foremost out of respect [*hörmət*] for my parents. Not to do so would be considered disrespectful not only by my parents, my relatives, but by myself too.

He continued to talk about the different value of family in Azerbaijan and Western countries which offered a very contrary approach to the freedom he emphasised in other contexts:

> I know that my attitude towards family life is kind of conservative. I
> don't like the European family model with one or two children while
> not even being married. Also, the lack of respect and commitments
> of children towards their parents I consider uncivilised.

When talking about women and gender relations, Anar strongly emphasised
the value of *hörmət*. His understanding of this notion, as involving respect
and honour, was explained in a way that resembled many similar accounts
from my male informants:

> In Azerbaijan, most men think that women should not work, drive a
> car, or deal with money. Instead, a woman should take care of the
> home and the family. This has nothing to do with domination but
> with respect [*hörmət*]. It is a sign of respect towards women, if men
> feel responsible for these issues. It actually expresses that a woman
> enjoys a much higher status than a man in our society. You know,
> working, driving, earning money are extremely stressful activities
> and it is a man's duty to protect his wife from such stress. This is
> also why women become older than men. Now there is the tendency
> that a lot of women want to lower themselves down to men by
> engaging in similar activities. I, personally, find that problematic. I
> want my future wife to enjoy the privilege of staying home, not
> having to work but instead taking care of my children.

For Anar this interpretation appears perfectly rational although it stands in
stark contrast to the Soviet state's ideology on the equal role of women in
society. In Anar's case, it does not seem that Soviet ideology was able to
replace traditional gender roles in the long run but merely constituted their
supplement in the disguise of modernisation discourse. The well-described
phenomenon of Soviet women's 'double burden' is an expression of such
developments.

My previous examples focused on aspects of how generations
negotiate everyday life against the ideals and values of a supposed traditional
lifestyle. My final example is less about the patriarchal bargain and more
about economic patriarchy and the strong emotional attachment in which
such kin-ideology is embedded – thus providing a fuller picture of how
patriarchy works on the ground.

Elbəy, whom I introduced previously was married to his wife at the
age of nineteen, a process which was largely directed by the young spouses'
parents. Living in Baku, but being originally from the town of Sabirabad, the
family has a rural background and entertains a strong and intimate
relationship with their local kin and community. According to Elbəy, there
was no question that his wife's family would be from the same region of
origin – a marriage preference that is commonly practiced in Azerbaijan. It is

a high value to marry a member of one's imagined 'local community' (*yerli camaat*), and Elbəy's family was in a position to assure such a marriage. Some time previously, Elbəy's father bought hectares of land and constructed large cowsheds in order to start a cattle-breeding business. The business was successful, and Elbəy's own high social and economic status and affluent lifestyle are essentially connected to his father's network and economic success. His father, too, was responsible for almost every crucial decision in Elbəy's life – something Elbəy did not perceive as control but rather as an admirable and respect-worthy achievement. This became comprehensible to me when Elbəy talked about his father as we were sitting in his car and enjoying the view over Baku from a parking place near the Baku TV Tower:

> There in Sabirabad, where my father constructed the cowsheds, I will breed cattle. I am doing that for him because his heart is devoted to his village but he doesn't have the energy and health anymore to engage in it himself. And although I would rather like to invest my time in starting a new business in İçəri Şəhər, I am ready to give that up for now.[82] My father wants me to focus instead on the agricultural business in our home-region. Thus, I thought of buying one hundred cows but for this I need experts who are not available here. Maybe you can recruit some people from Croatia or Germany who know all the procedures and who are able to supervise a *cadre* and to teach their knowledge to my people. They do not have to care for anything like food, car, living, good payment. I will provide them with everything. I have the money. My father isn't a millionaire but he is rich. Nevertheless, he is a *prostoi chelovek* [ordinary person]. You know, he bought me the latest Mercedes while he himself is driving an old Lada. He has been working all of his life, he earned *everything* on his own. He has two sons, he built a house for each of them and he married them successfully. He reached everything! But he cannot do without work and this is why he still works in his office until ten p.m. every day. Five years ago, he built all this agricultural infrastructure in his village. He loves his homeland [Az. *vətən*] and he wants it to prosper. So, it is my job to take care of that now. I do it for his well-being. I want him to feel good. You know, I never worked the way my father did. But I have been to a lot of places that he never got to know. I've been fifteen times to Europe, twenty times to Turkey, to Dubai and other places. And I have money. Already my grandfather was such a person. God loved him [*Allah*

---

[82] He once told me about a possibility to acquire real estate in İçəri Şəhər through his network. He wanted to buy there in order to open a restaurant.

onu sevirdi]. He reached everything in his life. I want to continue this tradition.

This very emotional account reflects the emic perspective of what Joseph has described as 'economic patriarchy' (1996: 15). Elbǝy's reference to his grandfather and constant praising of his father is embedded into the cultural ideology of the *nǝsil*. On a broader comparative level, such an ideology has been described recently by anthropologists as gendered memory within patrilines by introducing the concept of 'lineal masculinity' (King and Stone 2010). It describes a 'concept of (bio)cultural reproduction that [...] flows through time, through males to successive generations. Only sons pass it on' (King and Stone 2010: 323). Most important in the present context is that 'Each individual man builds on, maintains, or diminishes whatever lineal masculinity he has received from his lineage (most directly, his father)' (ibid.). On the level of cultural ideas regarding patrilineal descent, the concept encompasses identity categories like property, inheritance practices, and citizenship (ibid. 324). Although the aspect of time is central to their argument, the authors of the article overlook the important role of states and their identity politics of cultural nationalisation, which is of primary importance in the post-Soviet context, as I will show in the following.

Patriarchy and the State

Having come to Baku for doing fieldwork in Autumn 2013, the city was plastered with election posters for the upcoming presidential election on 9 October. (Unsurprisingly, the ruling New Azerbaijan Party (Yeni Azǝrbaycan Partiyası) of the President won with nearly 85 per cent of votes while the candidate of the united opposition parties, who recently joined under the name National Council of Democratic Forces, as well as the candidates of eight other parties, officially shared the rest). The seemingly democratic elections must have reminded many critics of a *pokazukha* deliberately staged by the government. However, the public representation of the president strongly connects to the country's recent history since independence, and to traditional role models and loyalties in family life. On my regular bus rides to the centre, one election poster stood out. On the background it depicted a map of the country, implicitly reminding the viewer of the decade-long territorial conflict with neighbouring Armenia, and appealing to each citizen's patriotism and national duty to support the New Azerbaijan Party. Further emphasis on the nation is added by the colours of the flag. The three lines written on the poster read: *sǝnin ailǝn, sǝnin vǝtǝnin, sǝnin prezidentin* (your family, your homeland, your president).

Plate 19. Election poster of the ruling New Azerbaijan Party during presidential elections in 2013.

That kinship and gender ideologies can serve as a powerful tool in the construction of national identities and state-citizen relationships has been well studied by anthropologists and others (e.g. Connor 1994; Delaney 1995; Joseph 1997; Yuval-Davis 1997; Bryant 2002). Usually, such values are seemingly constructed by the involved actors in an ahistorical way that makes them appear as eternal cultural givens. However, with regard to masculine domination, Pierre Bourdieu rightly states that 'what appears, in history, as being eternal is merely the product of a labour of eternalisation performed by interconnected institutions such as the family, the church, the state, [or] the educational system' (Bourdieu 2001: viii). The same holds true for patriarchy.

Though the Soviet state aimed to eradicate patriarchy, at least in its most simplified understanding as the domination of men over women, today, the socialist endeavour seems rather suspect. What could it have achieved if we look at 'the impressive speed and relative ease with which Soviet-era pronouncements and policies concerning gender equality were superseded by conservative gender ideologies in post-Soviet states' (Kandiyoti 2007: 602)? Instead of interpreting these current trends as being limited to ideologies of gender by overemphasising the changing social articulation of women's role alone, I want to shift attention to patriarchal ideology in a rather inclusive sense that exerts nuanced power on people across gender and age in everyday social, economic, political and other contexts. And although, the Soviets tried to do away with what they thought of 'patriarchy', many facets of this ideology (role expectations, support models, economic and moral responsibilities, and others) was not far at all from the just emerging shape of Soviet society and its welfare state. Thus, throughout the Soviet Union notions of patriarchy were constantly present and made the (re)appearance of 'patriarchy' so vivid in democratic nationalism. This provides a more comprehensive explanation as it accordingly includes men in the overall picture. Moreover, we know that the 'socialist paternalism' aimed towards gender equality was ambivalent.

This ideology in present Azerbaijan I see corresponding to Joseph's terms of *political patriarchy*. This kind of patriarchy is characteristic of states in which '[K]inship is central to the political system' and where 'the family, not the individual, is the basic unit of society'. Further, [B]y declaring the responsibility of the state to preserve the family as the basis of the nation, the constitutions use the family as the recruiting and training ground for citizenship' (1996: 16).

Azerbaijan's former president Heydar Aliyev came to power again in 1993. Before he was appointed, under Brezhnev, as First Secretary of the Central Committee of the Communist Party of Azerbaijan in 1969, he had been the deputy chairman of the Azerbaijani KGB and then its chairman (from 1967). In 1982 he became a member of the Politburo in Moscow. Today he is widely referred to by the Azerbaijani people as Heydər Baba (Grandfather Heydər). He fostered patriarchal and familial notions of the young nation and established his image as the father and saviour of the nation. The personality cult around his person is promoted actively and enacted in public state rituals under the government of Aliyev's son Ilham, who followed his father's footsteps as president in 2003 (for details see Roth 2013; Aivazishvili-Gehne 2018). In his humbly translated biography on the Heydar Aliyev Heritage International Online Library it is written that the:

> Historical destiny of Azerbaijan [...] was inseparably linked with the name of Heydar Aliyev. Revival in these years in all the spheres of socio-political, economic, and cultural life is connected just with his name. [...] Heydar Aliyev helped his native Azerbaijan, he persistently strived for progress. He was always proud of the rich culture and great historical past of the country. He was concerned about the future generations and made Azerbaijan overcome hard and terrible ordeals of time. Being an outstanding politician and statesman, indisputable leader of the nation, he was a live legend [...]. Heydar Aliyev, seeing the misfortune of his nation, accepted

the invitation and returned to great politics in Azerbaijan. People welcomed his return with hope and joy, and this day went down into history of the independent Azerbaijan as the Day of National Salvation.[83]

Like a responsible family father, he embodies the moral values and duty to care, to protect and to support his children (i.e. the people). Such implicit patriarchal notions of kinship in post-Soviet Azerbaijan became not only central to state-citizenship relations, but the family became defined as the basic unit of society in Article 17 of the Constitution. Furthermore, state institutions actively promote the role and responsibilities of the family. For instance, the State Committee for Family, Women, and Children's Affairs describes its main objectives and functions as, first, increasing the role of the family in society; second, the protection and promotion of national and moral values; third, passing them from generation to generation; and, fourth, the psychological preparation of young people to family life.[84] The committee's internet site is adorned with Heydər Aliyev's photograph and his aphorisms such as 'We should try to bring up our youth on the basis of moral national traditions of the Azerbaijani nation'. However, the promotion of such national values increasingly imparts and legitimates patriarchal practices and gender inequality in state institutions and the domestic sphere which, according to one of my informants in her forties who works for an NGO, represented a counter-development when compared to Soviet times:

> Today, national and moral values have become very different from Soviet times. With regard to equal treatment and the protection of civil rights there was always the possibility to write a complaint to the Communist Party in Baku or to the highest instance in Moscow. For instance, a man had to be more careful in how he treated his wife as she potentially could write a letter of complaint to responsible state ministries. This was a sensitive issue because when people used to get a job they had to submit an autobiography in which it was categorically indicated whether a person was married and morally stable. Being morally stable meant to be a good and stable family man. In case there was any official complaint in a person's autobiography, then he couldn't get a good job. I have lived in the Soviet Union and compared to now I can definitely say that there were much less traditional elements.

Such statement on a policy that promotes conservative family values as national-cultural mentality is accompanied by the contradiction of continuously cutting down citizens' former entitlements to social services,

---

[83] See http://lib.aliyevheritage.org/en/2169646.html. Last accessed 27 February 2016.

[84] See http://scfwca.gov.az/?cat=36&lang=en. Last accessed 17 September 2015.

health care, and state welfare – responsibilities which are increasingly outsourced to families. In practice this means that:

> The state utilized Azerbaijan's familial tradition to justify low levels of wages and social security, upholding the idea that nobody was completely on his or her own, and that if everyone in a family 'brought in a little' there now would be 'enough for all' (Rzayeva 2013: 57).

Although this has happened in all other post-Soviet republics as well, Azerbaijan is particular because it 'is underspending on public health care in the context of sufficient resources for allocation. [...] Ironically, in 2005 only one country in all of the former Soviet Union (Tajikistan) spent less on health care than oil-rich Azerbaijan' (Rzayeva 2013: 36). Although the health budget did rise significantly between 2007 and 2014, it remains low in comparison to the country's GDP (World Bank Group 2015: 7).

The state's increasing withdrawal from obligations that were once the defining characteristic of socialist welfare and its outsourcing to families constitute a paradox between the way state-citizen relations are promoted and articulated under the concept of nation and the factual support that the state provides on an everyday basis. While the low state performance with regard to the latter is perceived critically by many who nostalgically remember Soviet welfare, the institution and person of the president is, nevertheless, perceived by many as representing the ideals of a protective and supportive household head and father. In Chapter 2, I described the protests in Sovetski for fairer compensations by the government. I explained my observation that many were holding up photographs of Heydar and Ilham Aliyev in the hope that the president would bring justice to their unheard case.

In a way, this represents an inverted continuity of Kandiyoti's 'Soviet paradox' by which she referred to the 'combined and contradictory operations of a socialist paternalism' (2007: 602). While the Soviets supported and legitimated gender equality, other approaches like the 'command economy and nationalities policy [...] effectively stalled processes of social transformation commonly associated with modernity' (ibid.). In contemporary Azerbaijan, we encounter a similar paradox in relation to the representation of a modern nation: a patriarchal state whose authorities support and foster 'traditional' kinship and gender ideologies embedded in notions of solidarity, support, care, and loyalty as parts of 'cultural' and national identity. This also serves to legitimate a political system where wealth can be acquired by a few elite families following these principles in economic terms. For most others, loyalty and solidarity among kin is a requirement for facing economic uncertainties. The paradox is that, at the same time, the elite's politics and economic interests hinder the state from providing the deserved care to its citizens as members of the national family.

In the Soviet period, part of the modernising agenda towards gender equality was traded-off in the challenges of planned economy and nationality policy. Today, the government forgets about its cultural-national responsibilities: it promotes a father-state but does not reciprocate the loyalty it demands from its citizens in terms of national-territorial conflicts. The architectural display and future-oriented international representation follows the logics of different façade politics described in this book.

Conclusion

One of the aims in this chapter was to show that people's contemporary notions of property and their practices with regard to housing often contradict the legal framework that was established in the context of housing privatisation. Property is embedded within historically and 'traditionally' informed experiences and policies that made housing the primary device for distributing social entitlement and which strongly influences social relationships among family members. I partly agreed with other authors that, due to housing privatisation, patriarchal structures and parental control over that resource were increasing. Privatisation played an important role but not the only one. Another important factor was people's increasing lack of secure and well-paid employment. This is why housing for many households became the main source and most important basis for household security after the economic and political transformations in the 1990s. It constituted the major and sometimes the only asset in a new context where the state does not provide security in housing, employment, or income as in the past. Another important aspect to consider when talking about property in today's Azerbaijan was the concept of patriarchy which is not only about exerting power and control over the 'dominated' but that such power can be equally challenging for the 'dominators' as they, too, are influenced in their decisions by the very same patriarchal ideology. After socialism, the increased reliance on kin for housing, education, social services, and marriage partly reinforced patriarchal aspects in different spheres of everyday life. Patriarchy, I have argued, cannot be reduced to male domination but entails a variety of differing patriarchies in which implicit power relations are recognised and acknowledged by members of society because they constitute the moral order that became part of post-Soviet national ideology. Such processes of diffuse social, economic, and political patriarchy are enhanced not only through privatisation and generations' differential access to housing as a resource, but by the active promotion of traditional values by state representatives in bureaucratic and governmental institutions. My examples have also shown that there is great variation in how families deal with conflicting interests, and that patriarchal control appears in different forms and various disguises. Depriving others from legal rights and protection, registration politics, and engaging in fraud and blackmail to enforce individuals' and families' entitlements were among the rather extreme examples. But diverging interests surrounding marriage and housing are a common thing to deal with and are often negotiated in light of the several challenges of everyday life, even as they are usually embedded in commonly shared notions of traditional patterns and moral standards.

Chapter 7
Conclusions

This work has dealt with the role of housing in people's everyday life and its significance as a socio-cultural, economic, political, legal, and moral phenomenon in Baku's past and present. Due to these multiple dimensions of the house, one of my aims was to show that urban housing has been of primary importance in shaping the relations and interactions between families, citizens, the urban community, and the state. The different material and immaterial qualities and other relevant spheres of housing which I described in this book, such as architecture, ideology, modernity, the allocation of and access to housing, inequalities, state-citizens-interactions, bureaucracy, cosmology, family, marriage, support, morality, privacy, home-making, domestic display, property, and patriarchy are by no means exhaustive. But they suggest that the house/ home stands empirically and analytically at the crossroads of multiple phenomena of interest to social anthropologists and others. Therefore, I am advocating the heuristic value of approaching the house as a 'total social fact' (Mauss 1966 [1925]). Especially in the post-Soviet context, where the housing question has been transformed from being a state responsibility towards becoming a private responsibility in the contemporary market economy, it is of special relevance to look at how people's experiences of a past housing regime relate to the wider contemporary social, economic, and political developments in Azerbaijan. Each chapter has focused on different aspects of the house's totality and how it embodies different politics of representation.

During the Soviet period, some distinct neighbourhoods stood in sharp contrast to the Soviet modernisation discourse, housing policy, and politics of representation. The houses, vernacular architecture, and neighbourhoods of the 'other Baku' which challenged the official modernisation discourse had a strong impact on how their residents were represented in public, as both their material and social make-up were perceived by state and citizens alike as the ideological 'other' (Chapter 2). Throughout the Soviet period, housing became constitutive for collective 'socialist' identities, but at the same time represented spatial and social inequalities. As access to and allocation of housing were connected primarily to differently valued occupations and institutions, differentiated spatial patterns and inequalities in urban areas became inevitable (Chapter 3). Additionally, the Bolsheviks' demunicipalisation campaign in the early 1920s rather accidently reinforced spatial inequalities. Houses that were not of appropriate size and quality could be regained as private property by the previous owners. Homeowners could not anticipate the disadvantages that the return of this property would mean in the long run. The state control over building material and its continuous scarcity made the issue of maintaining privately owned houses a constant concern to dwellers. As my archival material demonstrated, people mobilised networks of kin and other trusted people, and applied various informal strategies to access housing and other related resources. In that regard, my material also pointed to the ambivalent role of state representatives, since housing authorities were often embedded in various relations within their local community. Thus, they had to negotiate, constantly, their loyalties to the state and to their private networks, which entailed the constant risk of being sanctioned by higher authorities. Citizens found ways to deploy the state's official propiska-regime in order to access the city, to obtain housing and work, and generally to increase their chances for receiving a separate apartment, especially since the 1960s. As I showed, people were often registered in different places than those in which they actually lived, hoping this would raise their family's chance for obtaining better housing. It constituted part of the long-term strategies by families and kin groups to secure and hoard the state housing which was inevitably perceived as a necessary requirement for marriage and the establishment of independent households in the younger generation. At the same time, marriage itself only legitimated access to separate housing and more autonomy from the parental household. Interestingly, this mutual relation between housing and marriage had long been part of pre-Soviet cosmology which, in principle, was equally applied by the Soviet state and the allocation of urban housing. In addition, the chronic public discourse of housing shortage reified and enhanced citizens' awareness for the scarcest but most valuable resource and fostered people's strategies for improving accommodation against the background of housing's socio-cultural and moral embeddedness.

With regard to the latter, the house reproduces the social and symbolic order of what is locally perceived as being associated with cultural and national values (Chapter 4). Here, the house at the same time includes notions of home; both notions are inextricably linked and brought together in the local concept *ev* which I have argued is only created by the ritual of marriage that unites the gendered aspects of one single concept. These gendered aspects of *ev* are symbolised by the gendered classes of gifts (house and dowry) provided for the young family by the bride's and bridegroom's family respectively. Such gift-giving expresses symbolically that only through marriage a house becomes a proper home and, last but not least, a family.

It is one thing to obtain a house or apartment, but making it a home is another. Hence, notions of home and materiality not only play an important role in local conceptualisations of gender, space, and privacy but also in practices of consumption, status, and impression management (Chapter 5). Thresholds that separate the private home from the public – such as walls, gates, doors, and curtains – not only protect the privacy of the home but equally display dwellers' aspirations towards status and impression management to the outside world. A distinctive feature here is the curtain (*pərdə*). Being not only an essential element of a proper home, it further constitutes a culturally-specific metaphor for appropriate and respectful ways of social interaction within the family as well as with the outside world. 'Maintaining the curtain' (*pərdə saxlamaq*) stands for people's constant concern to uphold family reputation within the community and structures interaction between people of different gender, age, and status. Embedded in notions of respect (*hörmət*), maintaining the curtain in social settings represents a skilful and mutually acknowledged negotiation of what has to remain unspoken and secret. Another issue I have discussed in that context are home-making activities and the importance that people attach to home renovations (*remont*) – a common practice all across the Soviet successor states, which, as I have argued, is significantly related to the socialist past and people's experiences of shortage amidst the state's approach towards socialist mass consumption in the late Soviet Union. Not only can home-making be interpreted as a person's striving for social distinction. As I demonstrated, such practices are deeply embedded in people's understanding and concerns for marriage, dowry, and hospitality – and these provide additional motivations for transforming domestic space into a home. These processes have been hardly acknowledged in home-making literature on socialist times.

By using the key-concepts of property and patriarchy, I have discussed finally how citizens' customary notions and practices of transferring ownership and property have contributed to increasingly patriarchal structures in family and society after privatisation. Social inequalities and potential conflicts were latent issues as privatisation turned housing into the most important and, sometimes, the only noteworthy asset or base that families had in times of economic and political uncertainty

(Chapter 6). It showed that entitlements to ownership were usually distributed and negotiated among family members in ways significantly different from the state laws on housing privatisation. This led, in some cases, to conflicts over and contestations of ownership rights which were also caused by bureaucratic hurdles due to people's informal registration practices in Soviet times that basically defined who was eligible to inherit use-rights over housing. Patriarchal biases, which have experienced a heyday under Azerbaijan's authoritarian post-Soviet government, have reinforced the power of traditional and national values and led to discrimination and everyday inequalities in the domestic sphere but also in encounters with state institutions.

One aim of this book was to contribute to postsocialist scholarship on urban transformation by focusing on the house as a heuristic category. From the outset, such an approach requires an inclusive perspective because as a *total social institution*, the house and therefore anthropological research unites aspects of social, economic, and political anthropology. Hence, I aimed at demonstrating the relevance and total (or holistic) character of houses and at demonstrating their applicability and explanatory value in (post)socialist urban contexts. By applying concepts and arguments by anthropologists having worked in very different temporal and spatial contexts than my own, I aimed at providing a fresh look and alternative way to explain dynamics of housing under post-Soviet conditions. A reconsideration of Lévi-Strauss's concept of house societies and a comparison with the Soviet housing regime enabled insights into the role of marriage, kinship, and affinity with regard to issues of solidarity and cooperation in hoarding and transmitting ownership and use-rights in urban contexts. In socialist state housing, it was not the inhabitants who owned property but the state. Nevertheless, a household's main tenant could ensure continuity of collective entitlements and use-rights to a dwelling by bequeathing his status to one of the co-registered household members. Although this was normatively considered to follow the paternal line (kinship/ descent), in practice such continuity could be upheld equally through marriage relations (affinity). Because unclaimed dwellings would fall back automatically to the state's disposal, dwellers ensured the continuity of their entitlements by whatever means were available, kinship or affinity. But legally, entitlements were connected to dwellings and not to people – a long lasting principle that has changed with housing privatisation. The strategic importance of family ties, whether based on descent or alliance, was essential in claiming, reproducing, and increasing the resource of urban accommodation.

This book therefore also addresses the crucial question of how families experienced and coped with the Soviet housing regime and its transformation from a socialist planned economy to a neoliberal market economy. Beyond that, it looks to re-examining the question of how successful the Soviet state and its modernisation efforts were in transforming prevalent notions, practices, and loyalties of family and kinship, as well as gender (i.e. 'patriarchy'). I have argued that, similar to what has been said for rural contexts, urban family solidarities were not weakened but reinforced during the Soviet past (Kandiyoti 1996). To 'cultivate kin' became among the most important strategies for families to cope with shortage and to prevent dwellings falling back to the state's disposal (Dragadze 2001 [1988]). At least in the sphere of housing, local ideas of kinship were strengthened because mobilising kin in urban contexts gained importance for family's housing security and access to other welfare benefits. Hence, the local importance of family, housing, and the norms of post-marital residence with their associated moral values have not diminished. According to what others have demonstrated in regard to the seemingly competing identities of being 'Soviet' and 'Muslim', there were no contradictions. Instead, each role had its own space (Tohidi 1996; Abashin 2014). What has significantly changed, though, is the state's active promotion of 'traditional' family values as part of national identity. First, these values, raised to the political level, serve to increase the loyalty of citizens to a patriarchal and authoritarian state by embedding the latter in highly valued notions of kinship. Second, the official promotion of these values naturalises the new role and responsibility of the family in matters of support, care, finding work, and – most important – housing, which were previously provided by the Soviet state (Chapter 6). Thus, present notions of modernity have shifted significantly from a focus on state welfare for citizens towards an emphasis on the national representation of progress and wealth increasingly uncoupled from most citizens' social and economic conditions (Chapter 2).

On a more general level this book has dealt with a range of phenomena described as 'politics of (mis)representation' or 'façade politics' in past and present Baku. Based on the notion of Potemkin villages (*Potemkinskie derevni*), its historical and social dynamics, I described tensions in the sphere of architecture, bureaucratic institutions, and social life between official public representation and the everyday realities that unfold behind the façade politics. In different contexts, I have introduced and discussed the related concepts of the Potemkin city, papereality, *pərdə*, and *pokazukha*. All these practices are characterised by what others have called the 'Potemkin village dilemma' that 'exposed the Soviet urge to plan, limit, and control what visitors did and saw' while the latter where well aware of and only expected to be presented 'Potemkin villages' (David-Fox 2012: 126). With regard to the material presented in this book, the same can be said for the interactions between state and citizens and between people within social communities in that the play with façades can be understood as an open secret between the involved parties. The concealed but open secret links the construction and renovation of architectural façades in the Potemkin city of Baku, *papereality* in the bureaucratic processes of socialist allocation of resources and housing, and the management of *pərdə* in people's daily interactions. In the end, politics of misrepresentation in the spirit of Potemkin villages have gained new relevance in the present international political landscapes. Negotiations about what is fake, or real, or revitalised have again entered political and social life. And new technologies of communication and impression management have shifted further the previously established relation between displayed and concealed realities in people's daily life around the globe.

Bibliography

Aalbers, M. B., and B. Christophers. 2014. Centring Housing in Political Economy. *Housing, Theory and Society* 31 (4): 373–394.

Abashin, S. 2014. A Prayer for Rain: Practicing Being Soviet and Muslim. *Journal of Islamic Studies* 25 (2): 178–200.

Abrahamian, L. 2007. Troubles and Hopes – Armenian Family, Home and Nation. In T. Darieva, and W. Kaschuba (eds.), *Representations on the Margins of Europe: Politics and Identities in the Baltic and South Caucasian States*, pp. 267–281. Frankfurt/M.: Campus.

Adams, L. 2010. *The Spectacular State: Culture and National Identity in Uzbekistan*. Durham: Duke University Press.

Aivazishvili-Gehne, N. 2018. "Der Staat ist der Präsident": Ingiloer und öffentliche Zeremonien in Aserbaidschan. *Paideuma* 64: 27–50.

Akiner, S. 1997. Between Tradition and Modernity: The Dilemma Facing Contemporary Central Asian Women. In M. Buckley (ed.), *Post-Soviet Women: From the Baltic to Central Asia*, pp. 261–304. Cambridge: Cambridge University Press.

Alexander, C. 2009. Privatization: Jokes, Scandal, and Absurdity in a Time of Rapid Change. In K. Sykes (ed.), *Ethnographies of Moral Reasoning: Living Paradoxes of a Global Age*, pp. 43–65. New York: Palgrave Macmillan.

------. 2012. Remont: Work in Progress. In C. Alexander, and J. Reno (eds.), *Economies of Recycling: The Global Transformation of Materials, Values and Social Relations*, pp. 255–275. London: Zed Books.

Alexander, C., V. Buchli, and C. Humphrey (eds.). 2007. *Urban Life in Post-Soviet Asia*. London: University College London Press.

Alexander, C., M. Hojer, and I. Koch. 2018. Political Economy Comes Home: On the Moral Economies of Housing. *Critique of Anthropology* 38 (2): 121–139.

Aliyeva, A. 1979. Kharakter razvitiia zhilishchnogo stroitel'stva v gorode Baku (The Character of Housing Construction Development in the City of Baku). In K. D. Kerimov et al. (eds.), *Sbornik materialov konferentsii molodykh uchenykh: Aktual'nye problemy razvitiia arkhitektury i iskusstva Azerbaidzhana* (Collection of Materials from the Conference of Young Scientists: Actual Problems of the Development of Architecture and Art in Azerbaijan), pp. 65–73. Baku: Elm.

Allina-Pisano, J. 2008. *The Post-Soviet Potemkin Village: Politics and Property Rights in the Black Earth*. Cambridge: Cambridge University Press.

Altstadt, A. 1992. *The Azerbaijani Turks: Power and Identity under Russian Rule*. Stanford: Hoover Institution Press.

Amin, A. 2014. Lively Infrastructure. *Theory, Culture & Society* 31 (7/8): 137–161.

Andrusz, G. 1984. *Housing and Urban Development in the USSR*. Houndmills: Macmillan.

------. 1990. A Note on the Financing of Housing in the Soviet Union. *Soviet Studies* 42 (3): 555–570.

------. 2002. Cooperatives and the Legacy of State Socialism. In D. Lane (ed.), *The Legacy of State Socialism and the Future of Transformation*, pp. 127–146. Lanham: Rowman & Littlefield Publishers.

Ashurbeili, S. 1992. *Istoriia goroda Baku. Period srednevekov'ia* (History of Baku. The Medieval Period). Baku: Azerneshr.

Attwood, L. 2010. *Gender and Housing in Soviet Russia: Private Life in Public Space*. Manchester: Manchester University Press.

Auch, E.-M. 2004. *Muslim–Untertan–Bürger: Identitätswandel in gesellschaftlichen Transformationsprozessen der muslimischen Ostprovinz Südkaukasiens (Ende 18. – Anfang 20. Jh.)*. Wiesbaden: Reichert.

Baberowski, J. 2003. *Der Feind ist überall: Stalinismus im Kaukasus*. München: Deutsche Verlags-Anstalt.

Baiar, O., and R. Blashkevich. 1962. *Kvartira i ego ubranstvo* (The Apartment and its Decoration). Moscow: Akademiia Stroitel'stva i Arkhitektury SSSR.

Barrett, T. 2014. Notes on the Moral Economy of Gas in Present-Day Azerbaijan. *Central Asian Survey* 33 (4): 517–530.

------. 2016. *Political Economy and Social Transformation in Baku, Azerbaijan*. Ph.D. dissertation, University of Cambridge.

Barry, D. 1969. Housing in the USSR: Cities and Towns. *Problems of Communism* 18 (3): 1–11.

------. 1977. Soviet Housing Law: The Norms and their Application. In D. Barry, G. Ginsburg, and P. Maggs (eds.), *Soviet Law after Stalin, Part I: The Citizen and the State in Contemporary Soviet Law*, pp. 1–32. Leyden: A. W. Sijthoff.

Bater, J. 1984. The Soviet City: Continuity and Change in Privilege and Place. In J. Agnew, J. Mercer, and D. Sopher (eds.), *The City in Cultural Context*, pp. 134–162. Boston: Allen & Unwin.

Beechey, V. 1979. On Patriarchy. *Feminist Review* 3 (1): 66–82.

Benda-Beckmann, F. von, K. von Benda-Beckmann, and M. Wiber. 2006. The Properties of Property. In F. von Benda-Beckmann, K. von

Benda-Beckmann, and M. Wiber (eds.), *Changing Properties of Property*, pp. 1–39. New York: Berghahn.

Berdahl, D., M. Bunzl, and M. Lampland (eds.). 2000. *Altering States: Ethnographies of Transition in Eastern Europe and the Former Soviet Union*. Ann Arbor: University of Michigan Press.

Beyer, J., and P. Finke. 2019. Practices of Traditionalization in Central Asia. *Central Asian Survey* 38 (3): 310–328.

Birdwell-Pheasant, D., and D. Lawrence-Zúñiga. 1999. Introduction: Houses and Families in Europe. In D. Birdwell-Pheasant, and D. Lawrence-Zúñiga (eds.), *House Life: Space, Place and Family in Europe*, pp. 1–35. Oxford: Berg.

Bissenova, A. 2014. The Master Plan of Astana: Between the 'Art of Government' and the 'Art of Being Global'. In M. Reeves, J. Rasanayagam, and J. Beyer (eds.), *Ethnographies of the State in Central Asia: Performing Politics*, pp. 127–148. Bloomington: Indiana University Press.

Bloch, M., and J. Parry. 1989. Introduction: Money and the Morality of Exchange. In J. Parry, and M. Bloch (eds.), *Money and the Morality of Exchange*, pp. 1–32. Cambridge: Cambridge University Press.

Bourdieu, P. 1976 [1972]. *Entwurf einer Theorie der Praxis auf der ethnologischen Grundlage der kabylischen Gesellschaft*. Frankfurt/Main: Suhrkamp.

—. 2001. *Masculine Domination*. Stanford: Stanford University Press.

Bouzarovski, S., J. Salukvadze, and M. Gentile. 2011. A Socially Resilient Urban Transition? The Contested Landscapes of Apartment Building Extensions in Two Post-Communist Cities. *Urban Studies* 48 (13): 2689–2714.

Boym, S. 1994. *Common Places: Mythologies of Everyday Life in Russia*. Cambridge: Harvard University Press.

Bray, F. 1997. *Technology and Gender: Fabrics of Power in Late Imperial China*. Berkeley: University of California Press.

Bridger, S., and F. Pine (eds.). 1998. *Surviving Post-Socialism: Local Strategies and Regional Responses in Eastern Europe and the Former Soviet Union*. London: Routledge.

Broudehoux, A.-M. 2007. Spectacular Beijing: The Conspicuous Construction of an Olympic Metropolis. *Journal of Urban Affairs* 29 (4): 383–399.

Brumfield, W., and B. Ruble (eds.). 1994. *Russian Housing in the Modern Age: Design and Social History*. New York: Woodrow Wilson Center Press.

Bryant, R. 2002. The Purity of Spirit and the Power of Blood: A Comparative Perspective on Nation, Gender and Kinship in Cyprus. *Journal of the Royal Anthropological Institute* 8 (3): 509–530.

Buchli, V. 1997. Khrushchev, Modernism, and the Fight against Petit-Bourgeois Consciousness in the Soviet Home. *Journal of Design History* 10 (2): 161–176.

——. 2002. Architecture and the Domestic Sphere: Introduction. In V. Buchli (ed.), *The Material Culture Reader*, pp. 207–213. Oxford: Berg.

——. 2007. Astana: Materiality and the City. In C. Alexander, V. Buchli, and C. Humphrey (eds.), *Urban Life in Post-Soviet Asia*, pp. 40–69. London: University College London Press.

Buckley, C. 1995. The Myth of Managed Migration: Migration Control and Market in the Soviet Period. *Slavic Review* 54 (4): 896–916.

Burawoy, M., and K. Verdery (eds.). 1999. *Uncertain Transition: Ethnographies of Change in the Postsocialist World.* Lanham: Rowman & Littlefield.

Caldwell, M. 2011. *Dacha Idylls: Living Organically in Russia's Countryside.* Berkeley: University of California Press.

Carrier, J. 1995. *Gifts and Commodities: Exchange and Western Capitalism since 1700.* London: Routledge.

——. 2003. Maussian Occidentalism: Gift and Commodity Systems. In J. Carrier (ed.), *Occidentalism: Images of the West*, pp. 85–108. Oxford: Clarendon Press.

Carsten, J. (ed.). 2000. *Cultures of Relatedness: New Approaches to the Study of Kinship.* Cambridge: Cambridge University Press.

——. 2004. *After Kinship.* Cambridge: Cambridge University Press.

Carsten, J., and S. Hugh-Jones (eds.). 1995a. *About the House: Lévi-Strauss and Beyond.* Cambridge: Cambridge University Press.

Carsten, J., and S. Hugh-Jones. 1995b. Introduction. In J. Carsten, and S. Hugh-Jones (eds.), *About the House: Lévi-Strauss and Beyond*, pp. 1–46. Cambridge: Cambridge University Press.

Castillo, G. 2010. *Cold War on the Home Front: The Soft Power of Midcentury Design.* Minneapolis: University of Minnesota Press.

Chernyshova, N. 2013. *Soviet Consumer Culture in the Brezhnev Era.* London: Routledge.

Cieraad, I. (ed.). 2006a. *At Home: An Anthropology of Domestic Space.* Syracuse: Syracuse University Press.

——. 2006b. Dutch Windows: Female Virtue and Female Vice. In I. Cieraad (ed.), *At Home: An Anthropology of Domestic Space*, pp. 31–52. Syracuse: Syracuse University Press.

Connor, W. 1994. *Ethnonationalism: The Quest for Understanding*. Princeton: Princeton University Press.

Constantine, E. 2007. Practical Consequences of Soviet Policy and Ideology for Gender in Central Asia and Contemporary Reversal. In J. Sahadeo, and R. Zanca (eds.), *Everyday Life in Central Asia: Past and Present*, pp. 115–126. Bloomington: Indiana University Press.

Creed, G. 1998. *Domesticating Revolution: From Socialist Reform to Ambivalent Transition in a Bulgarian Village*. University Park: Pennsylvania State University Press.

Crowley, D., and S. Reid. 2010. Introduction: Pleasures in Socialism? In D. Crowley, and S. Reid (eds.), *Pleasures in Socialism: Leisure and Luxury in the Eastern Bloc*, pp. 3–51. Evanston: Northwestern University Press.

Darieva, T., W. Kaschuba, and M. Krebs (eds.). 2011. *Urban Spaces after Socialism: Ethnographies of Public Places in Eurasian Cities*. Frankfurt/ Main: Campus.

David-Fox, M. 2012. *Showcasing the Great Experiment: Cultural Diplomacy and Western Visitors to the Soviet Union, 1921–1941*. Oxford: Oxford University Press.

Delaney, C. 1991. *The Seed and the Soil: Gender and Cosmology in Turkish Village Society*. Berkeley: University of California Press.

------. 1995. Father State, Motherland, and the Birth of Modern Turkey. In S. Yanagisako, and C. Delaney (eds.), *Naturalizing Power: Essays in Feminist Cultural Analysis*, pp. 177–200. New York: Routledge.

Demirdirek, H. 1993. *Dimensions of Identification: Intellectuals in Baku, 1990–1992*. M. A. Thesis, University of Oslo.

Dery, D. 1998. 'Papereality' and Learning in Bureaucratic Organizations. *Administration & Society* 29 (6): 677–689.

DiMaio, A. 1974. *Soviet Urban Housing: Problems and Policies*. New York: Praeger.

Douglas, M. 1966. *Purity and Danger: An Analysis of Concepts of Pollution and Taboo*. New York: Praeger.

------. 1987. A Distinctive Anthropological Perspective. In M. Douglas (ed.), *Constructive Drinking: Perspectives on Drink from Anthropology*, pp. 3–15. Cambridge: Cambridge University Press.

------. 1991. The Idea of a Home: A Kind of Space. *Social Research* 58 (1): 287–307.

Dragadze, T. 2001 [1988]. *Rural Families in Soviet Georgia: A Case Study in Ratcha Province*. London: Routledge.

Drieskens, B. 2008. Changing Perceptions of Marriage in Contemporary Beirut. In B. Drieskens (ed.), *Les métarmorphoses du marriage au Moyen-Orient*, pp. 97–118. Beyrouth: Presses de l'Ifpo.

Dunham, V. 1976. *In Stalin's Time: Middleclass Values in Soviet Fiction.* Cambridge: Cambridge University Press.

Efendizadeh, R. 1971. *Planirovka i zastroika zhilykh raionov Baku (1920-1967)* (Planning and Development of Residential Areas in Baku [1920-1967]). Baku: Elm.

------. 2012. *Azerbaijan's Architecture of late XIX – early XXI Centuries.* Baku: Sharg-Garb.

Endres, K. W. 2018. Making the Marketplace: Traders, Cadres, and Bureaucratic Documents in Lào Cai City. In K. W. Endres, and A. M. Leshkowich (eds.), *Traders in Motion: Identities and Contestations in the Vietnamese Marketplace*, pp. 27–40. Ithaca: Cornell University Press.

Engels, F. 1872/ 73. *Zur Wohnungsfrage.* http://www.mlwerke.de/me/me18/ me18_209.htm, accessed 31 May 2019.

------. 1986 [1884]. *The Origin of the Family, Private Property and the State.* London: Penguin Books.

Fatullaev, Sh. 1963. *Zhilye doma v zastroike gorodov Azerbaidzhana na rubezhe XIX–XX vekov* (Residential Buildings in the Development of Azerbaijani Cities at the Turn of the Nineteenth and Twentieth Centuries). Baku: Izdatel'stvo Akademiia Nauk Azerbaidzhanskoi SSR.

Fatullaev-Figarov, Sh. 1998. *Arkhitekturnaia Entsiklopediia Baku* (Architectural Encyclopaedia of Baku). Baku: Mezhdunarodnaia Akademiia Arkhitektury Stran Vostoka.

Fehérváry, K. 2013. *Politics in Color and Concrete: Socialist Materialities and the Middle Class in Hungary.* Bloomington: Indiana University Press.

Fehlings, S. 2014. *Jerewan: Urbanes Chaos und soziale Ordnung.* Münster: Lit.

------. 2015. Intimacy and Exposure – Yerevan's Private and Public Space. *International Journal of Sociology and Social Policy* 35 (7/ 8): 513–532.

Fitzpatrick, S. 1999. *Everyday Stalinism: Ordinary Life in Extraordinary Times: Soviet Russia in the 1930s.* New York: Oxford University Press.

Fox, L. 2002. The Meaning of Home: A Chimerical Concept or a Legal Challenge? *Journal of Law and Society* 29 (4): 580–610.

Gal, S. 2002. A Semiotics of the Public/ Private Distinction. *Differences: A Journal of Feminist Cultural Studies* 13 (1): 78–95.

Geertz, C. 1973. *The Interpretation of Cultures: Selected Essays*. New York: Basic Books.

Gerasimova, E. 2002. Public Privacy in the Soviet Communal Apartment. In D. Crowley, and S. Reid (eds.), *Socialist Spaces: Sites of Everyday Life in the Eastern Bloc*, pp. 207–230. Oxford: Berg.

Gerasimova, E., and S. Tchouikina. 2004. Obshchestvo remonta (Repair Society). *Neprikosnovennyi zapas* 2 (34). http://magazines.russ.ru/ nz/2004/34/ ger85.html, accessed 24 July 2015.

Ghannam, F. 2002. *Remaking the Modern: Space, Relocation, and the Politics of Identity in a Global Cairo*. Berkeley: University of California Press.

------. 2013. *Live and Die Like a Man: Gender Dynamics in Urban Egypt*. Stanford: Stanford University Press.

Gillespie, S. 2000. Lévi-Strauss: Maison and Société à Maisons. In R. Joyce, and S. Gillespie (eds.), *Beyond Kinship: Social and Material Reproduction in House Societies*, pp. 22–52. Philadelphia: University of Pennsylvania Press.

Gilmore, D. 1982. Anthropology of the Mediterranean Area. *Annual Review of Anthropology* 11: 175–205.

Goffman, E. 1959. *The Presentation of Self in Everyday Life*. New York: Doubleday & Company.

Goluboff, S. 2008. Patriarchy through Lamentation in Azerbaijan. *American Ethnologist* 35 (1): 81–94.

Goody, J. 1970. Marriage Prestations, Inheritance and Descent in Pre-Industrial Societies. *Journal of Comparative Family Studies* 1 (1): 37–54.

Grant, B. 2001. New Moscow Monuments, or, States of Innocence. *American Ethnologist* 28 (2): 332–362.

------. 2010. Cosmopolitan Baku. *Ethnos* 75 (2): 123–147.

------. 2014. The Edifice Complex: Architecture and the Political Life of Surplus in the New Baku. *Public Culture* 26 (3): 501–528.

Gregory, C. 1982. *Gifts and Commodities*. London: Academic Press.

Gronow, J., and S. Zhuravlev. 2010. Soviet Luxuries from Champagne to Private Cars. In D. Crowley, and S. Reid (eds.), *Pleasures in Socialism: Leisure and Luxury in the Eastern Bloc*, pp. 121–146. Evanston: Northwestern University Press.

Gudeman, S. 2008. *Economy's Tension: The Dialectics of Community and Market*. New York: Berghahn.

------. 2016. *Anthropology and Economy*. Cambridge: Cambridge University Press.

Gudeman, S., and A. Rivera. 1990. *Conversations in Colombia: The Domestic Economy in Life and Text*. Cambridge: Cambridge University Press.

Gudeman, S., and C. Hann. 2015. Introduction: Self-Sufficiency as Reality and as Myth. In S. Gudeman, and C. Hann (eds.), *Oikos and Market: Explorations in Self-Sufficiency after Socialism*, pp. 1–23. New York: Berghahn.

Guliyeva, N. 2011. *Family and Family Life of Baku's Urban Population in the 19th–20th Centuries*. Baku: Elm.

Gurova, O. 2006. Ideology of Consumption in the Soviet Union: From Asceticism to the Legitimating of Consumer Goods. *Anthropology of East Europe Review* 24 (2): 91–98.

Habeck, J. O., and G. Belolyubskaya. 2016. Fences, Private and Public Spaces, and Traversability in a Siberian City. *Cities* 56: 119–129.

Hamilton, E. 1993. Social Areas under State Socialism: The Case of Moscow. In S. G. Solomon (ed.), *Beyond Sovietology: Essays in Politics and History*, pp. 192–225. New York: M. E. Sharpe.

Hann, C. 1992. Radical Functionalism: The Life and Work of Karl Polanyi. *Dialectical Anthropology* 17 (2): 141–166.

------. 1993. From Production to Property: Decollectivization and the Family-Land Relationship in Contemporary Hungary. *Man* 28 (2): 299–320.

------. 1998. Introduction: The Embeddedness of Property. In C. Hann (ed.), *Property Relations: Renewing the Anthropological Tradition*, pp. 1–47. Cambridge: Cambridge University Press.

------. 2006. *'Not the Horse We Wanted!': Postsocialism, Neoliberalism, and Eurasia*. Münster: Lit.

Hann, C. (ed.). 2002. *Postsocialism: Ideals, Ideologies, and Practices in Eurasia*. London: Routledge.

Hardenberg, R. 2007. Das „einschließende Haus": Wertehierarchien und das Konzept der „Hausgesellschaft" im interkulturellen Vergleich. *Anthropos* 102 (1): 157–168.

Harris, S. E. 2013. *Communism on Tomorrow Street: Mass Housing and Everyday Life after Stalin*. Washington: Woodrow Wilson Center Press.

------. 2015. Soviet Mass Housing and the Communist Way of Life. In C. Chatterjee, D. Ransel, M. Cavender, and K. Petrone (eds.), *Everyday Life in Russia Past and Present*, pp. 181–202. Bloomington: Indiana University Press.

Heady, P. 2010. Family, Kinship and State in Contemporary Europe: Introduction to the Three-Volume Series. In H. Grandits (ed.), *Family, Kinship and State in Contemporary Europe, Vol. 1. The Century of Welfare: Eight Countries*, pp. 9–21. Frankfurt/ Main: Campus.

Heathershaw, J. 2014. The Global Performance State: A Reconsideration of the Central Asian 'Weak State'. In M. Reeves, J. Rasanayagam, and Judith Beyer (eds.), *Ethnographies of the State in Central Asia: Performing Politics*, pp. 29–54. Bloomington: Indiana University Press.

Hegedüs, J., and I. Tosics. 1983. Housing Classes and Housing Policy: Some Changes in the Budapest Housing Market. *International Journal of Urban and Regional Research* 7 (4): 467–494.

Henry, J. D. 1905. *Baku: An Eventful History*. London: Archibald Constable & Co.

Herzfeld, M. 2005 [1997]. *Cultural Intimacy: Social Poetics in the Nation-State*. New York: Routledge.

Heyat, F. 2002. *Azeri Women in Transition: Women in Soviet and Post-Soviet Azerbaijan*. London: Routledge.

Hirt, S. A. 2012. *Iron Curtains: Gates, Suburbs and Privatization of Space in the Post-Socialist City*. West Sussex: Wiley-Blackwell.

——. 2013. Whatever Happened to the (Post)Socialist City? *Cities* 32: S29–38.

Hooper, C. 2006. Terror of Intimacy: Family Politics in the 1930s Soviet Union. In C. Kiaer, and E. Naiman (eds.), *Everyday Life in Early Soviet Russia: Taking the Revolution Inside*, pp. 61–91. Bloomington: Indiana University Press.

Howell, S. 1995. The Lio House: Building, Category, Idea, Value. In J. Carsten, and S. Hugh-Jones (eds.), *About the House: Lévi-Strauss and Beyond*, pp. 149–169. Cambridge: Cambridge University Press.

Höjdestrand, T. 2003. *The Soviet-Russian Production of Homelessness: Propiska, Housing, Privatisation*. http://www.anthrobase.com/Txt/ H/Hoejdestrand_T_01.htm, accessed 25 March 2015.

——. 2009. *Needed by Nobody: Homelessness and Humanness in Post-Socialist Russia*. Ithaca: Cornell University Press.

Humphrey, C. 1997. The Villas of the 'New Russians': A Sketch of Consumption and Identity in Post-Soviet Landscapes. *Focaal* 30/ 31: 85–106.

——. 1998. *Marx Went Away but Karl Stayed Behind*. Ann Arbor: University of Michigan Press.

------. 2002. *The Unmaking of Soviet life: Everyday Economies after Socialism*. Ithaca: Cornell University Press.

------. 2005. Ideology in Infrastructure: Architecture and Soviet Imagination. *Journal of the Royal Anthropological Institute* 11 (1): 39–58.

------. 2008. The 'Creative Bureaucrat': Conflicts in the Production of Soviet Communist Party Discourse. *Inner Asia* 10 (1): 5–35.

Huseynova, S. 2015. Baku zwischen Orient und Okzident: Der Islam in der postsowjetischen Stadt. *Osteuropa* 65 (7–10): 569–586.

Huseynova, S., A. Hakobyan, and S. Rumyantsev. 2008. *Kyzyl-Shafag i Kerkendzh: Istoriia obmena selami v situatsii Karabakhskogo konflikta* (Kyzyl-Shafag and Kerhendzh: A Story of Village Exchange during the Karabakh Conflict). Tbilisi: Heinrich-Böll-Stiftung.

Ilkhamov, A. 2007. Neopatrimonialism, Interest Groups, and Patronage Networks: The Impasses of the Governance System in Uzbekistan. *Central Asia Survey* 26 (1): 65–84.

Ismailbekova, A. 2014. Migration and Patrilineal Descent: The Role of Women in Kyrgyzstan. *Central Asian Survey* 33 (3): 375–389.

Ismayilov, M. 2019. Azerbaijan's Russia Conundrum: Towards the Rise of an Unlikely Alliance. *Russian Politics* 4 (2): 242–267.

Joseph, S. 1993a. Connectivity and Patriarchy among Urban Working-Class Arab Families in Lebanon. *Ethos* 21 (4): 452–484.

------. 1993b. Gender and Relationality among Arab Families in Lebanon. *Feminist Studies* 19 (3): 465–486.

------. 1996. Patriarchy and Development in the Arab World. *Gender and Development* 4 (2): 14–19.

------. 1997. The Public/ Private: The Imagined Boundary in the Imagined Nation/ State/ Community. *Feminist Review* 57: 73–92.

Joyce, R., and S. Gillespie (eds.). 2000. *Beyond Kinship: Social and Material Reproduction in House Societies*. Philadelphia: University of Pennsylvania Press.

Kandiyoti, D. 1988. Bargaining with Patriarchy. *Gender and Society* 2 (3): 274–290.

------. 1996. Modernization without the Market? The Case of the 'Soviet East'. *Economy and Society* 25 (4): 529–542.

------. 2007. The Politics of Gender and the Soviet Paradox: Neither Colonized, nor Modern? *Central Asian Survey* 26 (4): 601–623.

Kettering, K. 1997. 'Ever More Cosy and Comfortable': Stalinism and the Soviet Domestic Interior, 1928–1938. *Journal of Design History* 10 (2): 119–135.

Kharkhordin, O. 1997. Reveal and Dissimulate: A Genealogy of Private Life in Soviet Russia. In J. Weintraub, and K. Kumar (eds.), *Public and Private in Thought and Practice: Perspectives on a Grand Dichotomy*, pp. 333–363. Chicago: University of Chicago Press.

Kiaer, C., and E. Naiman. 2006. Introduction. In C. Kiaer, and E. Naiman (eds.), *Everyday Life in Early Soviet Russia: Taking the Revolution Inside*, pp. 1–22. Bloomington: Indiana University Press.

King, D., and L. Stone. 2010. Lineal Masculinity: Gendered Memory within Patriliny. *American Ethnologist* 37 (2): 323–336.

Koch, N. 2015. The Violence of Spectacle: Statist Schemes to Green the Desert and Constructing Astana and Ashgabat as Urban Oases. *Social & Cultural Geography* 16 (6): 675–697.

Koch, N., and A. Valiyev. 2015. Urban Boosterism in Closed Contexts: Spectacular Urbanization and Second-Tier Mega-Events in Three Caspian Capitals. *Eurasian Geography and Economics* 56 (5): 575–598.

Konrád, G., and I. Szelényi. 1979. *The Intellectuals on the Road to Class Power: A Sociological Study of the Role of the Intelligentsia in Socialism*. New York: Harcourt Brace Jovanovich.

Kotkin, S. 1995. *Magnetic Mountain: Stalinism as a Civilization*. Berkeley: University of California Press.

Kuliyev, H. 2002. *Arkhetipichnye Azeri: liki mentaliteta* (Archetypical Azeris: Faces of Mentality). Baku: Yeni Nesil.

Laszczkowski, M. 2014. State Building(s): Built Forms, Materiality, and the State in Astana. In M. Reeves, J. Rasanayagam, and J. Beyer (eds.), *Ethnographies of the State in Central Asia: Performing Politics*, pp. 149–172. Bloomington: Indiana University Press.

------. 2016. *'City of the Future': Built Space, Modernity and Social Change in Astana*. New York: Berghahn.

Laszczkowski, M., and M. Reeves (eds.). 2017a. *Affective States: Entanglements, Suspensions, Suspicions*. New York: Berghahn.

------. 2017b. Introduction: Affect and the Anthropology of the State. In M. Laszczkowski, and M. Reeves (eds.), *Affective States: Entanglements, Suspensions, Suspicions*, pp. 1–14. New York: Berghahn.

Ledeneva, A. V. 1998. *Russia's Economy of Favours: Blat, Networking, and Informal Exchange*. Cambridge: Cambridge University Press.

Lenhard, J., and F. Samanani (eds.). 2020. *Home: Ethnographic Encounters*. London: Bloomsbury.

Lenin, V. 2017 [1917]. *The State and Revolution*. London: Aziloth Books.

Leutloff-Grandits, C. 2006. *Claiming Ownership in Postwar Croatia: The Dynamics of Property Relations and Ethnic Conflict in the Knin Region*. Berlin: Lit.

Lévi-Strauss, C. 1982 [1979]. *The Way of the Masks*. Vancouver: Douglas & McIntyre.

Liu, M. 2007. A Central Asian Tale of Two Cities: Locating Lives and Aspirations in a Shifting Post-Soviet Cityscape. In J. Sahadeo, and R. Zanca (eds.), *Everyday Life in Central Asia, Past and Present*, pp. 79–98. Bloomington: Indiana University Press.

———. 2011. Central Asia in the Post-Cold War World. *Annual Review of Anthropology* 40: 115–131.

———. 2012. *Under Solomon's Throne: Uzbek Visions of Renewal in Osh*. Pittsburgh: University of Pittsburgh Press.

Loos, A. 1898. Die Potemkin'sche Stadt. *Ver Sacrum: Organ der Vereinigung bildender Künstler Österreichs* 1 (7): 15–17.

Lovell, S. 2003. *Summerfolk: A History of the Dacha 1710–2000*. Ithaca: Cornell University Press.

Low, S., and E. Chambers. 1989. Introduction. In S. Low, and E. Chambers (eds.), *Housing, Culture, and Design: A Comparative Perspective*, pp. 3–9. Philadelphia: University of Pennsylvania Press.

Makarychev, A., and A. Yatsyk (eds.). 2016. *Mega-Events in Post-Soviet Eurasia*. New York: Palgrave Macmillan.

Mallett, S. 2004. Understanding Home: A Critical Review of the Literature. *The Sociological Review* 52 (1): 62–89.

Manderson, L., M. Davis, C. Colwell, and T. Ahlin. 2015. On Secrecy, Disclosure, the Public, and the Private in Anthropology. *Current Anthropology* 56 (12): 183–190.

Manning, P. 2012. *The Semiotics of Drink and Drinking*. London: Continuum.

Mars, G., and Y. Altman. 1987. Alternative Mechanism of Distribution in a Soviet Economy. In M. Douglas (ed.), *Constructive Drinking: Perspectives on Drink from Anthropology*, pp. 270–279. Cambridge: Cambridge University Press.

Marx, K., and F. Engels. 2009 [1848]. Manifesto of the Communist Party. In C. Calhoun et al. (eds.), *Classical Sociological Theory* (2nd Edition), pp. 96–111. Malden: Blackwell.

Matthews, M. 1993. *The Passport Society: Controlling Movement in Russia and the USSR*. Boulder: Westview Press.

Mauss, M. 1966 [1925]. *The Gift: Forms and Functions of Exchange in Archaic Societies*. London: Cohen & West.

------. 1979 [1904/05]. *Seasonal Variations of the Eskimo: A Study in Social Morphology*. London: Routledge & Kegan Paul.

Mazumdar, S., and S. Mazumdar. 2001. Rethinking Public and Private Space: Religion and Women in Muslim Society. *Journal of Architectural and Planning Research* 18 (4): 302–324.

Meneley, A. 2007 [1996]. *Tournaments of Value: Sociability and Hierarchy in Yemini Town*. Toronto: Oxford University Press.

Miller, D. 2001. Behind Closed Doors. In D. Miller (ed.), *Home Possessions: Material Culture Behind Closed Doors*, pp. 1–19. Oxford: Berg.

Militz, E., and C. Schurr. 2016. Affective Nationalism: Banalities of Belonging in Azerbaijan. *Political Geography* 54: 54–63.

Montefiore, S. S. 2001. *Prince of Princes: The Life of Potemkin*. London: Phoenix Press.

Morgan, L. H. 1995 [1877]. *Ancient Society*. Tucson: The University of Arizona Press.

------. 2010 [1881]. *Houses and House-Life of the American Aborigines*. Whitefish: Kessinger Publ.

Morton, H. W. 1980. Who Gets What, When and How? Housing in the Soviet Union. *Soviet Studies* 32 (2): 235–259.

------. 1984. Housing in the Soviet Union. *Proceedings of the Academy of Political Science* 35 (3): 69–80.

Mühlfried, F. 2006. *Postsowjetische Feiern: das georgische Bankett im Wandel*. Stuttgart: Ibidem.

------. 2014. *Being a State and States of Being in Highland Georgia*. New York: Berghahn.

Müller, M. 2015. The Mega-Event Syndrome: Why so much Goes Wrong in Mega-Event Planning and What to Do About It. *Journal of the American Planning Association* 81 (1): 6–17.

Müller, M., and J. Pickles. 2015. Global Games, Local Rules: Mega-Events in the Post-Socialist World. *European Urban and Regional Studies* 22 (2): 121–127.

Nelson, C. 1974. Public and Private Politics: Women in the Middle Eastern World. *American Ethnologist* 1 (3): 551–563.

Obertreis, J. 2004. *Tränen des Sozialismus: Wohnen in Leningrad zwischen Alltag und Utopie 1917–1937*. Köln: Böhlau.

Ong, A. 2011. Hyperbuilding: Spectacle, Speculation, and Hyperspace of Sovereignty. In A. Roy, and A. Ong (eds.), *Worlding Cities: Asian Experiments and the Art of Being Global*, pp. 205–226. Malden: Wiley-Blackwell.

Osteen, M. 2002. Gift or Commodity? In M. Osteen (ed.), *The Question of the Gift: Essays across Disciplines*, pp. 229–247. London: Routledge.

Papanek, H. 1973. Purdah: Separate Worlds and Symbolic Shelter. *Comparative Studies in Society and History* 15 (3): 289–325.

Panchenko, A. 1999. Potemkinskie derevni kak kul'turnyi mif (Potemkin Villages as a Cultural Myth). *Déjà vu*. http://ec-dejavu.ru/p/Potemkin_village.html, accessed 2 October 2018.

Parry, J., and M. Bloch (eds.). 1989. *Money and the Morality of Exchange*. Cambridge: Cambridge University Press.

Pelkmans, M. 2003. The Social Life of Empty Buildings: Imagining the Transition in Post-Soviet Ajaria. *Focaal* 41: 121–135.

Pfluger-Schindlbeck, I. 2005a. *Verwandtschaft, Religion und Geschlecht in Aserbaidschan*. Wiesbaden: Reichert.

––––. 2005b. Kinship, Descent Systems and State: The Caucasus. In J. Suad (ed.), *Encyclopedia of Women & Islamic Cultures, Volume II: Family, Law and Politics*, pp. 336–338. Leiden: Brill.

Pine, F. 2002. Retreat to the Household? Gendered Domains in Postsocialist Poland. In C. Hann (ed.), *Postsocialism: Ideals, Ideologies and Practices in Eurasia*, pp. 95–113. London: Routledge.

Pisano, J. 2018. Potemkin Villages (Russia). In A. Ledenova (ed.), *The Global Encyclopaedia of Informality: Understanding Social and Cultural Complexity* (Volume 2), pp. 278–280. London: University College London Press.

Prokhorov, A. M. 1972. *Bol'shaia Sovetskaia Entsiklopediia* (Great Soviet Encyclopaedia), Vol. 9. Moscow: Izdatel'stvo Sovetskaia Entsiklopediia.

Prost, A. 1991. Public and Private Spheres in France. In A. Prost, and G. Vincent (eds.), *A History of Private Life, Vol. 5: Riddles of Identity in Modern Times*, pp. 1–143. Cambridge: Harvard University Press.

Rasanayagam, J., J. Beyer, and M. Reeves. 2014. Introduction: Performances, Possibilities, and Practices of the Political in Central Asia. In M. Reeves, J. Rasanayagam, and J. Beyer (eds.), *Ethnographies of the State in Central Asia: Performing Politics*, pp. 1–26. Bloomington: Indiana University Press.

Read, R., and T. Thelen. 2007. Introduction. Social Security and Care after Socialism: Reconfigurations of Public and Private. *Focaal* 50: 3–18.

Reid, S. 2011. Building Utopia in the Backyard: Housing Administration, Participatory Government, and the Cultivation of Socialist Community. In K. Schlögel (ed.), *Mastering Russian Spaces: Raum und Raumbewältigung als Probleme der russischen Geschichte*, pp. 149–186. München: Oldenbourg.

––––. 2015. Everyday Aesthetics in the Khrushchev-Era Standard Apartment. In C. Chatterjee, D. Ransel, M. Cavender, and K. Petrone (eds.), *Everyday Life in Russia Past and Present*, pp. 203–233. Bloomington: Indiana University Press.

Robben, A. 1989. Habits of the Home: Spatial Hegemony and the Structuration of House and Society in Brazil. *American Anthropologist* 91 (3): 570–588.

Roberts, K., S. C. Clark, C. Fagan, and J. Tholen. 2000. *Surviving Post-Communism: Young People in the Former Soviet Union*. Cheltenham: Edward Elgar.

Roberts, K. et al. 2009. Young Adults' Family and Housing Life-Stage Transitions during Post-Communist Transition in the South Caucasus. *Journal of Youth Studies* 12 (2): 151–166.

Roche, S. 2017. The Family in Central Asia: New Research Perspectives. In S. Roche (ed.), *The Family in Central Asia: New Perspectives*, pp. 7–38. Berlin: Klaus Schwarz Verlag.

Roth, S. 2013. The Making of Home, the Making of Nation: Cultural Notions of Conflict and Displacement in Post-Soviet Azerbaijan. In S. Voell, and K. Khutsishvili (eds.), *Caucasus, Conflict, Culture: Anthropological Perspectives on Times of Crises*, pp. 169–194. Marburg: Curupira.

––––. 2019. Ideologies and Informality in Urban Infrastructure: The Case of Housing in Soviet and Post-Soviet Baku. In T. Tuvikene, W. Sgibnev, and C. Neugebauer (eds.), *Post-Socialist Urban Infrastructures*, pp. 54–71. London: Routledge.

––––. 2020. Curtains, Cars, and Privacy: Experiences of Dwelling and Home-Making in Azerbaijan. In J. Lenhard, and F. Samanani (eds.), *Home: Ethnographic Encounters*, pp. 45–57. London: Bloomsbury.

Rumyantsev, S. 2008. Neft i ovtsy: Iz istorii transformatsii goroda Baku iz stolitsy v stolitsu (Oil and Rams: On the History of the City of Baku's Transformation from Capital to Capital). In B. Cope, and N. Milerius (eds.), *P. S. Landshafty: Optiki gorodskikh issledovanii* (P-S Landscapes: Optics for Urban Studies), pp. 228–266. Vilnius: European Humanities University.

Rzayeva, S. 2013. Oil and Health Care in Post-Soviet Azerbaijan. *European Journal of Sociology* 54 (1): 33–63.

Safiyev, R. 2018. *Hinter der glitzernden Fassade: Über die Macht der Informalität in der Kaukasusrepublik Aserbaidschan*. Bielefeld: Transcript Verlag.

Salukvadze, J., and O. Golubchikov. 2016. City as Geopolitics: Tbilisi, Georgia – A Globalizing Metropolis in a Turbulent Region. *Cities* 52: 39–54.

Sántha, I., and T. Safonova. 2011. *Pokazukha* in the House of Culture: The Pattern of Behavior in Kurumkan, Eastern Buriatiia. In B. Donahoe, and J. Otto Habeck (eds.), *Reconstructing the House of Culture: Community, Self, and the Making of Culture in Russia and Beyond*, pp. 75–96. New York: Berghahn.

Sayfutdinova, L. 2018. Taş (Azerbaijan). In A. Ledeneva (ed.), *The Global Encyclopaedia of Informality: Understanding Social and Cultural Complexity* (Volume 1), pp. 82–85. London: University College London Press.

Scott, J. C. 1976. *The Moral Economy of the Peasant: Rebellion and Subsistence in Southeast Asia.* New Haven: Yale University Press.

Semenova, V. 2004. Equality in Poverty: The Symbolic Meaning of *Kommunalki* in the 1930s–50s. In D. Bertaux, P. Thompson, and A. Rotkirch (eds.), *On Living through Soviet Russia*, pp. 54–67. London: Routledge.

Semenova, V., and P. Thompson. 2004. Family Models and Transgenerational Influences: Grandparents, Parents and Children in Moscow and Leningrad from the Soviet to the Market Era. In D. Bertaux, P. Thompson, and A. Rotkirch (eds.), *On Living through Soviet Russia*, pp. 120–145. London: Routledge.

Sgibnev, W. 2015. *Remont*: Housing Adaption as Meaningful Practice of Space Production in Post-Soviet Tajikistan. *Europa Regional* 22 (1/2): 53–64.

Shevchenko, O. 2015. 'The Mirror with a Memory': Placing Photography in Memory Studies. In A. L. Tota, and T. Hagen (eds.), *Routledge Handbook of Memory Studies*, pp. 272–287. London: Routledge.

Shlapentokh, V. 1989. *Public and Private Life of the Soviet People: Changing Values in Post-Stalin Russia.* New York: Oxford University Press.

Sidikov, B. 2007. Barth, 'Yeraz', and Post-Soviet Azerbaijan: Inventing a New Sub-Ethnic Identity. In T. Darieva, and W. Kaschuba (eds.), *Representations on the Margins of Europe: Politics and Identities in the Baltic and South Caucasian States*, pp. 301–321. Frankfurt/Main: Campus.

Siegelbaum, L. H. 2008. *Cars for Comrades: The Life of the Soviet Automobile.* Ithaca: Cornell University Press.

Sillince, J. 1990. Housing Policy in Eastern Europe and the Soviet Union. In J. Sillince (ed.), *Housing Policies in Eastern Europe and the Soviet Union*, pp. 6–57. London: Routledge.

Simmel, G. 1904. Fashion. *The International Quarterly* 10: 130–155.

–––––. 1994 [1909]. Bridge and Door. *Theory, Culture & Society* 11 (1): 5–10.

Singerman, D. 1995. *Avenues of Participation: Family, Politics, and Networks in Urban Quarters of Cairo*. Princeton: Princeton University Press.

Singerman, D., and B. Ibrahim. 2001. The Cost of Marriage in Egypt: A Hidden Variable in the New Arab Demography. In N. Hopkins (ed.), *The New Arab Family*, pp. 80–116. Cairo: The American University in Cairo Press.

Smith, M. 2010. *Property of Communists: The Urban Housing Program from Stalin to Khrushchev*. DeKalb: Northern Illinois University Press.

Stronski, P. 2010. *Tashkent: Forging a Soviet City, 1930–1966*. Pittsburgh: University of Pittsburgh Press.

Struyk, R. J. (ed.). 1996. *Economic Restructuring of the Former Soviet Bloc: The Case of Housing*. Aldershot: Avebury.

Struyk, R., and K. Angelici. 1996. The Russian Dacha Phenomenon. *Housing Studies* 11 (2): 233–250.

Swietochowski, T. 1985. *Russian Azerbaijan, 1905–1920: The Shaping of National Identity in a Muslim Community*. Cambridge: Cambridge University Press.

Swietochowski, T., and B. C. Collins. 1999. *Historical Dictionary of Azerbaijan*. Lanham: The Scarecrow Press.

Szelényi, I. 1983. *Urban Inequalities under State Socialism*. Oxford: Oxford University Press.

Thelen, T., L. Vetters, and K. von Benda-Beckmann. 2014. Introduction to Stategraphy: Toward a Relational Anthropology of the State. *Social Analysis* 58 (3): 1–19.

Thompson E. P. 1971. The Moral Economy of the English Crowd in the 18th Century. *Past & Present* 50 (1): 76–136.

Timasheff, N. 1946. *The Great Retreat: The Growth and Decline of Communism in Russia*. New York: E. P. Dutton & Co.

Tohidi, N. 1996. Soviet in Public, Azeri in Private: Gender, Islam, and Nationality in Soviet and Post-Soviet Azerbaijan. *Women's Studies International Forum* 19 (1/2): 111–123.

Trifonov, Yu. 1983 [1969]. *Another Life and the House on the Embankment*. New York: Simon and Schuster.

Trudolyubov, M. 2018. *The Tragedy of Property: Private Life, Ownership and the Russian State*. Cambridge: Polity Press.

United Nations Economic Commission for Europe (UNECE). 2010. *Country Profiles on the Housing Sector: Azerbaijan*. New York: United Nations.

Urban, F. 2012. *Tower and Slab: Histories of Global Mass Housing*. London: Routledge.

Utekhin, I. 2004. *Ocherki kommunal'nogo byta* (Sketches of Communal Living). Moscow: OGI.

------. 2015. The Post-Soviet *Kommunalka*: Continuity and Difference? In C. Chatterjee, D. Ransel, M. Cavender, and K. Petrone (eds.), *Everyday Life in Russia Past and Present*, pp. 234–251. Bloomington: Indiana University Press.

Vainshtein, O. 1996. Female Fashion, Soviet Style: Bodies of Ideology. In H. Goscilo, and B. Holmgren (eds.), *Russia, Women, Culture*, pp. 64–93. Indiana: Indiana University Press.

Valiyev, A. 2013. Baku. *Cities* 31: 625–640.

------. 2014. The Post-Communist Growth Machine: The Case of Baku, Azerbaijan. *Cities* 41: S45–53.

Valiyev, A., and L. Wallwork. 2019. *Post-Soviet Urban Renewal and its Discontents: Gentrification by Demolition in Baku*. Urban Geography 40 (10): 1506–1526.

Van Gennep, A. 2004 [1909]. *The Rites of Passage*. London: Routledge.

Vasile, M. 2015. The Trader's Wedding: Ritual Inflation and Money Gifts in Transylvania. In S. Gudeman, and C. Hann (eds.), *Economy and Ritual: Studies of Postsocialist Transformations*, pp. 137–165. New York: Berghahn.

Veblen, T. 2009 [1899]. *The Theory of the Leisure Class*. Oxford: Oxford University Press.

Vera, H. 1989. On Dutch Windows. *Qualitative Sociology* 12 (2): 215–234.

Verdery, K. 1991. Theorizing Socialism: A Prologue to the 'Transition'. *American Ethnologist* 18 (3): 419–439.

------. 1995. *National Ideology under Socialism: Identity and Cultural Politics in Ceauşescu's Romania*. Berkeley: University of California Press.

------. 1996. *What was Socialism, and What Comes Next?* Princeton: Princeton University Press.

------. 1999. *The Political Life of Dead Bodies: Reburial and Postsocialist Change*. New York: Columbia University Press.

------. 2003. *The Vanishing Hectare: Property and Value in Postsocialist Transylvania*. Ithaca: Cornell University Press.

Voell, S., and I. Kaliszewska (eds.). 2015. *State and Legal Practice in the Caucasus: Anthropological Perspectives on Law and Politics*. Farnham: Ashgate.

Vom Bruck, G. 1997. A House Turned Inside Out: Inhabiting Space in a Yemeni City. *Journal of Material Culture* 2 (2): 139–172.

Weintraub, J. 1997. The Theory and Politics of the Public/ Private Distinction. In J. Weintraub, and K. Kumar (eds.), *Public and Private in Thought and Practice: Perspectives on a Grand Dichotomy*, pp. 1–42. Chicago: University of Chicago Press.

Werner, C. A. 1997a. *Household Networks, Ritual Exchange and Economic Change*. Ph.D. dissertation, Indiana University.

———. 1997b. Marriage, Markets, and Merchants: Changes in Wedding Feasts and Household Consumption Patterns in Rural Kazakhstan. *Culture & Agriculture* 19 (1/2): 6–13.

White, E. H. 1977. Purdah. *Frontiers: A Journal of Women Studies* 2 (1): 31–42.

Wolle, S. 1998. *Die heile Welt der Diktatur: Alltag und Herrschaft in der DDR 1971–1989*. Berlin: Ch. Links Verlag.

World Bank Group. 2015. *Azerbaijan Partnership Program Snapshot*. http://www.worldbank.org/content/dam/Worldbank/document/Azerbaijan-Snapshot.pdf, accessed 7 March 2016.

Yalçın-Heckmann, L. 2001. The Political Economy of an Azeri Wedding. *Working Paper* 28. Halle/ Saale: Max Planck Institute for Social Anthropology.

———. 2010. *The Return of Private Property: Rural Life after Agrarian Reform in the Republic of Azerbaijan*. Berlin: Lit.

———. 2012. Rethinking Citizenship in the South Caucasus. *Europe-Asia Studies* 64 (9): 1724–1738.

Yanagisako, S., and C. Delaney. 1995. Naturalizing Power. In S. Yanagisako, and C. Delaney (eds.), *Naturalizing Power: Essays in Feminist Cultural Analysis*, pp. 1–22. New York: Routledge.

Yunusov, A. 2009. *Migration Processes in Azerbaijan*. Baku: Adiloglu.

Yurchak, A. 2006. *Everything Was Forever, until it Was No More: The Last Soviet Generation*. Princeton: Princeton University Press.

Yuval-Davis, N. 1997. *Gender & Nation*. London: Sage.

Zakharova, L. 2010. Dior in Moscow: A Taste for Luxury in Soviet Fashion under Khrushchev. In D. Crowley, and S. Reid (eds.), *Pleasures in Socialism: Leisure and Luxury in the Eastern Bloc*, pp. 95–119. Evanston: Nortwestern University Press.

Zavisca, J. R. 2012. *Housing the New Russia*. Ithaca: Cornell University Press.

Zuo, J. 2016. *Work and Family in Urban China: Women's Changing Experience since Mao*. London: Palgrave Macmillan.

Index

Halle Studies in the Anthropology of Eurasia

1 Hann, Chris, and the "Property Relations" Group, 2003: *The Postsocialist Agrarian Question. Property Relations and the Rural Condition.*

2 Grandits, Hannes, and Patrick Heady (eds.), 2004: *Distinct Inheritances. Property, Family and Community in a Changing Europe.*

3 Torsello, David, 2004: *Trust, Property and Social Change in a Southern Slovakian Village.*

4 Pine, Frances, Deema Kaneff, and Haldis Haukanes (eds.), 2004: *Memory, Politics and Religion. The Past Meets the Present in Europe.*

5 Habeck, Joachim Otto, 2005: *What it Means to be a Herdsman. The Practice and Image of Reindeer Husbandry among the Komi of Northern Russia.*

6 Stammler, Florian, 2009: *Reindeer Nomads Meet the Market. Culture, Property and Globalisation at the 'End of the Land'* (2 editions).

7 Ventsel, Aimar, 2006: *Reindeer,* Rodina *and Reciprocity. Kinship and Property Relations in a Siberian Village.*

8 Hann, Chris, Mihály Sárkány, and Peter Skalník (eds.), 2005: *Studying Peoples in the People's Democracies. Socialist Era Anthropology in East-Central Europe.*

9 Leutloff-Grandits, Caroline, 2006: *Claiming Ownership in Postwar Croatia. The Dynamics of Property Relations and Ethnic Conflict in the Knin Region.*

10 Hann, Chris, 2006: *"Not the Horse We Wanted!" Postsocialism, Neoliberalism, and Eurasia.*

11 Hann, Chris, and the "Civil Religion" Group, 2006: *The Postsocialist Religious Question. Faith and Power in Central Asia and East-Central Europe.*

12 Heintz, Monica, 2006: *"Be European, Recycle Yourself!" The Changing Work Ethic in Romania.*

26 Cash, Jennifer R., 2011: *Villages on Stage. Folklore and Nationalism in the Republic of Moldova.*

27 Köllner, Tobias, 2012: *Practising Without Belonging? Entrepreneurship, Morality, and Religion in Contemporary Russia.*

28 Bethmann, Carla, 2013: *"Clean, Friendly, Profitable?" Tourism and the Tourism Industry in Varna, Bulgaria.*

29 Bošković, Aleksandar, and Chris Hann (eds.), 2013: *The Anthropological Field on the Margins of Europe, 1945-1991.*

30 Holzlehner, Tobias, 2014: *Shadow Networks. Border Economies, Informal Markets and Organised Crime in the Russian Far East.*

31 Bellér-Hann, Ildikó, 2015: *Negotiating Identities. Work, Religion, Gender, and the Mobilisation of Tradition among the Uyghur in the 1990s.*

32 Oelschlaegel, Anett C., 2016: *Plural World Interpretations. The Case of the South-Siberian Tyvans.*

33 Obendiek, Helena, 2016: *"Changing Fate". Education, Poverty and Family Support in Contemporary Chinese Society.*

34 Sha, Heila, 2017: *Care and Ageing in North-West China.*

35 Tocheva, Detelina, 2017: *Intimate Divisions. Street-Level Orthodoxy in Post-Soviet Russia.*

36 Sárközi, Ildikó Gyöngyvér, 2018: *From the Mists of Martyrdom. Sibe Ancestors and Heroes on the Altar of Chinese Nation Building.*

37 Cheung Ah Li, Leah, 2019: *Where the Past meets the Future. The Politics of Heritage in Xi'an.*

38 Wang, Ruijing, 2019: *Kinship, Cosmology and Support. Toward a Holistic Approach of Childcare in the Akha Community of South-Western China.*

39 Coşkun, Mustafa, 2020: *Improvising the Voice of the Ancestors. Heritage and Identity in Central Asia.*